D0900815

Women and
Culture Series

The Women and Culture Series is dedicated to books that illuminate the lives, roles, achievements, and status of women, past or present.

Fran Leeper Buss
Dignity: Lower Income Women Tell of Their Lives and Struggles
La Partera: Story of a Midwife

Valerie Kossew Pichanick
Harriet Martineau: The Woman and Her Work, 1802–76

Sandra Baxter and Marjorie Lansing
Women and Politics: The Visible Majority

Estelle B. Freedman
Their Sisters' Keepers: Women's Prison Reform in America, 1830–1930

Susan C. Bourque and Kay Barbara Warren
Women of the Andes: Patriarchy and Social Change in Two Peruvian Towns

Marion S. Goldman
Gold Diggers and Silver Miners: Prostitution and Social Life on the Comstock Lode

Page duBois
Centaurs and Amazons: Women and the Pre-History of the Great Chain of Being

Mary Kinnear
Daughters of Time: Women in the Western Tradition

Lynda K. Bundtzen
Plath's Incarnations: Woman and the Creative Process

Violet B. Haas and Carolyn C. Perrucci, editors
Women in Scientific and Engineering Professions

Sally Price
Co-wives and Calabashes

Patricia R. Hill
The World Their Household: The American Woman's Foreign Mission Movement and Cultural Transformation, 1870–1920

Diane Wood Middlebrook and Marilyn Yalom, editors
Coming to Light: American Women Poets in the Twentieth Century

Leslie W. Rabine
Reading the Romantic Heroine: Text, History, Ideology

Joanne S. Frye
Living Stories, Telling Lives: Women and the Novel in Contemporary Experience

SALLY PRICE is winner in the Hamilton Prize competition for 1982. The Alice and Edith Hamilton Prize is named for two outstanding women scholars: Alice Hamilton (educated at the University of Michigan Medical School), a pioneer in environmental medicine; and her sister Edith Hamilton, the renowned classicist. The Hamilton Prize competition is supported by the University of Michigan and by private donors.

Co-wives and Calabashes

Co-wives and Calabashes

SALLY PRICE

Ann Arbor

The University of Michigan Press

Copyright © by The University of Michigan 1984
All rights reserved
Published in the United States of America by
The University of Michigan Press and simultaneously
in Rexdale, Canada, by John Wiley & Sons Canada, Limited
Manufactured in the United States of America

1987   1986   5   4   3   2

Library of Congress Cataloging In Publication Data

Price, Sally.
  Co-wives and calabashes.

  (Women and culture series)
  Bibliography: p.
  Includes index.
  1. Women, Saramacca (Surinam people).   2. Saramacca
(Surinam people)—Social life and customs.   3. Art,
Primitive—Surinam.   I. Title.   II. Series.
F2431.S27P74   1984   305.4′88960883   83-16929
ISBN 0-472-10045-9
ISBN 0-472-08045-8 (pbk.)

Jacket or cover photo: Saramaka girls, dressed up and bearing dishes,
on their way to serve a meal to their play husbands.

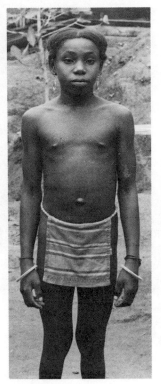

To the Saramaka women of Moina's generation and to their future

968

1974

1978

Acknowledgments

The contribution of the Saramakas among whom I have lived should be apparent on every page of this book. I am deeply grateful to them for teaching me about their way of life and for offering me their friendship.

Richard Price has, over the past twenty years, provided a model of fieldwork and scholarship that has molded my entire approach to anthropology. He has encouraged my work at every step and commented thoughtfully on my writing, often suggesting subtle reorientations of my arguments that have clarified their meaning and expanded their significance.

Sidney W. Mintz has enriched my understandings about Afro-America and the Caribbean, and offered detailed comments on a draft of the manuscript.

William C. Sturtevant contributed to the development of the ideas in this book by sharing his insights on the study of art and material culture.

Diane Vernon, whose knowledge of Djuka culture has cast light on my own understanding of Saramaka life, gave generously of her time and sensitivities in exploring mutual interests.

Pauline Randolph Hamlin brought me up as enough of a seamstress so that Saramaka techniques of embroidery, patchwork, and crocheting were possible for me to learn.

Niko and Leah Price both participated in this project according to their individual strengths; Niko shared in the fieldwork experience with special enthusiasm, and Leah offered insightful criticisms of a near-final draft of the manuscript.

Fieldwork and museum research for this book have been supported by grants from the Fulbright-Hays Doctoral Dissertation Research Abroad Program, the Johns Hopkins Program in Atlantic History and Culture, and the Tropical South American Program of the University of Florida, as well as a fellowship from the National Science Foundation. The writing was completed while I was a NATO Postdoctoral Fellow affiliated with the Rijksuniversiteit Utrecht (Netherlands).

Translations from Dutch, French, Saramaccan, and Spanish are my own. I am grateful to Gerlind Wolinsky for helping me with German translations.

Contents

The Suriname Maroons

The Suriname Maroons, Afro-Americans who live in the tropical rain forest of northeastern South America, are divided into six politically distinct groups—the Saramaka, Matawai, and Kwinti in central Suriname and the Djuka, Aluku, and Paramaka in eastern Suriname and western French Guiana. The ancestors of all these peoples, who came from a wide range of societies in West and Central Africa, were imported in chains to the young Dutch colony of Suriname and held in slavery on the plantations of the coastal plain. During the late seventeenth and early eighteenth centuries many slaves escaped and fled far inland, where they joined other runaways in setting up new and independent communities. After a century-long war of liberation, the Maroons were finally sued for peace by the colonists, who recognized the Maroons' territorial rights in the interior and agreed to supply periodic tribute in the form of cloth, pots, guns, and other coastal goods. Once the provision of tribute was phased out by the colonial government in the mid-nineteenth century, Maroon men began spending time as boatmen, loggers, and laborers on the coast in order to provide the imports needed for their life in the interior. The general history of the Suriname Maroons is spelled out in R. Price 1976, which also provides a comprehensive bibliography. The early history of the Saramaka is recounted in more detail, through the words of twentieth-century tribal elders, in R. Price 1983a.

Because there has often been confusion among outsiders about the various terms that designate these groups, collectively and individually, and about the various languages that are spoken by them, I begin with a few remarks on terminology and language.

Most writers have attempted to convey their admiration for the Maroons through the terms they use for them, but many have fallen victim to misunderstandings and have settled on choices that, from a Maroon perspective, range from the offensive to the meaningless. Morton Kahn adopted a particularly pejorative choice in his book about the Saramaka, entitled *Djuka* (1931), not realizing that coastal Surinamers used the term *Djuka* in this generalized sense (rather than its proper sense as the name for one of the six tribes) as an expression of contempt. The term *Bush Negro*, which is found frequently in the literature, comes closest to the Saramakas' own designation for themselves and other groups of similar historical origin (*Búsinêngè*), but the abandonment of *Negro* elsewhere in the Americas has made this term less acceptable to outsiders in recent years. In the 1960s, attempts by coastal Afro-Surinamers ("Creoles") to gain the political solidarity of their newly enfranchised compatriots in the interior led to the coining of the Dutch term *Boslandcreolen* (Bushland Creoles), despite the objection of many Saramakas that it erased the important distinction between people whose ancestors had accepted slavery (Sar. *Nêngè*, Dutch *Creolen*) and those whose ancestors had valiantly liberated themselves (Sar. *Búsinêngè*, Dutch *Bos[ch]negers*). Most recently, two U.S. Afro-Americans in search of their roots, after being corrected in their use of the term *Djuka,* decided that their brothers and sisters in the rain forest were best described as *Bush Afro-Americans,* a term that conveys both exoticism and a shared heritage to audiences in the United States, but that has no past history in Suriname and no equivalent among the people it labels (Counter and Evans 1974; 1981). In this book, which is largely concerned with members of a single tribe, I generally use the proper name for that group, Saramaka; in discussing realities that apply also to the Djuka, Aluku, Paramaka, Matawai, and Kwinti, I refer to Maroons. This latter choice is intended to reflect the heritage of heroism that the term *maroon* connotes in Suriname, Jamaica, Cuba, Haiti, and elsewhere in the Americas. (For a discussion of the etymology of this term and the history of its alternatives, see R. Price 1976:2–3.)

In terms of language, the Maroons are divided into two groups; the Djuka, Paramaka, and Aluku speak variants of one creole language (known in the literature as Ndjuka), and the Saramaka, Matawai, and Kwinti speak variants of another (known as Saramaccan). These languages reflect the complex cultural experiences of the Maroons' early ancestors. Both Ndjuka and Saramaccan combine elements from the languages of the whole range of West and Central African societies that provided slaves to Suriname, other elements from the languages of the early English settlers (1651–67) and of the subsequent Dutch colonists, and still others from the Amerindian languages spoken by the various Carib and Arawak groups in the area. Saramaccan also has a strong Portuguese component, inherited in part from the language of the Brazilian Jews who owned most of the plantations from which the Saramakas' early ancestors escaped. Although Dutch is the official language of Suriname, Sranan-tongo (sometimes referred to in the popular literature as "Taki-Taki") is the main language spoken by non-Maroons, and this is learned as a contact language by Maroon men, who spend time on the coast as laborers. For a bibliography of linguistic studies on the Suriname Maroons up to 1975, see R. Price 1976:60–62.

In transcribing Saramaccan words, I employ a modified version of the orthography developed by Voorhoeve (1959). Its essential features include the following: vowels have "Italian" values except that *è* represents the vowel in the English word *met* and *ò* represents that in the English word *all;* vowel extension in speech is indicated by vowel repetition in writing; and high tones are indicated by acute accents, while low tones are left unmarked. In the spelling of proper names for people and places, I follow the current Suriname convention of omitting diacritical marks.

Chapter One

Opening Images

Throughout their history, the Suriname Maroons have excited the romantic imagination of outsiders—from the eighteenth-century soldiers who fought against them to the twentieth-century anthropologists who have lived among them, and from the coastal Surinamers who see them walking barefoot in the streets of the capital city to the tourists who sign up for one-day "jungle excursions" to the interior. Observers have been fascinated by the Maroons' heroic struggle for freedom, by their independence in the rain forest, by the vitality of their cultural institutions, and by the visible debt of their way of life to the societies of their African ancestors.[1]

The place of women in these societies has been one area of particular interest. Maroon kinship is strongly matrilineal, and this fact has often inspired outsiders to speculate about the political and ritual influence of Maroon women within their communities. Furthermore, Maroon women are strikingly independent in many respects. Each lives in a house of her own rather than sharing one with her husband; she grows most of her own food in an individually owned garden; she often raises children as a single parent; and, in the most literal sense, she paddles her own canoe. Perhaps not surprisingly, this independence has led to conjectures about the power of women over men in domestic matters.

Noticing that women are the people through whom the basic structure of social relations is defined, visitors to the Maroons have often gone on to assume that women must also play a central role in running social life itself; matriliny has been misread as matriarchy. Moreover, they have often assumed that if women in such a society are independent in terms of housing, subsistence activities, childrearing, and transportation, it must be because they choose to be. Independence has been misread as a Western-style women's liberation. As a result of such speculations, the image of Maroon women in the literature has been dominated by characterizations of the following sort:

> The women essentially rule the entire people because they are the main ones who deal with the gods and are possessed by them. [Kersten 1770:137]
>
> It is chiefly the women who see that the ancestral and village customs are enforced. They are the guardians of the ancient traditions and customs of the race. [Kahn 1931:98]
>
> The Maroon woman, . . . jealous of her independence from the man, places her pride in being able to get along on her own. [Hurault 1961: 158]
>
> The women . . . participate fully in the . . . major decisions about village life. Women sit on the high councils, equal to the men. [Counter and Evans 1981:92]

This image of Maroon women, frequently reinforced by an ideologically motivated glorification of Maroon society, has sometimes led to ironic distortions. The custom of menstrual seclusion, which is explicitly designed to protect men's ritual powers from pollution and is viewed by Maroon women as one of the more distasteful and inconvenient necessities of their lives (see chap. 2), inspired one recent example. Two visitors, whose only verbal contact with Maroons had been through a male interpreter from Paramaribo, stood the periodic banishment of women from society on its head and presented the menstrual hut as the location of a kind of feminist escape from the burdens of daily life, asserting that

> rules governing the practice [of menstrual seclusion] are made by the women themselves. . . . The women seem to enjoy this opportunity to get away from the village chores and family and join their friends in the woman's *oso* [house] for several days of gossip and laughter. [Counter and Evans 1981:133]

Like the subject of women, the subject of art has consistently attracted the interest of visitors to the Maroons and has resulted in a massive body of literature in Dutch, English, French, German, Spanish, and Swedish. Many studies of Maroon art have been quite detailed, but attitudes toward women—on the part of both ethnographers (who have almost always been men) and their informants (also almost always men)—have tended to distort our overall understanding of Maroon arts and of their role in social life. Popular and scholarly accounts alike have defined Maroon *têmbe* (art) in terms of the elaborate wood carvings that the men produce as gifts for the women they love, and they have speculated at length on the ways in which the designs communicate the men's feelings of affection and desire. In this much-repeated vision of Maroon artistic life, women are painted as passive and admiring recipients. Melville Herskovits, while conceding weakly that "[the Maroon] woman . . . is not deprived of an opportunity to show her skill in ornamentation" (1930:159) and briefly mentioning the existence of women's calabash carving, patchwork textiles, and decorative cicatrizations, nevertheless devoted his entire study of "Bush-Negro Art" (1930) to men's wood carving. Justifying this decision with a quotation in pseudo-Saramaccan, Herskovits declared that " '*Tembe no muje sundi*,' . . . 'Wood-carving is not a woman's affair' " (1930:159). Other studies have followed in this same tradition, erroneously equating the Maroon concept of *têmbe* exclusively with men's wood carving (see, for example, Dark 1954; Hurault 1970; Kahn 1931; and Muntslag 1966). In this literature, women's artistic skills—if they are acknowledged at all—tend to be presented as a kind of "doodling" (Dark 1951:59). Summing up the published materials on Maroon arts and sex roles, one commentator was led to conclude quite generally that "the role of the men is primarily concerned with creation, that of the women with appreciation" (Dark 1951:57).

The failure of most observers to recognize the richness of women's artistry can be traced at least in part to ideas about a woman's "place" that are common to both Maroon and Euro-American cultures. These ideas have affected every stage of the research process, from interviews in Maroon villages to the analysis of Maroon artifacts in museums. Because of strong traditions in our own society, it has been men more than women who have traveled to the Suriname rain forest and written about their experiences. And because of related and equally strong traditions in Maroon societies, it has been men who have almost always served as their guides, interpreters, and informants. Maroon ideas about language learning have created a formidable barrier to the equal coverage of men's and women's interests, for men are expected to learn a contact language (Sranan-tongo) and women are not. Since relatively few outsiders take the time to master the languages of the Maroons, most of the ethnographic statements on record have been provided by men.

My own experience with Maroons over the past seventeen years has not called into question the view of Maroon women as personally independent, self-assertive individuals and as admiring connoisseurs of men's art. At the same time, however, it has contradicted the received wisdom about Maroon women and their participation in artistic life in certain ways. First, the image that the women project of themselves is not one of defiantly independent matriarchs, running council meetings, ruling over social and religious life, and delighting in the conviviality of the menstrual hut. Rather, when they speak of their participation in public life, it is with recognition of the dominant role of men as social and religious leaders. When they speak of menstrual seclusion, it is with resignation rather than joy. And the great bulk of their conversations center on their involvement in a polygynous marriage system strongly tilted in favor of men. (I might add that during my field stays their daily life offered ample support for these views, in the form of countless specific incidents.) Second, in terms of art, it became clear that artistic creativity and productivity are not confined to men, and that women have developed forms of artistic expression that are every bit as richly elaborated as those of their brothers.

This book represents an attempt to communicate a view of Maroon social and artistic life that respects the insights and perceptions of the people who first stimulated me to think about the relationship between gender and aesthetics— Saramaka women in the villages of the Pikilio (see fig. 1). Through a detailed examination of their artistic expression (especially calabash decoration, textile arts, and popular songs), it explores the ways in which cultural ideas about the sexes influence their artistic life and analyzes the complementary contributions that the most important artistic media make to their social life. Its special emphasis on women's conjugal experiences, within the broader realm of their personal involvements, stems from my goal of exploring the links between art and social relations, for it is chiefly the institution of marriage that brings together these two aspects of life in Maroon villages.

In 1966, Richard Price and I traveled to Suriname to explore the possibility of conducting long-term fieldwork with the Saramaka. After a brief stay in the capital city of Paramaribo, our three-day trip to the Pikilio in a motorized dugout canoe was an exciting journey of

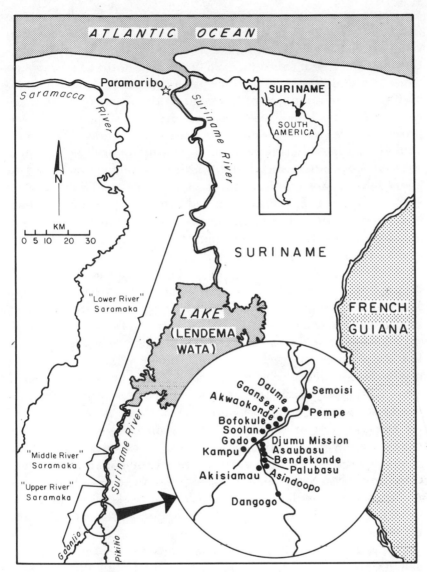

Fig. 1. The sixty-odd Saramaka villages, strung out along the Suriname River, are conceptualized locally as being divided into three regions. The circle inset shows the location of villages in the area most directly described in this book.

discovery, and by the time we reached Asindoopo, the village of the tribal chief, we were eager to turn our superficial fascination into serious understanding. During that first month-long stay in the interior, we were granted occasional audiences with Chief Agbago (Aboikoni) and were befriended by his thirty-year-old grandson, who lived upriver in the village of Dangogo. With this man and his three older sisters, we began to learn about hunting, fishing, and food processing; we spent a few days in a small horticultural camp several hours upstream; we participated in a feast in honor of an ancestor; and our speech began to shift from Sranan-tongo (which we had learned in preparation for our trip) into Saramaccan. By the time we returned to the United States, we had made arrangements to come back for a two-year stay in Dangogo, where a standard one-room house with an earth floor and palm-leaf walls and roof was being constructed for us.

After a six-month period devoted to library research on Maroons and an intensive course in Dutch, we flew to Suriname and began our immersion in Saramaka life. The complex negotiations that were conducted on our behalf with the main oracle of Dangogo eventually produced a conditional acceptance of our presence by the ancestors, but it was made very clear that our "Saramakanization"—especially my rigorous compliance with the complex rules of menstrual seclusion—was a prerequisite for that acceptance. Because of Saramakas' close association of both work and travel with the male world, I was automatically cast in the role of an accompanying wife. It was assumed that my function there was to cook, wash clothes, and provide companionship for my husband who, in contrast, had come in a wage-earning capacity. I was taught to dress properly, to launder our hammock at boulders in the river, to balance large buckets of water on my head for the walk from the river to our house, to serve attractive men's meals, to participate in gossip sessions, and otherwise to conduct myself as an artificial approximation of a properly socialized Saramaka woman.

In contrast to Richard Price's fieldwork, which alternated between participation in village life and day-long interviewing in our house, my own learning during the first year appeared to Saramakas to focus more exclusively on "practical" knowledge. I did not generally write notes in the presence of others; I refrained from asking questions that could not be worked into a natural conversation; and I spent a great deal of time in the company of Saramaka women, engaged in women's work— from harvesting rice and skinning animals to sewing clothes and carving calabashes.

After about a year, we were comfortable in Saramaccan and had achieved a basic working knowledge of Saramaka life that covered everything from kinship structure and political history to the classification of the nine stages in the growth of a rice plant. In my case, the steady experience of participation had been especially crucial both to my own socialization and to Dangogo's acceptance of me, and it paved the way for my second year, when I devoted more time to intensive interviews on a wide range of topics, from marital histories to possession spirits, with an emphasis on art, material culture, and women's life experiences.

During the 1970s, we returned several times to Suriname for summer field trips. Although these visits included some time in Dangogo, we conducted most of our work in Asindoopo. As the seat of tribal government and the main "contact point" for visiting coastal officials, Asindoopo was in certain ways less representative of Saramaka culture, but it offered conveniences, such as electricity and opportunities to purchase food, that allowed us to take maximal advantage of our more limited time in the field. These later research trips represented focused attempts to refine particular pieces of the ethnographic patchwork that had resulted from our earlier immersion in the life of the Dangogo community.

Even in years that did not include fieldwork, our lives became focused on Saramaka in other ways. In 1968, just after we returned from Dangogo, a friend from that village came to live with us in order to learn English and begin his education, and our household was largely Saramaccan-speaking for the first six months that he spent with us. Our research and writing—on a range of topics from history and emigration patterns to music and personal names—kept our thoughts turned toward Saramaka on a daily basis. The three different years we spent in the Netherlands were motivated by Saramaka interests, as we delved into archives and museum storerooms, consulted with others who had lived in the Suriname interior, and kept up on news of our friends in Saramaka through their relatives who were living in Dutch cities. During the late 1970s we took on a project that eventually allowed us to return the hospitality of several of the people who had so many times been our hosts on the Pikilio; we became curators of a major exhibition of Maroon arts that traveled across the United States from October 1980 through January 1982. During its appearance in Baltimore, with the support of the National Endowment for the Humanities, we invited eight Saramaka men and women to our home for a ten-day visit, to present performances of music and dance to audiences in Baltimore, New York, and Washington. For ten days the Suriname flag flew over our front door as our friends—including the man who had first invited us to stay on in Dangogo—explored the world that they had asked us about so often in Suriname.

Since our first trip to the Pikilio in 1966, many changes have taken place. Saramakas have begun to vote in national elections; air travel between Saramaka and the coast has become more affordable than canoe trips on the river; electricity has been introduced to some villages; more boys, and even some girls, are attending mission schools; women are being allowed to accompany their husbands on long-term trips to the coast; and the toddlers we knew from our early visits are now parents many times over. Like other Surinamers, our friends on the Pikilio became citizens of an independent republic in 1975. And though they have been relatively isolated from the aftermath of the military takeover in 1980, their future now seems far from certain, for as this book goes to press the full dimensions of the current turmoil in the nation's capital have yet to be assessed.

The imminent demise of Maroon cultural life has repeatedly been forecast by outsiders over the full course of Maroon history, and countless observers have convinced themselves that theirs is the last account of a once-proud people who are losing their cultural identity and being absorbed into the Western world. My most recent encounter with friends from the Pikilio, during their trip to the United States, reminded me of how much of Saramakas' ideology, social perspectives, religious beliefs, sense of humor, motor habits, culinary preferences, technical skills, musical style, and aesthetic ideas remains, even in the face of persistent external pressures for assimilation into another way of life. It is true that an increasing number of Saramakas are being exposed to the campaigns of Christian missionaries; others are apparently being introduced to drugs and prostitution in the streets of Paramaribo; men are clearing gardens with gasoline-powered chain saws as well as axes; women are learning plastic macramé as well as embroidery; and children are growing up with a stronger sense than their parents had of the larger world beyond Saramaka and of their need to be able to operate in it. But these changes are still taking place in the context of an ongoing, dynamic cultural life, and the end is not yet in sight. As Saramakas watch their cultural life change, they sometimes lament the abandonment of things they enjoyed in their youth and sometimes criticize modern trends, but they never forget (as outside observers sometimes do) that their society's cultural vitality is based not only on customs established by its original members, but also on the new ideas and interests of their living descendants.

Chapter Two

A Woman's Place

Kinship lies at the heart of the Saramaka social system, and women lie at the heart of Saramaka kinship. A matrilineal ideology pervades Saramaka understandings about the world, and its influence is felt in every aspect of life, from residence and fosterage to marriage and inheritance. When people pray to ancestors for offspring, they lay explicit emphasis on girl children, since they are the ones who will "make the lineage" for future generations. In the Saramaka system, a kin group without daughters is doomed to extinction.

This focus on women in defining the structure of social relations should not be misinterpreted, however, as a focus on women in social life itself. While women are seen as responsible for perpetuating social groups, it is largely men who carry on the business of managing them, and Saramaka notions of gender include an unchallenged understanding that men are more qualified for these responsibilities than are women.

Men's and women's lives differ equally sharply in terms of their access to material goods, and this aspect of Saramaka understandings about the sexes has a strong influence on the nature of men's and women's arts and on their various contributions to social life. Except for cultivated products (garden crops and the fruits of certain domestic trees) and some forest products (such as palm nuts), virtually everything that women own must be provided for them by men. Even in terms of food, men supply the most desirable elements of the diet through fishing (in which the techniques used by men yield larger fish than those used by women) and, above all, hunting. Men build women's houses, canoes, and furniture, and they fashion out of wood most of the implements that women need for subsistence tasks, such as mortars, pestles, winnowing trays, food stirrers, and laundry beaters. Men also provide all imported manufactures that women use—from needles and hammocks to buckets and lanterns—as well as other essential products imported from the coast, such as salt, soap, and kero-

11

sene. Finally, certain coastal imports are kept in the possession of men
altogether. Saramakas consider watches, tape recorders, eyeglasses,
sewing machines, and outboard motors, for example, to be male possessions. In this context, women act mainly as processors rather than
providers of materials.

The implications of these facts for Saramaka artistic understandings will become clear in later chapters. Let us begin, however, by
looking at some of the more fundamental understandings about the
sexes that help shape the life experiences of Saramaka women.

Growing Up Female

In Saramaka ideology, the conceptual distinction between male and
female is pervasive and unambiguous, and sexual identity influences
every aspect of a person's life, beginning at birth. As soon as a baby of
either sex is "thrown to the ground," the umbilical cord is carefully
measured to reach the infant's knee before being severed with a
razor, but it must be the right knee for a girl and the left for a boy.[1]
While Saramakas are unanimous that the token clothing they assign
to infants is intended primarily to affirm the distinction between
people (who are clothed) and animals (who are naked), it also serves
to mark the distinction between males and females; girls wear a string
of commercial beads around their waist, while boys wear a black or
navy cord made of twisted cotton cloth. And as soon as they can walk,
Saramaka children become responsible for observing the distinction
between the special men's paths and women's paths that have been
established in many villages.

Little children are constantly reminded in a playful way about
their sex, most often by adults of their grandparents' generation, but
also by others. Men tease girls from infancy on by grabbing at their
"breasts" and genitals, and women often pull playfully at a little boy's
penis, interrogating him about whether he really knows how to use it
and whether he thinks it is big enough to satisfy them. A favorite way
of engaging a two- or three-year-old boy is to ask after his pregnant
wife or, for a girl, to inquire whether her recent labor pains were
severe, and children are expected to provide appropriate answers.
When three- or four-year-old children play at sexual intercourse,
adults are generally amused, expecting them to learn discretion in
these games as they grow older.

Young children of both sexes are always entrusted to the care of a woman (usually, though not always, their own mother), but this arrangement poses no special threat to the sexual identity of a boy, because he is consistently and explicitly assigned a "man's role" from a very early age.[2] While girls have infants tied onto their backs or are sent off to the river with dirty dishes to wash, boys are told to catch some fish for the next meal. And in traveling with children on the river, women start having their sons sit in the rear of the canoe as soon as possible (usually when the boy is about eight), since it is more appropriate for a canoe to be steered by a man than by a woman.[3]

Children's play is clearly molded by gender expectations (fig. 2). Beginning when they are two or three, little girls play at being preg-

Fig. 2. Children play at adult dress. *Left,* a skirt, cape, and waist-kerchief for girls and *right,* hunting gear for boys

nant, giving birth, nursing babies, tying "children" (gourds or, occasionally, a kitten) on their backs, and making formal visits to their "husbands' villages" (see, for example, the three girls on the jacket or cover of this book). Little boys stalk lizards and small birds, pack imaginary suitcases for trips to the coast, and drive scraps of wood along the ground, pretending that they are motorboats. And while all children like to practice the dances, songs, and speech patterns associated with the spirit world, little girls most often find themselves possessed by snake gods and little boys by warrior gods, reflecting the sex-typed distribution of actual spirit mediumships among men and women (to be discussed later).

Sex-typed skills are mastered at an early age. By the time boys are nine or ten, they have already tried their hand at wood carving on combs and food stirrers and may even have constructed a small open-sided cooking house for one of the women in their lineage. They help in clearing areas of the forest for gardens, supply small fish for the women who cook for them, and occasionally bring in birds or other small animals they have killed with a slingshot. By the age of ten or eleven, most boys have been allowed to fire a shotgun under the supervision of an older kinsman. Girls who are eight or nine know how to cook a full meal over a wood fire, crochet calfbands, harvest rice, and gather many wild forest products. They help in the tedious production of palm oil, care for young children, and on some days do as much dishwashing, laundry, and water carrying as their mothers.

The experiences of boys and girls on the Pikilio are also sharply divided in terms of their exposure to the outside world. During most of this century, it has been traditional for boys to be taken to the coast for an extended period by their father or another male kinsman at about the age of eight or ten. They would learn to speak a little Sranan-tongo, to buy things in a store, and to cross city streets, and they would acquire some familiarity with the ways in which Maroon men adapted to their temporary role in coastal society. In contrast, girls were usually taken on a very short buying trip to Paramaribo during their early teens, most often by their father. The express reason for such a trip was for the girl to "view the city" at least once in her life. Even this token trip has not always been considered essential to a girl's socialization; in 1968, eight of the forty-eight Dangogo women whose travel experience I asked about in detail had never been out of tribal territory. The introduction of mission schools into many areas has also affected boys differently from girls. In Dangogo in 1968, most of the school-age boys, but none of the girls, attended classes at the nearby mission. A Western education (which meant a rudimentary literacy in Dutch and some elementary arithmetic) was seen by many Saramakas as a possible advantage to young men in finding work on the coast, but only as a distraction from more useful pursuits for girls. Since the 1960s, both coastal trips and school attendance have increased slightly for Saramaka girls, but the sexual imbalance is still very great.

By the age of ten or eleven, Saramaka girls have already tasted almost every ingredient of a woman's life. They have participated in gardening alongside their older kinswomen (preparing the ground, planting, weeding, and harvesting crops). They have processed palm oil, winnowed rice, cleaned fish, skinned game, and cooked full meals. They have spent countless hours scrubbing pots and laundering clothes and hammocks at the river. They have cared for babies and young children, sometimes carrying them in a cloth tied onto their backs. They have danced for snake gods and forest spirits and participated in all communitywide ritual events. They have become relatively skillful at singing popular songs and telling folktales. They have sewn patchwork (or, since the 1970s, cross-stitch) textiles and crocheted their own calfbands. They have learned to navigate the river on their own. They have adopted the full range of address terms, including those for (classificatory) husband's kin. All have had some kind of sexual experience, most commonly digital penetration, and about half of them are formally betrothed to an older man. Unlike the boys of their age, who are still a decade or so away from social manhood, prepubescent girls are well aware that the responsibilities of marriage and child rearing will be theirs within a few short years (fig. 3).

Becoming a Woman

Around this time, the girl's father's lineage determines (in theory by watching the development of her nipples, which should have begun to protrude slightly) that she is ready to be socially recognized as an "apron girl" (koyó muyêè miíi), and a simple, brief ceremony is held in which one of them presents her with an unsewn piece of cloth that she will sew into an adolescent apron. Although she continues to wear

Fig. 3. *Left,* a girl taking care of her younger cousins in 1968 and *right,* one of her own children in 1974

such aprons until her first marriage, their size increases gradually, and by the time she is ready to receive the skirts of womanhood her apron may reach almost to her knees. In talking about teenage girls, people often specify their age by a comment on the size of their apron, and this has apparently been true for centuries. Tribal historians date Fankia, the woman known among Saramakas as the last survivor of their war of liberation, by the fact that she wore a very large apron when she participated in a downriver migration shortly after peace was concluded with the colonists (see R. Price 1983*a*:6).

The next several years are an unusually carefree time of life, and Saramakas recognize this in their formulaic phrase for its activities— "rejoicing with an apron" (*wái ku koyó*). Apron girls have most of the pleasures of adulthood and few of the responsibilities. They remain answerable to the person who has been raising them (whether their mother, their father, or another relative), and they continue to make a substantial contribution to domestic chores. But they also have a great deal of free time and lose few opportunities to enjoy the attention they are given by men, who generally consider them to be at the height of their sexual attractiveness. Apron girls are often teasing and flirtatious and enjoy alternating between seductive coyness and brash sassiness.

Close friendships with other women are especially important during the "apron" years. Although among adults it is men more often than women who establish formal friendships (addressing each other by the term *máti*, "friend," paying special visits, and exchanging periodic gifts), the declared friendships that I have heard about among teenagers all involved girls. Typically, an apron girl is attracted to a woman a few years older than she, declares her "love," and formally proposes the relationship, which lasts for several years. In addition to exchanging gifts and addressing each other as *máti*, they may cook together, wear matching clothes, braid each other's hair, and, in some cases, share a single hammock once in a while.[4]

During the apron years, girls also begin preparing their bodies for adult sexuality by having cicatrization designs incised (see R. and S. Price 1972*a*). Younger girls traditionally have two or three "seeds" cut on a forearm, just to introduce them to the pain they must be willing to bear. But it is only after the apron is given that a woman will carefully lay out decorative patterns on the girl's chest and belly with a kaolin and water solution, cut small gashes in the skin with a razor blade, and rub in irritants to encourage the buildup of scar tissue (fig. 4). Although these designs will need to be "wakened" by being recut periodically over the subsequent years before they attain the desired beadlike effect, and although the more explicitly erotic designs have yet to be cut on the buttocks and thighs, these first designs mark an important step toward sexual maturity.

Saramaka ritual practices recognize the special status of the apron stage of life in several ways. Apron girls are exempt from the important and complex rules of menstrual seclusion. During menstruation, an apron girl is expected simply to insert a small piece of cloth in her vagina and to continue her normal activities. And in large-scale rituals, apron girls are sometimes assigned a special role, partly because of the theory that their menstrual fluids cannot contaminate medicinal powers as those of socially mature women do. For example,

Fig. 4.   A woman whose facial cicatrizations
are quite typical for her generation

it is apron girls rather than socially mature women who must pound
and winnow the rice that is eaten at certain types of ritual feasts.

As with the transition from girlhood to adolescence, the development of a girl's breasts provides the traditional mark of readiness for
the rites of womanhood. People say that ideally a girl should be
passed from adolescent aprons to adult skirts as soon as her breasts
begin to "fall to the heart." In practice, many extenuating circumstances may hasten the event. If a girl is betrothed, her husband-to-be
often tries to persuade her kinsmen that she is ready to be married,
and he is sometimes successful. If an apron girl becomes pregnant,
she is given skirts and married immediately. Even without becoming

pregnant, a girl may be given skirts because she is sexually active. A
major scandal was caused during my first stay in Dangogo by a girl
who, according to local gossip, was inviting men to "Come fuck me.
I'm as hot as can be!" and it was considered resolved only when her
family reluctantly gave her skirts.[5] There are also rare cases in which
a young apron girl becomes possessed by a spirit and is immediately
given skirts so that she can serve properly as its medium.

No matter when the skirts are given, the timing of a girl's social
maturity presents a rich opportunity for village gossip. People enjoy
debating the wisdom of particular decisions—that of a physically im-
mature girl who was given skirts only because her precocious younger
sister was receiving them, that of a girl who did not begin menstruating until a year after she was given skirts, that of a girl whose elderly
stepfather delayed her marriageability so that he could enjoy clandestine sex with her, and so on.

Actual plans for giving a girl her skirts are made in great secrecy,
for she is expected to try to escape and must be grabbed by surprise.
Amid screams and physical struggling, she is dressed in two unsewn
skirt-cloths and a woman's waistkerchief is tied on top. She is then
presented with several other skirt-cloths and a few waistkerchiefs, and
a libation is poured to the ancestors to inform them that she has
become a woman. For most girls, the screams of protest reflect cultural tradition more than personal feeling. Although older Saramakas
say this rite once signaled the end of childhood freedom and the onset
of adult burdens, young girls now tend to view it more in terms of the
increased sexual liberty it implies.

Regardless of when a girl reaches menarche, it is only after the
skirt-giving ceremony that she is first introduced (ritually "pushed")
into the communal menstrual hut by a female relative, who admon-
ishes her to observe the rules of seclusion beginning with her next
menstrual period. During her first several-day stay in the hut, older
women provide some of her food, and they mark her emergence
from the polluted state by whitening her with kaolin and placing a
special fiber tie around her neck. After that, her observance of menstrual prohibitions is exactly like that of older women.

Girls are expected to marry soon after the skirt ceremony, and in
fact most have husbands within the year. In the brief period between
recognition of their marriageability and the marriage itself, girls'
dress carries a subtle recognition of the transition. At this stage, a girl

wears one rather than two skirt layers,[6] she continues to wear her waist tie and adolescent apron underneath, and her skirt is significantly shorter than those of married women. The rites of marriage symbolize the completion of a girl's passage to womanhood through the cutting of the waist tie. The husband, after lifting the girl out of her own hammock and into his, breaks the string and puts both it and the apron into his hunting sack.

On the occasion of her first marriage, the girl's older kinswomen present her with a beaded belt that carries special significance (see S. and R. Price 1980a: fig. 110). Composed of several strands with differently colored commercial beads, this "wrestling belt" will be worn only for lovemaking. Like the cicatrizations that the girl will now begin to have cut on her buttocks and inner thighs, the beads provide an important tactile stimulation and are intimately associated with her eroticism. A woman never shows her wrestling belt to men other than her lovers, and she may send it off with her husband when he goes to the coast to work, as a symbol of her intended fidelity. Although she may restring it at some point in her life, perhaps even reducing the number of strands as she gets older, she will never give it away. After death, it must be laid into her coffin along with the rest of the clothing required for a proper burial.

By about the age of sixteen, most girls have married and assumed full adult status. At this point, a young woman's behavior during menstruation, her participation in rituals, her manner of dressing, and her acquisition of body cicatrizations all reflect the completion of her passage from adolescence to womanhood. In most cases, her closest personal relationships continue to be with matrilineally related women (sisters, mothers, mother's sisters, and so on), but in addition to the house where she lives in their neighborhood, she is expected to have another in her husband's village.[7] She also becomes independent in terms of producing, storing, and managing food supplies. Rather than cooperating with her mother, sisters, and mother's sisters, she now works a garden cleared specially for her. Finally, she is making one of the most socially significant passages of her life by entering her childbearing years.

The remaining sections of this chapter explore Saramaka women's place in religious life, their contribution to the food supply, and their role in the raising of children. Chapter 3 then describes some of the ways in which their lives are affected by relationships with husbands, co-wives, and affines.

Pollution, Possession, and Power

Saramaka women's reproductive functions both define their major contribution to the society and circumscribe their participation in it. Women's children "make" their lineages, and women's uterine fluids endanger almost all ritual powers.

A belief in the polluting force of childbirth and menstruation stands behind an extensive range of ritual prohibitions. Both phenomena are carefully isolated from men and their ritual powers, which means that women's involvement in ritual life is restricted in important ways. The contamination of a house in which a baby is delivered is threatening to men, but not to women. During the birth, the men sit outside, well away from the house where a group of women are assisting with the labor. The men may help by praying or consulting oracles about the cause and solution of problems, but they never approach the house. After the birth the house must be specially purified before any man may enter it.

During menstruation, women may not approach any structure except those specially designated for menstruating women. Villages have one or two such houses (*faági*), which are built and maintained by women once men have set the corner posts, and sometimes an open-sided cooking shed as well (fig. 5). Each horticultural camp also includes some kind of shelter for this purpose (fig. 6). Some of the more serious ritual involvements of men (e.g., serving as the "priest" of certain oracles) place a permanent prohibition on physical proximity and verbal contact with menstruating women; and men, women, and children who have participated in ritual ablutions are frequently enjoined from speaking with them until the next day. It is the woman's own responsibility to see that these restrictions are respected. When in doubt, she does not answer a greeting directly, but looks away and announces that she is "outside" (*a dôò*). The fact that menstruating women are segregated from much social life encourages them to spend time at their horticultural camps, and it is rare for a woman to stay in her husband's village while she is menstruating unless she has no other convenient alternatives. Menstruating women must walk around, rather than through, the palm-leaf structures that mark village entrances, and in each village there are particular areas and paths that are banned to them as well. Menstruating women may not sit on stools, touch small babies, burn a garden site, plant crops, wash clothes at designated stones in the river, hand anything to a

Fig. 5.   The Dangogo menstrual hut

man, skin game or cook food for men, travel in a canoe with a man, or
carry water that will be used by others. Reference to the menstrual
hut as the "bad house" (*taku ósu*) and the fact that a single expression
(*dê a baáka*) means "to be in menstrual seclusion" and "to be in mourning" are true reflections of the tone of a woman's life during those
times.[8]

A woman's emergence from menstrual seclusion is marked in
several ways. She removes her belongings from the menstrual hut,
launders the hammock she slept in, and bathes. Special greetings are
reserved for the occasion. A woman still in the menstrual hut may ask,
"Are you going to Saramaka?" (*I nángó a Saamáka?*) and others often
comment, in a culinary/sexual double entendre, "Feast today!" (*Gaán
nyán tidé!*), since the woman is expected both to cook a special meal for
her husband and to sleep with him that night. In Saramaka understandings, it is immediately after a menstrual period that a woman can
become pregnant, and a man whose wife has just emerged from the
menstrual hut should sleep with her in preference to any of his other

Fig. 6.   A house (*left*) and shelter for menstruating women (*right*) in a horticultural camp

wives who are available. ~~This is considered a special time in terms of sex, and it is sometimes enhanced by a renewal of some of the woman's cicatrization designs on her last day of seclusion, since the scars are thought to be particularly erotic when freshly cut.~~ Emergence from menstrual seclusion is also marked in marriage customs for a girl who was betrothed during adolescence. On the day that she leaves the hut after her first stay there (that is, at the conclusion of her first menstrual period as a socially recognized adult), a messenger is dispatched to the prospective husband, who comes that night to consummate the marriage.

Compliance with menstrual prohibitions is understood as a serious moral responsibility, and women on the Pikilio are quite rigorous in their observance of them, even when it means personal hardship. A woman may be forced to cancel a trip she had arranged to make in a motorized canoe because of the ban on traveling with a man, to postpone an important ritual because her god cannot be summoned while she is menstruating, or to relinquish a planned night with her husband and watch him go off instead to meet a lover or sleep with another of his wives. When a man from the Pikilio takes a wife from a "missionized" village downstream (where the practice of menstrual seclusion has been abandoned), his kin and neighbors invariably object on the grounds that she will "hide" her state and destroy the power of local medicines.[9]

Partly because of beliefs about female pollution, women are ineligible for most positions of authority in Saramaka ritual life. While men have many outlets for their religious energies, including village oracles (*sóói-gádu*), individual possession spirits (*gádu a hédi*), powers dating from the war of liberation (*gaán óbia*), political/religious positions recognized by the Suriname government (chief, headman, assistant headman), and various aspects of ancestor worship (from the *papá* funeral cult to the supervision of ancestral feasts), women's opportunities for specialized ritual roles are confined largely to their involvements with possession spirits. Not surprisingly, then, men tend to regard possession spirits as a relatively minor force in the overall life of the community, while women view them as a unique opportunity for power and prestige.

As an example of this difference in the concerns of men and women, let us look briefly at the distribution of ritual positions in the village of Dangogo. The single most important religious authority in the community is *Gaan Tata* (Great Father), an oracle bundle imported from Djuka villages on the Tapanahoni River in the final decades of the nineteenth century. Gaan Tata is interrogated about virtually all village problems—from sickness and accidents to marital disputes and the raising of children. The twice-weekly sessions in which Gaan Tata is consulted, as well as the other rituals in which he participates, are conducted exclusively by men. Although women are present, men always serve as the "priests" of the cult, as the interrogators at oracle sessions, and as the bearers of the bundle itself. Furthermore, since the most stringent prerequisites for Gaan Tata's ongoing assistance in village problems concern the observance of menstrual prohibitions, women are periodically restricted even from approaching the area of the village where this oracle resides. In the Niukonde section of Dangogo (located on the east side of the river—see fig. 1), Gaan Tata's local equivalent—*Mama Gadu* (Mother God)—exerts almost as great an influence, and is likewise handled exclusively by men. (For a photograph of this oracle bundle supervising a ritual, see S. and R. Price

1980*a*:pl. VI.) Men also serve as the priests of Dungulali, a richly elaborated cult housed in the Niukonde section of Dangogo that established separate paths for men and women there and has for several decades provided important medicines for all Dangogo residents. Among its many services, Dungulali furnishes medicinal leaf mixtures that are bottled and used for a wide range of symptoms, as well as other leaf mixtures that are used in jewelry for ritual protection, in water for purificatory washings, and in special pipes that produce curative smoke. Political positions are likewise filled only by men— except for the recently created post of "Female Assistant" (*muyêè basiá*), whose duties consist of cooking and sweeping at community events. And after a death, it is the men of the community who orchestrate the complex sequence of communal events in which the body is buried, the village purified, the cause of death determined, the inheritance distributed, and a new ancestral persona established.

Even when we focus attention on the cults of possession spirits, in which women as well as men can serve as specialists, we find that sex figures importantly in the distribution of power.

First, more women than men become mediums for possession gods. Not only do more gods speak through women than men, but it is largely women who act as multiple mediums—sometimes taking on as many as four or five different spirits. Among lineage members in Dangogo in 1968, for example, about one-half of the women but only one-sixth of the men served as mediums. The distribution was as follows.

	Number of Mediumships per Person				
	0	1	2	3	4
Men	38	7	1	0	0
Women	29	17	5	3	2

Second, the characteristics of certain possession gods that tend to be associated with women differ from those that are more closely associated with men, and this defines different social roles for their respective mediums. In Saramaka there are many different kinds of possession spirits—dead people; forest spirits; water gods; several types of gods that live in the bodies of snakes, caymans, jaguars, and other animals; and a number of others as well. Among these, the only type that does not speak through both male and female mediums is *komantí*—the warrior gods that live in jaguars or, more rarely, buzzards.[10] *Komantí* mediums wield machetes, eat broken glass, walk on fire, and perform other feats of strength, and their spirits are, without exception, identified as males. Saramakas say that *komantí* gods have wives but that these female *komantí* never interact with human society because their husbands make them stay at home, deep in the forest. *Komantí* (also referred to simply as *óbia,* "ritual medicine"), are best known for their curing powers, which are used mainly for serious illnesses. Saramakas recall the occasion upon which a particular individual was cured by a *komantí* medium as a major event in that person's life, and the cure is commemorated by the person's permanent observance of *komantí* ritual prohibitions.

Women have no class of gods that is exclusively under their control, and they may serve as mediums for any type of god except a *komantí,* but at the same time there is a strong association, both statistical and conceptual, between women and two general classes of gods—snake gods and forest spirits. Of the forty-four spirits that spoke through female mediums in Dangogo in 1967–68, thirty-seven belonged to these two classes; twenty-six were snake gods, and eleven were forest spirits. *Vodú,* snake gods that live in the bodies of boa constrictors, are the most closely associated with the women's world. Even the drum used for snake-god rituals—the *agidá*—is conceptualized as female and "dressed" in a woman's skirt. In contrast to *komantí* gods, which serve chiefly as benefactors, *vodú* gods are avenging spirits and more often interact with Saramakas as aggressors who demand appeasement. *Vodú* become active in Saramaka life only after they have been molested, usually through the inadvertent killing of their boa constrictor body during the burning of a woman's garden site. Once the death is discovered, complex funeral rites are held and the remains of the snake are buried in a special coffin. From that time on, the god takes periodic revenge on the lineage of the person responsible for its death and demands frequent rituals of appeasement, communicating its wishes to the community through a particular human medium. Women play an important role in *vodú* rituals, performing the graceful, fluid dance of the snake gods whether or not they serve as a medium. In Dangogo, twenty-four of the twenty-six *vodú* gods had female mediums, and the two that spoke through men were considerably less active than the rest.

In a sense, *vodú* constitute a more self-contained part of Saramaka culture than *komantí*. While the cults of both classes of gods are equally visible aspects of Saramaka ritual life, the activity of *vodú* gods tends to be more focused on the infliction of minor sicknesses (which are later cured through rituals conducted in their honor), the announcement of dissatisfactions and demands, and participation in the elaborate ritual complexes necessary to redress the offenses against them. In contrast, the role of *komantí* gods is conceptualized more in terms of the positive influence they exert in life-and-death situations. Although the specific powers of each individual *komantí* are slightly different, this class of gods generally intervenes in cases of serious illness, gunshot wounds, and machete accidents; *komantí* provide special protection in physical fights; and during the last stage of funeral rites they are important agents in expelling the ghost of the dead person from the village. Hence, while *vodú* are more numerous and more lavishly feted, and while their mediums enjoy the personal status, power, and ritual attention that result from special access to these active spirits, Saramakas tend to perceive *komantí* as embodying a more powerful and more positive force. As one middle-aged man commented, after declaring that he would like to be possessed by a *komantí* but not by a *vodú*, "With a *vodú*, you have to take care of the god; it doesn't take care of you. It causes more harm than good. But women love so much to have *vodú*, because those gods like to dress in fancy clothes and strut around—just like women!" It is clear from remarks made among men that while both sexes cooperate closely to produce the rituals required by *vodú*, men are inclined to see these, within the context of their other religious and political obligations, as a relatively minor form of social action.

Women and Their Gardens

The most important material contribution that women make to Saramaka life is the growing and processing of rice, which is the daily staple. The word for cooked rice (*nyanyá*) serves also as the general word for food, and when Saramakas talk about periods of "hunger," they are referring explicitly to a poor rice harvest.[11] The two main meals of the day (in the morning and evening) consist of heaping bowls of rice and smaller amounts of meat, fish, or vegetable sauces. Other cooked dishes (e.g., plantains, taro, sweet potatoes, palm fruits, corn, and manioc) are known as "little foods" (*pikí nyanyá*), and are generally served only at midday, as a secondary supplement to the rice-based meals.

The gardens where women grow both rice and "little foods" are usually located at some distance from their villages, and every able-bodied woman transports herself back and forth between village and camp in her own canoe (figs. 7 and 8). Small groups of women (for example, an older woman, some of her adult daughters, and one or two of her daughters-in-law) share a single camp, though each works her own garden(s). Travel to these camps typically begins with a several-hour canoe trip up the river to a creek leading into the forest. Once the canoes are tied at a landing area, people continue on narrow and overgrown paths that often pass through creeks and swampy marshes. The entrance to a camp, like that to a village, is protected by an open palm-leaf gateway, and the ground itself is kept carefully scraped of all vegetation. Each woman has a small house, and there

Fig. 7.   A Saramaka woman harvesting rice in her garden

are open-sided structures for cooking and crop storage as well as some kind of shelter that serves as a menstrual hut. There are generally no men's houses, for men are guests rather than residents in Saramaka horticultural camps. Their visits are intended to provide specific services, such as felling the trees for a new garden or helping to build a new house and, even with extra time for hunting and fishing in the surrounding forest, these visits rarely last more than a few days.

For Saramakas, the atmosphere of such camps differs in many ways from that of the villages. While villages are generally built close to the river itself, most camps are located farther into the forest near a small creek. Isolated clearings in a vast tropical rain forest, camps constantly ring with the cries of birds and monkeys; forest animals, from turtles and sloths to jaguars and peccary, are occasional visitors; and the paths that connect the houses with individual gardens are darkened by canopies of tropical flora that partially shut out the light of day.

Fig. 8.   A Saramaka woman paddling her canoe

Life in the camps is at once more demanding and more relaxed than life in the villages. I have seen women spend as much as twelve hours in the tropical sun harvesting rice, breaking only briefly for a midday meal, and other tasks—such as weeding gardens, planting crops, or processing manioc—are done with a similar intensity. Nevertheless, women consistently express a preference for camp over village life. They cite the freedoms they enjoy—to wear ragged clothes if they like, to be less exacting about the etiquette of meals, and even to enjoy a relaxed evening of folktales, which are prohibited in the village except during funeral rituals. They also talk about being exclusively in the company of close kin, away from the social tensions of the larger community.[12] And they view the camp as a bounteous storehouse: the whole range of domestic crops is readily available; useful forest products, from edible palm fruits to roofing materials, are close at hand; the trees felled for garden sites provide a convenient supply of firewood; and the yields for every kind of fishing and hunting are many times greater than they are around the villages.

The Saramaka ideal is for each woman to have a "dry season garden" (deéwéi goón) and a "New Year's garden" (yái goón). New sites are selected in July. During the major dry season (August to mid-November), the lower vegetation is cut with machetes, the large trees are felled with axes, and the area is burned in preparation for planting—first of "little foods" and later of rice. For a dry season garden, the rice is planted in March, April, or May and ripens during the following dry season. New Year's gardens are usually second plantings of previously cultivated areas, but they may also be small sites cleared at the outskirts of the woman's village; in these, rice is planted in January and harvested the following May or June. Second plantings (woóko kákísa, "working the chaff") may also follow the timing of a dry season garden, though this is less frequent.

The standard division of labor is for a man to select the site (after considering the ritual restrictions that apply to different areas and discussing alternatives with the woman who will work it), cut the underbrush, fell the trees, and finally burn the garden. Women then take over, hoeing the ground and planting, weeding, and harvesting the crops. However, women sometimes cut the underbrush themselves (for example, when they have no husband and their brothers and uncles are busy with other gardens), and it is not at all rare for a woman to burn her own garden site. In general, women are more conservative than men about the strategy for burning gardens. Men prefer to gamble on the rains and wait until a site is fully dried by several weeks of strong sunshine, but women often "throw fire" on the site earlier, because of anxiety about the onset of the rains. Women recount with great satisfaction the cases in which a woman's decision to burn a garden site was followed immediately by a heavy rain.

The horticultural cycle not only structures the pace of women's work in the camps, but also influences the content of daily conversation in the villages. At the end of the dry season, for example, women help each other keep careful track of how many days have elapsed since the clearing of various gardens belonging to them and their neighbors and kinswomen. There are animated discussions about exactly when the rains are due to begin, and people comment at length on the success or failure with which each garden site burns. Later, the progress of each garden continues to be a matter of public knowledge within a several-village area, as people remark, for example, on which women are planting rice on a given day, whether or not a particular field is being reused for a peanut crop, or how a certain woman's rice is being devoured by birds because she is visiting her husband and has not had time to begin harvesting it.

What this means is that the potentially monotonous business of growing and processing food—which requires every woman to master the same skills as every other and to repeat them year after year for her entire active life—has become a highly individualized pursuit. Not only do people express interest in the variables that make each woman's garden subtly different, but they also enjoy individualizing the crops themselves. Saramaka women distinguish (and have names for) about fifteen to twenty varieties each of okra, sweet potatoes, yams, taro, bananas, and manioc.

They also differentiate a vast number of rice varieties and maintain the origin of each as part of their cultural knowledge. I have elicited the names for seventy-four varieties (of which many have multiple names and twenty are further divided into named subvarieties), but because I still encounter new varieties each time I ask, I have no reason to believe that I have even approached a complete list. Each variety is classified as "red" or "white" (depending on the darkness of its grains), and associated with details of its appearance, the time it takes to ripen, the difficulty with which it is hulled, and the history of its introduction to the region. Furthermore, each woman maintains separate seed supplies of many different varieties, and sows these in different sections of her garden to create a patchwork effect. While her preferences for some varieties over others often reflect practical considerations (e.g., when they ripen or how hard they are to hull), her arrangement of them within the garden is primarily an aesthetic matter, in which an explicit attempt to juxtapose "red" and "white" varieties combines with attention to plant height, grain size, shape, density, and other visible variables. Like other aspects of horticultural life, the layout of rice varieties in particular gardens is of general interest, and the fact that each one is named enriches the detail with which people discuss women's activities. They comment, for example, that one woman's *tjêke muyêè* (an early-ripening variety) is saving her from a serious rice shortage, that another woman has finished harvesting all but her *alêkesoóla*, or that another's *wáta dágu* is being eaten by birds.[13]

It is worth noting that this vast array of rice varieties is a recent development. People born in the 1920s assert that there were no more than four or five varieties when they were adolescents—"forest rice" (*mátu alísi*— used mainly in rituals), "true rice" (*alísi seéi*), a red variety of "true rice" (*bè alísi seéi*), and one or two types of "little rice" (*pikí alísi*). The rapid proliferation of "little rice" types has been fueled from the coastal region of Suriname, where individual Saramakas learned about them, one by one, from East Indians and Javanese and began trying them out in their own gardens once they returned to Saramaka. This phenomenon represents one example (among many) of the fact that while Saramaka contact with the outside world has sometimes led to the gradual demise of particular cultural traditions (e.g., men's cicatrizations), it has also sometimes contributed to the gradual *creation* of other (equally rich and uniquely Saramaka) cultural traditions.

The harvesting of crops is followed by their transformation into edible foods, and this too is the responsibility of women. Saramaka women spend many hours a week pounding rice in a wooden mortar and winnowing it on a large round tray. On most days they cook rice in the morning and again in the evening, rinsing it first in several waters and later shaping it carefully into the smooth hemispheres required for men's meals, piling it loosely into large bowls for their own and their children's meals, and moistening the crust at the bottom for later consumption, usually by children.

Women also devote very large amounts of time to the processing of other foods. One example is cooking oil. Women gather palm nuts from the forest and, once the thin edible layer has been eaten as snacks and the pits have been dried for several weeks in the sun or over a fire, they begin the laborious process of converting them into cooking oil. First, the pits are cracked between two rocks and the white nutmeat is picked out in bits and pieces with a small knife—a task that takes place in a leisurely fashion over many days. These nutmeats are then winnowed (to remove any pieces of pit that may be mixed in), cooked over a wood fire in a sawed-off oil drum, and pounded in a mortar. Finally, this mashed substance is boiled in water and the oil itself is skimmed off the surface. It is perhaps not surprising that women often include a bottle of cooking oil in formal gift presentations to their husbands, even though men do not use it themselves, for oil rendering (like a smoothly mounded bowl of rice) epitomizes women's work, and the final product is viewed by Saramakas as an important symbol of wifely devotion and conscientiousness.[14]

Women and Their Children

A conventional piece of Saramaka wisdom likens women to hearthstones and men to axe handles. Once a set of hearthstones is fashioned and placed in a house, it is never moved away, just as a girl who is born into a community is expected to stay there and, eventually, produce children for her own lineage. In contrast, an axe handle, carried from place to place, is simply thrown away wherever it happens to break, just as a boy is raised to travel all around, providing offspring for others but leaving none for his own lineage.

This image nicely highlights the social value of women in Saramaka, for it is only the women of each lineage who can assure its perpetuation. Through their children, it is women who "make the lineage." In both prayers and informal discussions, Saramakas repeatedly stress this aspect of their social organization and make clear that, although male and female offspring are both desired, it is girls who are "most essential." At the news of a birth, there is a special aura of excitement if the child is a girl. One reaction to a boy's birth is hopeful speculation that, by the law of averages, the woman's next child will be a girl. And when children play house, the girls who become pregnant

and give birth to little gourd dolls invariably identify them as
daughters.

Abortion accusations also reflect the strength of attitudes about
girls versus boys. Two of the three cases that I heard about during the
1960s involved personal clandestine rituals designed to abort the
pregnancy if it was a boy, but to bring it to term if it was a girl. While
everyone expressed shock and outrage at the notions of birth control
and abortion, the idea that anyone could want not to produce a future
lineage daughter was almost inconceivable.

As each girl grows up, she is constantly reminded of her importance as a childbearer and provider of lineage members. Once she is
physically mature, her relatives' motivation to give her the skirts of
adulthood and her first husband is explicitly linked to their desire for
children. Young women whose husbands stay away on the coast for
more than a year or two are often encouraged to take another husband so that they can begin to produce children, and infertile women
are similarly coaxed to divorce and remarry in the hope that another
husband might be able to make them pregnant.

Within this context, the state of pregnancy assumes great significance, and pregnant women are treated with special attention. Many
steps are taken to assure the proper development of the fetus. The
father of the child has a responsibility (considered especially crucial
for a woman's first pregnancy) to nurture it through frequent intercourse, and he is expected to adjust his plans (e.g., to cancel a planned
trip to the coast) in order to fulfill it.[15] Many spiritual powers are
called upon during the course of each pregnancy to diagnose and
cure various problems and complications. Oracles are interrogated,
possession gods summoned, and minor forms of divination consulted.
Their responses lead to special prayers, offerings to gods and ancestors, ritual washings and sprayings, the making of medicinal necklaces, and so on. Furthermore, both parents-to-be take on a complex
set of prohibitions for the duration of the pregnancy. The man, for
example, may not hunt deer or tapirs, do the hammering for a new
canoe, construct a house frame, use a shovel, harvest coconuts, help
with a burial, or take on a new wife. The woman must observe the *táta
tjína* (father's ritual prohibition) of the unborn child, refrain from
eating the fish known as *nduyá*, and switch from hot to cold water for
her morning ablutions.[16] If a woman's husband dies while she is
pregnant, she follows none of the customary procedures for mourn-

ing, and is even offered (though she invariably declines) the sexual services of one of the man's brothers in order to nurture the baby's development. In large-scale ritual washings, it is often specified that pregnant women must be washed before anyone else. Not only is the well-being of these women of special concern to the community, but they are considered more vulnerable to supernatural aggression. As one man commented, in explaining the constant bustle of ritual activity that attends a pregnancy, this is a phenomenon that causes every hostile power to perk up and take notice.[17]

Whenever possible, childbirth takes place in a house in the village and is attended by a woman experienced in helping with deliveries, as well as by a variety of kinswomen. Seated on a rolled-up cloth on the dirt floor, the woman in labor is supported by someone sitting behind her, while the "midwife" sits facing her, ready to grasp the child as it begins to appear.[18] The births I have witnessed have been dominated by loud and animated discussions about techniques and customs—when to do what, how to deal with complications, whether divination is necessary to diagnose a particular problem, and so on. The woman may be rubbed with oil, sprayed with rum, fed with broth, or even suspended upside-down for a few moments. Possession gods may make brief appearances through their mediums, and, outside the house just within earshot, the baby's father sits with a group of men, ready to raise oracle bundles or perform rituals as they are called for.

Once the baby is born, there are further ritual procedures, with the details varying according to the personal experience of the woman in charge. The child may be rubbed with the pulp of a smashed calabash fruit, washed in various waters, and blown on. There are libations, verbal thanks to different gods, formal hand clapping, and celebratory drinks of rum and soft drinks. A spontaneously composed song may be sung in honor of the child. One or two names may be called out for the child by older men and/or women. The afterbirth is prepared for burial by being set on a bark dustpan and covered with special leaves, and the house is ritually purified.[19] The father of the baby presents a cloth to his wife and performs special chores for her. He cuts a large supply of firewood, carries water from the river for her to bathe in, and then goes hunting, for meat and fish are considered essential for the "power" of her breast milk.

The baby is kept in the house for periods varying from a week to three months (depending on personal preference, regional custom, and circumstances of the birth) and then is presented to the community in a ceremony known as "bringing [the baby] outside" (*púu a dôò*). As relatives sit around on stools outside the house, a person carrying the baby steps over the threshold and draws back twice, emerging the third time to walk along a white line drawn in kaolin and to hand the baby to its mother. Oracle bundles often supervise this ceremony (see S. and R. Price 1980*a*: pl. VI), in which the mother and child are ritually washed and given a special solution to drink. The baby's bottom is playfully "bumped" against the ground, the roof of the house, and other places, as a ritual encouragement of the child's physical liveliness in the coming years. The baby is also tied onto its mother's back for the first time, explicitly to set a precedent (*púu tjína* —literally, "remove the ritual prohibition"). Finally, rum and soft drinks are served and gifts are exchanged among the mother, father, and others present (see chap. 4).

For the first several years, the child stays with its mother constantly, sharing her hammock, nursing, and spending much of its time tied onto her back as she goes about her daily tasks. Anyone visiting with the woman is given the baby to hold for a while and young girls are occasionally asked to "distract" (*ganyá*) it when the woman needs a few moments to herself (see fig. 3 left), but otherwise mothering is a full-time responsibility. Once children learn to walk, they receive their first hammock, though they continue to nap on their mother's back during the day and to nurse at her breasts. Three- and four-year-old children are generally still under the care of their mothers, but may be taken by other adults for a day or two when, for example, the mother attends a funeral, spends a day cutting rice, or gives birth to a new child.

Past infancy, there is no automatic assumption that a child will remain with its mother, and "parenting" may be provided by any relative. A five- or six-year-old child with a younger sibling or two, for example, may start to spend days with her grandmother. This eases the mother's busy life and provides companionship and domestic help for the grandmother, for the child can already assist with tasks such as washing dishes and bringing water from the river. Or a nine-year-old boy may be taken on a coastal trip by his father or mother's brother and then stay on with that person when he returns to Saramaka. Some such relationships work out well for both the adults and the children and continue for many years. Others develop tensions or are discontinued for situational reasons—for example, when a woman moves into a new husband's village and the girl she is raising wants to remain near her mother's kin.

Whether such parenting relationships are established suddenly or take definition gradually, they are always negotiated, confirmed, and legitimized through community discussion and consultation of the gods and ancestors. In Dangogo, for example, where the oracle of Gaan Tata serves as a powerful voice in village affairs, decisions about the parenting of individual children are always subject to his influence and approval. Doubts about a particular woman's devotion to her own children, concern that a twelve-year-old boy has not yet experienced coastal life, attention to the needs of an older woman who can no longer provide her own water supply, disputes between divorcing parents about the future of their children, and so on, inevitably pass back and forth between village gossip and formal oracle sessions. Over time, different viewpoints are laid out and debated and eventually an arrangement is established.[20]

For women, bearing a child and raising a child are significant for different reasons. A woman who gives birth is seen as providing the most precious "good" that can be given—a new person for her lineage. Declarations that children are the most valuable "commodity" pepper prayers and oratorical statements. This attitude represents an unshakable cornerstone of Saramaka thinking. The relationship between mother and child becomes, in this context, the most structurally important relationship in the society, exerting more influence than any other factor on the child's social network, residence possibilities, and marriage constraints. From the mother's point of view, it is by producing children that she guarantees for herself not only care in her old age, but also prominence as an ancestor, once she dies.

Raising a child (whether or not it is her own biological offspring) brings rewards on a more daily level. Although Saramakas frequently engage in animated discussions about the naughtiness, disobedience, irresponsibility, laziness, and contentiousness of the children growing up around them, and although disciplinary whippings are a source of great entertainment, women are also unanimous that life without children would be lonely and difficult indeed. Women prefer not to travel alone or to sleep alone in a house. They benefit from the services that even a fairly young child can provide, and they develop real pride as they watch the child grow up under their care and become a functioning member of the adult community. Between a woman and the child she has raised there is affection and strong solidarity that is based in the mutual voluntariness of their relationship.

We have seen in this chapter that the life experiences of Saramaka women are strongly influenced by cultural assumptions about femaleness, by the matrilineal foundation of their kinship system, by understandings about pollution and the distribution by sex of ritual powers and privileges, by the division of labor and the calendar of subsistence activities, and by expectations about their role in bearing and raising children. The Saramaka institution of marriage reflects all these influences and provides the only context within which a woman can fulfill the role expected of her. Yet Saramaka women spend more time apart from husbands than with them, and most end their lives without a husband at all. Chapter 3 will introduce the relationships that Saramakas expect women to develop as a result of their conjugal histories and will explore some of the rewards and frustrations of married and unmarried life.

Chapter Three

Wives, Husbands, and More Wives

It used to be that all the men of the world lived in one village and all the women in another. No man had ever ventured into the women's village and survived, but one day Anasi the Trickster-Spider devised a clever and mischievous scheme. Hiding on his back in a hollowed-out log that the women stepped over on their way to the river, and working through a discreet hole that he made just large enough to accommodate his penis, he surreptitiously introduced every one of them to the pleasure of sex. The entertaining Saramaka folktale that describes this escapade honors Anasi as the founding father of sexual relations, and remarks that "That is how our present way of life began."[1]

The idea of one man having sexual access to many women is a primary determinant of Saramaka social life. Although both men and women characteristically have a number of lovers and spouses in the course of their lifetime, the imbalance between men's and women's sexual opportunities exerts a profound influence on conjugal relations and on the character of social interaction more generally. This chapter explores some of the ways in which women's lives are shaped by the Saramaka definition of sex and marriage by examining sexual relationships, men's attitudes toward women, women's relationships with their husbands' kin and other wives, and the ways in which opportunities for sex and marriage change with age. These materials constitute essential background for the subsequent chapters on artistic production and exchange for, as we will see, the meeting ground of Saramaka social and artistic life is, incontestably, the institution of marriage.

Affairs and Marriages

Sexual banter is enjoyed by Saramakas of all ages. Toddlers are frequently teased about sex and encouraged to develop their verbal wit in this direction, elderly women love to issue brash sexual challenges and to reminisce about the days of small breechcloths when, given the correct angle, you could enjoy a good view of a man's testicles, and so on. When this kind of joking is exchanged between sexually active people, it often ends in a clandestine rendezvous. A teenager whose husband had gone to the coast a few months earlier, for example, once complained to a young man in my presence that she had not been feeling well. He offered to diagnose the problem for her, describing at length how he would have to feel all around until he arrived at a certain place that God had given her. "What place is that," she inquired coyly. "A very special place that was made to be shared with others," he replied. He then amused her with tall tales about the size of his penis. Even if they slept at opposite ends of the village, he boasted, he would still be able to make her pregnant. In the course of the conversation, she mentioned casually that she always slept alone in her house, and the stage was set.

Partly as a result of such exchanges, nights are a time of active travel on the Suriname River and its tributaries, as men quietly paddle through the darkness to villages where lovers await them. A woman whose husband was away for the night once remarked, "All men 'walk about' [have affairs] too much. As soon as night falls, they're out there on the water, and they just keep fooling around until dawn, without even sleeping." Although sexual adventures may be initiated by either the man or the woman, men seem to take special pleasure in recounting experiences in which they played a passive role and were seduced by an extraordinarily beautiful (and often anonymous) woman. In some, the encounter culminates in the discovery that the woman had been a female forest spirit disguised as a human being. In all, it is the man's personal irresistibility that drives the woman mad with desire and leads her to pursue him. I cite here two variations of a favorite theme that were told during a men's meal in Dangogo.[2]

One man related how an attractively fat Saramaka woman once got off a bus with him in the coastal village of Balen. Walking along, they came to a creek, where she asked him to hold her towel while she bathed. He stood motionless on the bank and watched as she removed first her dress, then her slip, and finally her underpants. There were her beadlike cicatrizations, glistening in the sun! Then she went to the side of the stream where she defecated and then urinated, he said, providing graphic sound effects for each bodily function. After she bathed, she put on her underpants, her slip, and her dress and said,

"Let's go." She took him to her house and told him that she slept there all alone. Unfortunately, he said, he was recovering from a hernia operation, so he simply told her good-bye and walked away.

Inspired by this episode, an older man followed it with the story of a local woman who once asked him to accompany her upstream to her garden. At dawn they met at a designated bend in the river. She then joined him in his canoe, and they continued to the landing place of her horticultural camp. Halfway along the forest path, she announced that she was hot and tired and would like to wash off in the creek. The man telling the story detailed the removal of each piece of clothing and, like his younger friend, stressed that he watched the entire process without moving or making a sound. When she was finished bathing, they went to her house in the camp. There he sat down on a stool and stared and stared at her until he could stand it no longer, and they finally made love.

An extramarital relationship may continue secretly for some time because of various kinds of obstacles to marriage. A woman who is having an affair while her husband is on the coast would be giving up a great deal if she remarried before he returned and distributed the supplies that he bought there. Lovers whose kinship ties or ritual involvements could cause them problems often try to keep their affair from becoming public. Members of a single lineage, for example, or people whose lineages are linked by an avenging spirit are loathe to announce a desire to marry.[3] And a man who is sleeping with a woman in a village or lineage where he has a past history of adultery is particularly careful to keep out of sight of the woman's kinsmen and neighbors. If an affair continues over time, however, it inevitably enters into the stream of village and regional gossip. The woman's young child may refer innocently to the man's visits; someone may see him leaving her house before dawn; something he owns may be noticed in her house; or she may become pregnant. However it leaks out, an affair that becomes public knowledge is a matter of concern to the relatives of both participants, and efforts are made either to terminate it (not an option if it has resulted in pregnancy) or to have it recognized as a legitimate marriage.

Marriages that are not preceded by extensive discussion, controversy, and negotiation are extremely rare in Saramaka. The number of people who feel entitled to raise objections, together with the range of social and ritual problems that can be cited, put almost any relationship in a potentially questionable light. But it is also rare for the objections not to be manageable through some combination of persuasion, divination, prayer, ritual action, and compensatory payments. Pregnancies constitute an especially forceful incentive for the resolution of problems. The man's kin take pride in his ability to provide the other group with a new member, and the woman's kin are eager to legitimize the relationship for the sake of the child's well-being.

The recognition of a marriage—through a formal announcement to the ancestors and the exchange of special gifts (see chap. 4)—establishes partnerships that vary greatly in their stability and tone. At one extreme, a pregnant woman whose lover fulfills his conjugal duties only reluctantly and minimally and then leaves her after the child is born is described as having taken a *fèndi mánu*—a "husband for [nothing but] sex." At the other extreme, a woman may spend her whole life with a single husband, living primarily in his village, gardening with his mother and sisters, and sharing the raising of her children with him and his kin; and a man may offer the kind of emotional commitment and material security to a wife that gradually builds a relationship of total and lifelong solidarity. Most conjugal relationships not only fall somewhere in between these extremes, but also vacillate through time. A woman may alter her primary residence according to the husband's changing involvements with other wives. Strained relations between in-laws may discourage either partner from visiting the other's village. Personal obligations such as attention to a possession god or mourning for a close relative may cut into the time they have together. A joint trip to the coast may strengthen the marriage. And a couple may divorce and remarry later, sometimes with different spouses in the interim, as they play out the passions and frustrations of a stormy love relationship.

Individual people also vary considerably in the kinds of marriages they are inclined to develop. Some men acquire reputations as die-hard monogamists, either out of personal preference or from an inability to manage the jealousies of rival co-wives, while others are referred to as "many-wife-ers" (*hía-muyêè-ma*) because of their preference for having four or more wives at a time. One Dangogo man was widely criticized for divorcing wives too readily, while his nephew was mocked for keeping wives who were known to be unfaithful. One thirty-year-old woman was devoting her adult life to the pursuit of a man who had rejected her after a brief marriage, following his activities from day to day, baring her soul to any of his relatives who would listen, and gossiping heatedly about his continuing marriages. Another woman was famous for marrying anyone who could supply her with tobacco and, by menopause, had had eight recognized marriages, five of which lasted less than a year. Because styles of marrying are one of the many ways in which Saramakas play out their individuality, the remaining sections of this chapter should be understood as defining a range of culturally acceptable arrangements within which people experience very different selections and find very different kinds of satisfaction.

A Man's-Eye View of Marriage

The emotions that are felt between Saramaka marriage partners are as varied as the individual personalities themselves, ranging from admiration to condescension, trust to suspicion, fulfillment to frustration, and lively passion to near indifference. But some of these feelings are promoted more strongly than others by cultural convention, traditional wisdom, and popular consensus.

One of these latter is a husband's distrust of his wife. Saramaka men are encouraged to view wives as potentially untrustworthy, and to protect themselves by taking wives into their confidence only partially and with real caution. A folktale about a legendary hunter, Basi Kodjo, describes how he was nearly lured to his death by the Bush Cows that he had been killing when one of them assumed the form of a beautiful woman and became his wife. Like a Saramaka Mata Hari, she used her extraordinary sexual charms to pry out the secrets of his success and of his invulnerability to attack. It was only at the very last moment that his wise grandmother intervened, warning him against revealing his final secret, and setting up the bloody confrontation in which he foiled the treachery of his seductive wife and slew the entire Bush Cow population.[4] Although this tale serves as a caution against trusting outsiders, it is also explicitly understood by Saramaka men as a warning about women and, in particular, wives. Men all agree in principle that it is foolish to tell wives about their protective "medicines." One supported this view by describing what could happen if he were to reveal to a wife the rituals with which he protected his hunting dog from jaguars, explaining that in a later moment of jealous rage, for example over a co-wife, she would be in a position to kill the dog out of spite by transgressing one of the special prohibitions required by the protective ritual. Men are also concerned with protecting their possessions from their wives, and it is customary for a man to lock his house and take the key whenever he leaves the village so that his wives will not help themselves to supplies such as kerosene or soap.

Men recognize that such fears are more justified in some cases than in others, and some attempt to "test" each of their wives through systematic experimentation. One man left a jar of pomade in his wife's house each time he married, to see whether she would take any of it while he was away with his other wives. And trivial demands are sometimes made by men expressly to reassure themselves of a wife's reliability and obedience.

Men also like to think that women must be "trained" by their husbands in order to become fully accomplished in the art of wifely service. One man took pleasure in describing how one of his wives had not realized, until he took the time to explain it to her, that pieces of manioc cake should be served with the patterned side facing up. Another made a point of correcting the way a young wife tied up her hammock when it was not in use. In general, men address many criticisms directly to their wives (about their dress, their social behavior, their cooking, and so forth) of a sort that would be entirely inappropriate for the women to reciprocate.

In Saramaka ideology, only a man is entitled to make direct demands on a spouse. He may tell her to cook when he is hungry or to prepare heated water for him to bathe in, but she must never be the one to suggest that he go hunting or fishing. He may send her on small errands as he wishes, but when she needs some service from him, she must make a formal plea for his cooperation, often with the help of a member of his family who is in a position to ask him favors on her behalf.

A man may also place restrictions on his wife's social life. One man, for example, forbade his wife to visit her classificatory sister who lived in another section of his village, on the grounds that it was improper for a woman to wander about in a husband's village as if it were her own. Oral accounts of the eighteenth-century celebration of peace, concluding a century of warfare against the colonists, suggest that this has long been a Saramaka man's prerogative:

> When they finished this celebration, . . . one woman said to another, "Child, with the size of our 'play,' with that fantastic *aléle* dancing, how come you didn't show up?" [The other] said, "Oh, the man [my husband] locked me up and left me in the house. That's why I didn't come. . . . That *gbêlè-kísi-gbáda* [expletive] Kwasi didn't want me to come."[5]

The way in which spouses address and talk about each other reinforces the asymmetry of their relationship. A husband may use any of his wife's several names freely, both when speaking to her and when talking about her. In contrast, it is generally only an older woman who has been married to the same man for many decades who feels audacious enough to call out his name. Proper etiquette prescribes avoidance of a husband's name and requires the use of respectfully elliptical substitutions such as "that man there."

Men's and women's meals are another reflection of the nature of husband-wife relations. To Saramakas on the Pikilio, the separation of the sexes during meals is an essential principle of daily life, and the way in which men expect to be served relates directly to cultural ideas about male and female roles. Descriptions by resident eighteenth-century missionaries make clear that Saramaka meals have always been segregated by sex:

> A Negro woman never eats in the presence of her husband, nor does the man eat in the presence of his wife. This custom . . . is very important to them. In order not to eat alone, they eat with their neighbors. . . . Even though a group of people of one sex might be in proximity to a group of people of the other sex, places are chosen so that one group will not see the other. [Staehelin 1913–19, 3.2:272]

Today as well, visual isolation continues to be the critical variable. To Saramakas, one of the most exotic features of Western culture is the custom of women eating within sight of their husbands. The segregation of the sexes is as strongly embedded in Saramaka concepts of propriety for meals as it is in Western notions about public bathrooms.

In this context, men's meals are seen as a crucial test of the success with which each woman fulfills her role as a wife. While a woman eats her own meals informally, often directly out of cooking pots, she lavishes the utmost care on those she prepares for her husband. When men's meals are concerned, Saramakas are extremely attentive to the shape and color of manioc pieces, the immaculateness of the dishware, the coolness and clarity of the water, the whiteness of the rice and the smoothness with which it is mounded, and the amount of bone and fat included in the meat or fish.[6] The proper arrangement of men's meals is carefully specified. The calabash hand-washing bowl must cradle the calabash drinking bowl, with a metal spoon placed inside; each food dish must have a cover; and the water must be served in a sparkling aluminum teapot. These displays are the symbolic culmination of Saramaka women's work, for behind each meal that a woman serves her husband lie her horticultural efforts, her skills at various kinds of food processing and cooking, her attention to cleanliness, and her mastery of the etiquette of meal service itself. Even her artistic sensitivities are in evidence, for the calabash bowls must be handsomely carved, and a colorfully embroidered cloth ideally covers the entire setting until the men sit down to eat.

Conventions of sexual behavior also reflect the Saramaka view that men should be less accountable to their wives than women are to their husbands. As one man noted,

> Men are more difficult [*môò ógi*—literally, "fiercer"] than women. If you're a man, you can interrupt an evening chat with your wife and say, "Well, good night. I'm going over there [to your other wife's house]." The wife will just say good night. But if a *woman* tried that, she'd never set foot in that house again! That's just the way men are made.

This image accurately portrays the usual behavior, if not the emotions, of Saramaka wives. I once saw a young woman looking on, for example, as her husband loaded a marriage basket to present to a new wife. Her resentment remained largely under control, expressed only in the bitter remark, made under her breath, that his excessive passion for this new woman was going to drive him to carry water from the river for her (a task that Saramaka women normally perform for their husbands).

A man requires his wife to tolerate not only his other marriages, but also his affairs, and may even ask her help in getting together his best clothes for a night out in an undisclosed woman's hammock. The number of different women that a man sleeps with over the course of a lifetime may easily run into the hundreds. My neighbor Naai once lamented that one of her great-grandsons was going to have a hard time finding himself a wife because almost all of the eligible women on the Pikilio had already either been married to his brother or had an affair with him. As one of the older brother's wives listened quietly, she discussed how, since two brothers should not "take" the same woman, the younger one's only option was betrothal with an apron girl. (I know from other sources that her assessment of the older brother's love life was no exaggeration, and her prediction for the younger brother was equally on target, since the two women whom he married later that year were, indeed, an apron girl and a woman from a village far downstream on the Suriname River.)

For a married woman, the main deterrent against having an affair is the understanding that her husband will leave her if her infidelity is discovered. But more direct means of control are said to be used by some men who are particularly concerned about keeping their wives to themselves. One man prepared for a trip to Paramaribo by aggressively forbidding everyone except one old, crippled woman from approaching his house during his absence, in order to assure his wife's fidelity. And some individuals allegedly know how to make ritual preparations that can prevent a woman from having intercourse with men other than her husband—most commonly when the latter is on the coast. Some of these operate by rendering her lover impotent, others by making her unable to say yes to another man's advances. There are also said to be solutions that a couple can rub on their bodies in order to make their marriage last forever. All such preparations are considered extremely dangerous to use, and stories of cases in which they backfired and killed one or another of the people involved are frightening enough to make most men vow never to try them.

A Husband's Family

Among her husband's kin, a woman is always considered an outsider, a "woman-come-to-a-husband" (*muyêè-kó-a-mánu*), and her guest status in their village is symbolized in many ways. She does not leave her house without the double layer of skirts and the decoratively sewn cape required for fully proper women's attire. She does not go visiting in the village without having a specific errand to do. She does not cook in an open-sided structure (*gangása*), which is the generally pre-

ferred type of cooking house for Saramaka women. She refrains from
singing and dancing at community "plays." She does not bathe in the
river when any of her husband's relatives are within sight. She often
contributes cooked food to an ancestral feast without attending or
partaking of the food herself. And in countless other ways, her behavior is required to communicate deference and respect to her hosts.
A popular song of the late 1960s expressed this principle quite
clearly.

Ná wáka pidí tabáku môò;	Don't walk around begging for tobacco anymore;
A mánu kôndè, wè, i dê.	[Bear in mind that] you're in your husband's village.

A woman who has spent little time with her husband's kin must be
particularly careful about her demeanor in his village. But even when
a woman has spent most of her life in a husband's village, she remains
a "woman-come-to-a-husband," and although her interactions with
other villagers become increasingly relaxed over the years, her behavior is still judged in terms of the rules for that status. For example, a
woman who had been living almost exclusively in Dangogo for four
years once mentioned in passing that she had never set foot in the
neighborhood immediately adjacent to her husband's. And another
cited the fact that she was in her husband's village to explain why she
decided to tolerate a painful menstrual disorder rather than to seek
the help of a woman in another neighborhood who knew special
remedies for it.

In addition to the general conventions for their behavior, women-
come-to-husbands are often subjected to special restrictions imposed
at a more local level. One village on the Suriname River has designated certain boulders at its landing, considered particularly desirable
for laundering clothes and hammocks, as off limits to female affines.
The lineage members of one horticultural camp on the upper Pikilio
reserve their heaviest rice pestle for the wives who work there, and
claim that they do not allow wives to use any other. And residents of
the Pikilio like to say that a woman must be willing to "swallow rocks"
if she marries a man from the upper Gaanlio, because of the various
hardships imposed on wives in those villages.

Women often devote conversations to the analysis of their feelings about living in their husband's village versus their own, and

about gardening with their husband's kinswomen versus their own, for these influence important ongoing decisions in their lives. A married woman's residence is always divided; she is never expected to declare a permanent arrangement, but rather adapts it to particular needs as they develop through time. Her residence pattern may change when she becomes the medium for a possession god based in her own village, when her aging mother needs to be cared for, when a sister she feels close to alters her primary residence or gardens, when her husband divorces a wife or takes on a new one, when he goes off to the coast for a few years, and so on.

The woman's husband and his kin invariably press her to spend as much time as she can in their village and to garden in their camp. A kin group's ability to attract and hold onto affinal women adds to their prestige and power within the community.[7] At the same time, however, the relationships between a woman and her husband's kin (especially his female kin, with whom she interacts most frequently) are, more often than not, distinctly strained. It is so common for women to contrast the relaxation they feel when living "sister-with-sister-with-mother" with the tensions of life among a husband's kinswomen that they can effectively convey their thoughts by saying very little. One woman gave a friend the following summary of the relationships she had in her husband's village (the names are pseudonyms):

> There's one woman named Yimba [her husband's mother] and I'm [barely] on speaking terms with her. There's another woman named Bodibo [a sister-in-law]. Even though she kills me [with malicious gossip], I still speak to her.

Although she said nothing more, her friend understood that she was citing these as the warmest relations that she had in her husband's village. And the powerful emotion behind another woman's distillation of her husband's village relations was carried fully by her tone of voice, as she declared cryptically, "One mother-in-law is with me there, along with one sister-in-law!" Such statements, heard frequently in women's conversations, represent a rhetorical form (used also to characterize co-wives) that carries meaning with little need for further elaboration.

Some discussions, however, provide more detail on the kinds of problems that women perceive. One common accusation is material

hardship. Women often complain about being left out when the results of a local man's hunting or fishing efforts are distributed. One
woman accused her mother-in-law of intercepting conjugal gifts that
her husband was sending her from the coast. Another woman told
how she was forced to build her own storage house in an affinal camp
even though she had a husband and four able-bodied brothers-in-law
in Saramaka. And another ranted that only divine intervention forced
her sisters- and mother-in-law to leave her the last few of the several
dozen manioc cakes that she had baked in their camp. Support of a
rival co-wife is also frequently cited as evidence of hostility (though I
have never heard the co-wives in question acknowledge such solidarity). The most common allegation against a husband's kin, however, is malicious gossip. Women repeatedly present themselves as the
victims of false rumors spread by their husband's relatives. This frustration contributes importantly to women's gossip sessions and, as we
will see in chapter 7, is a central subject for women's popular songs as
well.

    Although women often discuss their husband's kin as a collective
body, they also entertain distinct expectations about the relationships
they will have with those in particular kinship positions. The relationships that are most frequently cast in terms of cultural stereotypes are
those between a woman and her husband's mother and sisters.[8]

    A woman and her mother-in-law exercise great restraint with
each other, and there is no expectation that feelings of real warmth
will develop between them. Women see themselves as being under the
thumb of their husband's mother when they are in the same village.
Mothers-in-law are said to enjoy the prerogative to make specific
demands on their daughters-in-law (e.g., to carry water or cut firewood) and even though such services are more often offered by the
younger woman than demanded by the older, the principle looms
large in Saramakas' abstract image of this relationship. When, to cite
just one example, a woman said she intended to explain to a recently
married younger woman that she was her (distant classificatory)
mother-in-law, the woman she was talking to chimed in supportively,
"Yes, just bring her all the rice you need pounded and she'll understand." The aspect of my life in the United States that Saramaka
women were most curious about was the nature of my relationship
with my mother-in-law. Did I ever say her name out loud? Did I ever
walk behind her while she was bent over doing laundry at the river? If

a photo was taken of me, would I show it to her? And so on. Specific rules of etiquette reinforce this image. For example, a woman should not sit on a stool that belongs to her mother-in-law, and a mother-in-law may not be the one to help a new wife unload the special basket that she brings on her first formal visit to the husband's village.

In contrast, sisters-in-law are supposed to offer friendship and solidarity. In relationships with me, which were unusual in having no basis in (even very distant classificatory) kinship, most of the women I knew chose to define me as a sister-in-law, and this was an explicit gesture of cordiality and friendship. Unlike mothers- and daughters-in-law, sisters-in-law spend significant amounts of time together— eating, gardening, sewing, raising children, gossiping, and so forth. And unlike the tensions between co-wives or between mothers- and daughters-in-law, strains between sisters-in-law are viewed as individual difficulties in living up to "normal" standards of friendship and solidarity. The ideal relationship between a woman and her brother-in-law (either husband's brother or sister's husband) is similarly defined. Addressing each other repeatedly by the term *suági*, they play a game of exaggerated affection—embracing liberally, exchanging compliments, and in general carrying on a platonic and highly stylized flirtation.

The interactions between a woman and the people who are classified as her husband's grandparents are also specially defined. Addressing each other by the terms for husband and wife (*mánu, muyêè*) or, for two women, by a special adaptation (*kambó*) of the term for co-wife (*kambósa*), affines in alternate generations "play" with each other at being husbands, wives, and co-wives.[9] The teasing that goes on between a woman and her husband's grandparents is more cautious than that allowed for her own grandparents, more circumscribed by expectations of deference and distance, and more heavily complemented by small gifts and services. But there is often real warmth, and the kinds of interpersonal conflicts that mar other affinal relationships rarely intrude on the fictive "marriages" of alternate-generation affines.

Although women tend to cast their husband's kin in a distinctly negative light, they also like to discuss the pleasures of life in a husband's village, which are as unanimously agreed on as the tensions. Their guest status there implies not only restrictions, but also a kind of preferential treatment. Although having to wear "good clothes" all the time is seen as part of the formality and lack of relaxation in a husband's village, it carries to Saramaka women a sense of festivity as well. Women often describe a visit to their husband's village in terms of the special clothes they wore, the elaborate hairdo they had braided, and the sweet dishes that they cooked and presented to their affines. Ideals for the treatment of "women-come-to-a-husband" center on praise and extreme cordiality, and even when these ideals are not fulfilled on the level of actual feelings, they may still be reflected in the rhetoric with which affines interact with each other.

Women often cite the festive atmosphere of a visit to a husband's village as their motivation for not wanting to marry men from their own village. The image of loading a basket carefully with special foods plays a central role in glowing descriptions of these trips, and reference is frequently made to elaborate hairdos for the occasion. One man summed this up by noting that Saramaka women love the "*Ké baáa!*" of a separate husband's village; when they arrive there, he explained, their sisters-in-law will call out, "*Ké baáa!* [here, an exclamation of surprise and pleasure] Sister-in-law has come to visit!" In contrast, conjugal visits within the woman's own village, with people who have known her since childhood, are said never to inspire the same kind of excitement. On a more practical level, a woman's presence in her affinal village allows her both to spend time with her husband and to compete actively with her co-wives over his affection, conjugal services, and material resources, and this is a central motivation in decisions about residence and gardening. Because of the current definition of residence alternatives, a woman cannot expect her husband to spend more than a few days at a time visiting her in her own village, so that the days she spends in his village constitute almost her only opportunities to be with him.[10]

While the actual amount of time women spend in their husband's village may be quite slight, their residential base there carries great symbolic importance. A woman who simply uses an affinal relative's house rather than having one of her own while she is visiting her husband is seen as having a distinctly tenuous conjugal arrangement. And the clearest way for a woman to declare her decision to divorce a husband is to "pack up her things" (*pú lái*)—that is, to remove her clothing and kitchenware from her house in his village (see chap. 7, song 46). Because of this understanding, a man may accuse his wife of leaving him if she takes too many of her pots and pans back to her own village. Even when a husband dies, the proper procedure is for the woman to leave "one plate" in his village for the period of mourning. After a respectable amount of time, she then returns to sleep in her house there for a couple of nights before completing her withdrawal from his village and the termination of the marriage.

A Husband's Wives

Saramakas explicitly equate the relationship between a man's wives with outspoken hostility. In dyadic interactions, a standard synonym for the verb "to fight" (*féti*) is "to make [act like a] co-wife" (*mbéi kambósa*), and the current gossip in any village contains ample support for this association. Although there are a few famous instances in which co-wives became friendly with each other, solidarity between them is far from an expected development.[11] Rather, the ideal image of co-wife relations centers on the control of hostile feelings and on the relatively peaceful maintenance of separate lives. Saramakas feel strongly that each wife should have her own house (ideally not too near the others') and serve her own dishes in the house where the husband is eating. Expectations of cordiality are generally phrased in terms of a willingness to say a cool good morning to a co-wife if she should happen to walk by. The commentary of a missionary living among Saramakas in the eighteenth century suggests that this attitude dates to the society's earliest years.

> . . . the wives must live as separated from each other as possible. They call each other Gambossa (co-wife) and try to avoid meeting face-to-face, since they harbor a constant and deadly animosity. [Riemer 1801:252]

From the time they are first introduced—in a cryptic and visibly tense announcement of the new wife's arrival on the scene—co-wives are expected to interact, at best, with an icy cordiality. Saramakas describe the "traditional" (in this case, early twentieth-century) presentation of the new co-wife as requiring the following formal exchange.

First wife:	*Sísa ódi.*	Sister, greetings.
New wife:	*Tangí sísa.*	Thank you, sister.
First wife:	*Fá i dê?*	How are you?
New wife:	*Mi dê áfu sô.*	I'm all right.
First wife:	*I kó akí?*	You've come here?
New wife:	*Mi kó akí.*	I've come here.

A member of the husband's lineage would then admonish the two of them not to harbor bad feelings, but to cook and carry water and cut firewood "with joy."

By the 1960s, this phrasing had become obsolete, but the tone of the greeting was continued through more current modes of address. One meeting between co-wives that I witnessed in Dangogo, for example, was held at the request of the husband's grandmother, who summoned the new wife to her house to meet one of the man's other wives. Avoiding the otherwise-normal use of address terms, they responded to the older woman's request that they "say how do you do" (*ákísi i dê*) with the following conversation, during which the first wife kept her head turned toward the wall, away from the new wife:

First wife:	*I dê nô?*	How are you?
New wife:	*Mi dê-o.*	I'm fine.
First wife:	*I kó akí?*	You've come here?
New wife:	*Mi kó akí-o.*	I've come here.

The husband's grandmother then asked the new wife if she would sit down, but the latter declined and withdrew silently from the house. The introduction was over.[12]

Saramaka ideals for conjugal relationships stress the man's responsibility to treat all his wives equally. When more than one wife is present in his village, he is supposed to sleep with one of them for three nights, then go on to the next one's house for three nights, and so on, maintaining as regular a rotation among them as circumstances allow. When a man distributes presents, such as cloth or kitchenware, there should be equal amounts for each wife. And the results of his fishing and hunting efforts should be given evenly to whichever wives are in the village. In Saramaka ideology (even if not in some men's personal feelings), there is no "principal" wife.

Not surprisingly, most co-wife quarrels involve accusations that one woman is trying to maneuver herself into a privileged position, and the most frequent conjugal complaint heard from women is that their husband is favoring another wife. Each woman does her best to keep track of her husband's sleeping arrangements in order to know whether she is receiving her fair share of his time. If she feels she is being slighted, she does not generally broach the problem with the husband directly, but rather discusses it with her husband's sisters or others in the neighborhood, who may eventually bring it up with the husband. Women also make it their business to find out the nature and quantity of all conjugal gifts that their co-wives receive. And they do their best to keep track of the distribution of their husband's major hunting kills as well.

Women discuss their grievances readily with their own kinswomen, mimicking their co-wives' actions and ways of talking, and laying bare their feelings without restraint. There is strong supportiveness expressed in such sessions, for nearly every woman has had similar experiences. I cite just one representative example, using pseudonyms.

Ndolia was talking with Moninge, a woman from another lineage in her village. Ndolia's lineage had recently denied her permission to join her husband in Kourou, French Guiana, where he was working in a construction crew. He had already set the posts of a house for her there, she explained, and now her co-wife from a downstream village would probably end up living in it instead. She felt as though she had died; her coffin was already made, and all that was left was to be buried properly. But there was one particular incident that hurt the worst of all. Since it happened, she had been unable to eat; she wanted to do nothing but cry and cry. She had just visited her husband's village to clear the ground in front of her house there, and saw her co-wife, who approached her with a broad grin and inquired effusively about whether she was busy making preparations for her trip to the coast. That woman not only knew very well that Ndolia wasn't going; the husband's sisters said that she had been celebrating for two solid days! The whole experience was painful, but it was her co-wife's smile of satisfaction that hurt the worst of all. In the course of relating all this to Moninge, Ndolia mentioned the names of the six women who were traveling in the large motor-driven canoe that she would have taken downriver on her way to Kourou. One was a former co-wife of Moninge's. "Woman," said Moninge, "I divorced that husband of mine a long time ago, but even now when I hear that *that woman* is joining him in French Guiana, it really hurts, do you hear? It hurts me a lot, woman. It hurts me still."

Even when women are not describing particular problems, many of their conversations reflect general feelings toward their co-wives through their choice of words. In contrast to most Saramaka modes of personal reference, which are intended to communicate either respect or affection, the terms that are used for co-wives are charged with sarcasm and bitterness. "Your friend" is commonly used when talking to a woman about her co-wife, and any derisive term is considered appropriate for a woman to use in speaking of her husband's other wives—from "that other one" to "that slut of mine." A woman may also convey her feelings about a co-wife in the way she chooses to talk about her husband. For example, one woman began referring to her husband derisively as "Gogo-a-kini's husband," after the man expressed his love for a new wife through the creation of a highly complimentary play name, Gogo-a-kini.[13]

Co-wife rivalries are most commonly expressed in conversation and, as we will see in chapter 7, through song. But there are other outlets as well. The standard method of attacking a co-wife through supernatural means is to straddle a dish of food that she has prepared, thus polluting it so that it must be thrown out. I have heard stories of this technique being used by young and old women from various villages and with various consequences. In one well-known case, the co-wife threw out her polluted food without comment but later, once the other woman had served her own food and the husband was about to eat it, it is said that she grabbed a machete and with one swift blow "split the bowl in half," at which the man's *komantí* god cried out "*hooo hooo*" and he ran off into the forest.

Physical fights are also not rare among co-wives. For example, when one woman, who felt her husband was neglecting her, brazenly called to him in his other wife's house and "informed" him that he had more than one wife, the other woman sprang up, burst out of the house, and fought with her. In another famous case a woman attacked her pregnant co-wife, ripping off her outer skirt and forcing her to run off in just her underskirt. And the only large-scale fight among kinswomen that occurred during my fieldwork was described by Saramakas in part as a "practice" for fighting with co-wives. Although magical preparations were banned because of the close kinship ties involved, the women did engage in other techniques that are associated with co-wife fights—biting each other, clubbing each other with sticks, and urinating on each other. Co-wife fights provide a lively topic of conversation, as people reminisce about particularly fierce confrontations or women evaluate their chances of coming out on top if they attack a rival. Supernatural aids (*féti óbia*) play an important role in these discussions. For example, women generally explain the decision not to fight a co-wife by asserting that the other woman has purchased specially prepared body lotions that will assure her victory through magical means.

When a woman dies, her present (and, to a lesser extent, her former) co-wives are required to go through a period of intense mourning which functions in part to protect them from accusations of having contributed to her death. They wear old clothes which they may not launder, their hair is cropped close to their heads by the dead woman's kin, their possession gods may not come to them, and they may not have sexual intercourse. Of all the sets of mourning regulations that Saramakas recognize, only those for a husband or wife are more stringent than those for a co-wife.

Living without a Husband

Between the ages of about fifteen and thirty-five, most women spend very little time unmarried. When they become divorced or widowed, they remarry quickly, for they are attractive, physically strong, and at the height of their childbearing potential. Being married, however, does not always mean having access to a husband's companionship and services, for men spend long periods of their lives in money-earning trips outside of Saramaka territory, and the wives have always—until exceptions began to be made in the late 1960s—stayed behind.

A woman whose husband is away on a work trip is careful to maintain her social position as his wife. She keeps her furniture and dishware in the house that she has in his neighborhood, comes to sleep over with his family when there are major events in their community, and is especially conscientious about attending and contributing to any funeral rituals that are held for his relatives. Furthermore, she stays in contact with him through both messages and gift exchanges. She may ask an uncle on his way to the coast, for example, to deliver a bottle of palm oil and an embroidered cape, as a sign of her affection. And when a friend of the husband returns to Saramaka from the coast, he may be given a cooking pot, some cloth, or other commercial goods to bring to each wife. Both tape-recorded messages and letters (dictated to a literate acquaintance and written in Sranantongo or, sometimes, Dutch) are sent in both directions, carrying greetings, current news, thanks for gifts, and requests for needed supplies.

During these periods, a woman depends largely on her own kinsmen for meat and fish as well as for help in clearing garden sites, building houses, and performing other tasks that would otherwise be provided by her husband. She may take over parts of these jobs herself, for example repairing a leaking roof to maintain it provisionally until her husband can put on a new one. As time goes on, she may gradually use up many basic supplies such as soap, salt, and kerosene. Then her own kinsmen, and to a lesser extent the kinsmen of her husband, help out with small contributions, but she may also have to get along with a somewhat lower standard of living.

While a woman's husband is away, she has fairly limited possibilities for sexual gratification. Masturbation is only rarely acknowledged, and Saramakas consistently deny the existence of lesbian relations in their villages (though all men have heard about homosexuality, largely during work trips to French Guiana). The longer a woman's husband is away, the more tolerance there is of her accepting a lover. If the husband returns after a year or two and finds that his wife has been sleeping with another man, her lineage may either authorize the husband and his kinsmen to give the man a beating or help to extract a payment from him. By either course of action, the wronged husband "gives" the woman to the other man and fully terminates his relationship with her.[14] If, however, the husband returns after four or five years to find his wife with another man, the woman's lineage tends not to support his claims to compensation. After that amount of time, people generally agree that a woman's needs fully justify her decision to take a new husband. Cited most prominently is her lack of the material goods that a husband supplies.[15]

Most women go through several marriages in the course of a lifetime and, although some end with the husband's death, many more are terminated by divorce. As a woman reaches her forties and fifties, the period between one marriage and the next tends to lengthen and her chances of remarrying at all (as measured both by actual statistics and by Saramaka expectations) decline sharply. In Dangogo in 1968, although 80 percent of women aged forty-five or younger were married, only 32 percent of those who were over forty-five had husbands, and there were no cases of women who had entered new marriages when they were past the age of menopause.[16]

Older women who have no husbands tend to become nostalgic about the pleasures of their earlier years. There is no longer the joyful "*Ké baáa!*" of visits to a husband's village, there are no more massive presentations of conjugal gifts, there is more difficulty in persuading someone to clear a garden site or build a new house, and there are many more meals without meat or fish. On the other hand, older women often take on special roles in their villages—both because of their apical position in a matrilineal kin group and because of the ritual knowledge that they have accumulated over the years. Older women can contribute actively to community life as midwives, overseers of various possession cults, tellers of folktales, and, in general, as authorities on matters of tradition. Many are also given a young child to raise—partly in order to provide help with domestic chores. And all are actively involved in the social life of the community through daily visiting by children and adults, who make a point of keeping them up-to-date on current events.

Whether thinking of a young woman who is temporarily without a husband or an elderly woman who has no prospect of remarrying, Saramakas tend to define the main problem of unmarried life in terms of material poverty. While some of the goods that are provided by husbands outlast the marriage itself (especially carved wooden objects such as stools, trays, and peanut-grinding boards), most represent consumed rather than accumulated wealth. Women without husbands see the rarity of meat and fish in their diet as a basic concern. They must be very careful in their use of kerosene, salt, and soap. They learn to live with leaks in their canoe and eventually without a canoe of their own. And they must resign themselves to more torn and faded skirts, because the trade cotton that is imported to Saramaka from the coast wears out quickly. It is not rare, then, for an older woman to own exquisite wood carvings that date from earlier marriages but to be suffering real hardship in terms of diet and housing.[17]

Chapter 4 examines the nature of Saramaka economic life in more detail, focusing special attention on the role of conjugal gift exchanges. It also explores the role of art in this context—how artistically designed objects contribute to the flow of goods between men and women and how at the same time they reflect and reinforce important cultural understandings about the sexes.

Chapter Four

Giving and Receiving

In Saramaka as in other societies, people use material objects to symbolize their relationships with other people. The etiquette of gift giving and exchange, as well as the value of the object itself, are strongly influenced by the social roles of giver and receiver and by the social context of the transaction. Decoratively embellished objects offer a particularly valuable means of expressing solidarity, affection, and commitment between people, since they represent a clear "extra effort," an explicit attempt to extend an object's value beyond that of its straightforward utilitarian function. In Saramaka, the special focus on marriage as the social context in which gifts, especially artistically designed gifts, are presented reflects fundamental understandings about relations between men and women.

Indeed, the very delineation of the Saramaka domain of "art" is informed by the role of art in social life. The Saramaccan term used to refer most generally to the decorative arts is *têmbe*. Like many Saramaccan words, *têmbe* can function as several parts of speech. As a noun, it refers to "art" or "decoration." As an adjective, meaning "artistic," it refers to a person's artistic skills (rather than to an object's artistic quality), and may be used either in isolation (*a têmbe* meaning "he/she is artistic") or with the suffix *-ma* (*têmbema* meaning "artistic person"). The word *têmbe* specifically implies human motivation and skill; it does not refer to beauty in natural phenomena such as scenery or in commercially manufactured objects such as tape recorders. But the domain covered by this term may vary according to social context. For example, we will see that even the preparation of palm oil, which is normally considered a straightforward subsistence task, may be talked about as a kind of *têmbe* when the oil is intended to accompany other conjugal gifts such as decorative textiles or calfbands.

This chapter begins by laying out some very generalized features of exchange in Saramaka and tracing their development through time. It then considers the Saramaka concept of reciprocity and its

61

implementation in social life, particularly in the context of conjugal relations. Finally, it explores the ways in which Saramakas' understandings about men, women, and reciprocity influence their understandings about art and aesthetics.

Unless otherwise indicated, the ethnographic materials in this chapter describe the period between about 1870 and 1970, after which the position of Maroons within Suriname underwent fundamental changes that have begun to have direct and important consequences for the organization of life in Saramaka villages. During the 1970s there were, for example, increases in the opportunities for men to earn money within Saramaka, in the opportunities for women to spend time with their husbands on the coast and sometimes even to earn money there, and in the use of money to pay for both goods and services in Saramaka villages. As will be shown, these and other related changes are currently redefining Saramaka expectations concerning gift giving, food sharing, and the provision of services within a whole range of social relationships, from husbands and wives to members of co-resident lineage segments. And the influence of such developments is also beginning to be perceptible in the ways that Saramakas think about and use their arts.

Patterns of Exchange in Saramaka History

Because Saramakas have incorporated into their daily life neither a currency nor markets, they depend very heavily on socially motivated exchange for the allocation of goods. Throughout their history, it has been distributions and gift giving, rather than barter or buying and selling, that have spread material resources within the community.

Saramaka patterns of exchange have passed through two distinct stages and are now entering into a third. During the war years and early independence, while some goods were given or exchanged by individuals (to spouses, children, and so forth), a centralized system of distribution, administered by village headmen, was ultimately responsible for the material well-being of the community as a whole. Once labor opportunities opened up for Maroon men in the mid-nineteenth century, this pattern shifted to one in which individual men distributed goods within ego-centered networks of social ties focused on wives and, to a lesser extent, lineal kin. And during the past decade or two, a selective use of money within Saramaka villages has been encouraging an even more individualistic system, in which buying and selling are beginning to be substituted (as yet in limited contexts) for earlier modes of cooperative sharing.

Although our knowledge of how Maroons allocated resources before making peace with the colonists is somewhat sketchy, it is clear that the exigencies of long-term warfare—of constant vulnerability to attack from outside—encouraged strong centralized authority within each band, and that the provision of material goods was seen as a communal responsibility. When villages and gardens were destroyed by colonial soldiers, it was a communitywide loss, and reconstruction involved a communitywide effort. Many of the spoils from plantation raids were also treated as a generalized resource for communal survival. Once peace was concluded with the colonists, this centralized structure was continued in the form of tribute distributions. Goods provided by the colonial government to the newly liberated Maroons were sent to village headmen, who were responsible for overseeing their distribution within their respective groups.

During the nineteenth century, as the colonial government began to phase out its tribute to Maroon communities and as opportunities for wage labor emerged in coastal areas of the colony, economic patterns underwent a subtle but important change. The centralized distributions of goods that had been administered by village leaders ceased, leaving responsibility for the provision of imported goods in the hands of individual men, who acted as both earners and providers within smaller social networks. Men returned from the coast with goods that they had acquired through individual efforts, and the distribution of these goods, rather than being generalized within the community, reflected social networks that were different for each man. Ego-centered distribution, which had always been an option for the provision of locally made products such as garden produce, fish, game, and wooden objects, thus came to channel the flow of goods from external sources as well. The delineation of these ego-centered networks and the ways in which distribution was handled within them were, of course, based on cultural understandings shared by the community as a whole. But the responsibility for interpreting these understandings and executing the actual distributions was now divided among individual men rather than entrusted to a few village leaders.

Since the opening of wage labor opportunities in the nineteenth century, the image of men as providers of imported material goods has been a central component of Saramaka cultural assumptions. A man's house is often referred to as a "house of [imported] goods" (*gúdu ósu*) and the frequently heard term "person of [many imported] goods" (*gúduma*) is used only to refer to men. A very large portion of every Saramaka man's life is devoted to the accumulation of imported goods, and because there has been no tradition of barter or purchase in Saramaka, the subsequent distribution (and sometimes redistribution) of these goods has been intimately tied into social life, both reflecting and maintaining the entire range of social relationships.

During the late 1960s, the understanding that women in Pikilio villages had of Suriname's currency was extremely rudimentary. They had heard the names of many of the denominations (the equivalents of nickels, dimes, and quarters), but because they had some trouble remembering the place each one had within the system, they figured values only in terms of one of them, just as an American unfamiliar with British money might have heard of shillings and pence but prefer to think only in terms of pounds. Women who sold garden produce, eggs, chickens, and so forth often declined to deal with amounts other than whole Suriname guilders. With eggs valued at ten for a guilder, for example, a woman who had only nine might be unwilling to sell them until she found another, and a woman with eleven would sell only ten. There was also some confusion about amounts of money versus number of coins. A woman once showed me her matchbox of money, which contained one twenty-five-cent coin and four ten-cent coins, and asked whether her savings were "up to" a half-guilder. When I told her that she had even more, she wanted me to show her which one was the half-guilder coin and was troubled when there was none. The most frequent solution to the difficulties women experienced with currency was to phrase transactions purely in terms of goods, even if money had been involved at some stage. Women often referred to guilders (*kólu*) as skirt-cloths (*koósu*), which sold at that time for one guilder and provided a more meaningful way for them to envision values.[1] And women who had earned pocket money—for example by selling ground peanuts to the local mission or by sending a bucket of rice to Paramaribo with a kinsman on his way to Kourou—remembered the profit for each transaction in terms of the particular enamel bowl, piece of cloth, or other item that it had allowed them to purchase.

The system of distribution in which the use of currency was con-

fined largely to an external contact situation and individual men acted
as providers within ego-centered networks was unchallenged until
about 1970. Between the 1860s and the 1960s, the amounts of goods
that were flowing through this system varied significantly with
changes in labor opportunities and in the world market, but the conceptual framework and the principles of distribution remained relatively stable. Events of the past decade or two, however, have begun to
alter the system, making it less accurate now than it once was to
characterize Saramaka villages as having a nonmonetary economy.[2]
The primary catalysts for this change were the introduction of new
forms of transportation, the construction of a hydroelectric project in
Saramaka territory, and the government's decision to include Maroons in national elections—all of which served to bring Saramakas
into closer contact with the society of coastal Suriname. But the full
range of changes has been extensive and all can be seen to form a
complexly interrelated whole. Relations with the coast (which, while
important throughout Saramaka history, had always operated within
narrowly defined and carefully regulated contexts) began to expand
during the late 1960s with a new rapidity and flexibility, in terms of
both Saramakas' access to the coast and the introduction of elements
of coastal culture into Saramaka villages. The cumulative effect of the
changes of the past fifteen to twenty years has been to begin altering
both patterns of material resource allocation within Saramaka communities and, ultimately, the ideas about social life that underlie those
patterns.

During the 1960s, despite the repeated resistance of village
oracles and of other voices of community conservatism, Saramakas on
the Pikilio began to accelerate their acceptance of new introductions
such as radios and zinc roofing materials, part-time electricity was
planned by the government for the Tribal Chief's village, a Paramaribo radio station began broadcasting a weekly news summary in
Saramaccan, young boys began to attend the newly established school
at the local mission, women's opposition to giving birth under the care
of a physician when complications arose began to soften, and a few
men became actively interested in national politics. The flooding
caused by the hydroelectric dam, while not displacing Pikilio
Saramakas themselves, did relocate many of their downstream relatives in government-built towns in coastal territory, thus increasing
the familiarity of *all* Saramakas with features of coastal life, from

motorbikes and plumbing to unemployment and urban crime. Modes of transportation also opened new links to the coast. Outboard motors, which were introduced in the late 1950s and became increasingly common during the 1960s, allowed men easier access to the coast than they had had before. In 1950, a trip between Paramaribo and the Pikilio required two weeks of arduous paddling; in 1960 it took about four days with an outboard motor; and in the early 1970s it even became possible to make the trip in an hour's travel by light plane. As access to the coast became easier, men started putting pressure on affinal lineages to allow their wives to accompany them on coastal trips. After a number of unsuccessful petitions in the mid-1960s, village oracles began to acquiesce to their demands, and in the 1970s it became quite common for a man to send for one of his wives to join him once he was set up on the coast.

In many areas, it became possible in the 1960s for some Saramakas to earn money without leaving tribal territory. The expansion of Moravian and Roman Catholic mission stations meant that Saramakas were needed to cook, launder, mow lawns, clean hospital rooms, supply transportation from the mission to villages and airstrips, and provide fish, meat, and garden produce. The interest of national political figures in securing Maroon votes also led to the creation of a few steady jobs in the interior—for example as mechanics and operators of boats for the tribal chief—and increased the small stipends paid by the government to the chief, the headmen, and the assistant headmen. These developments meant that many men, and even some women, had access to modest amounts of cash in the villages. A few men took advantage of this situation by converting routine subsistence tasks, such as hunting or garden clearing, into money-making specialties. And others, encouraged by the increased accessibility of coastal resources, built tiny stores that stocked cloth, enamelware, costume jewelry, and canned foods.

These various changes have all begun to contribute to a new role for money in Saramakas' lives. For men, money had always represented a "foreign" substance, amassed outside of tribal territory as efficiently as possible, converted into useful goods within a several-day period of intensive buying in city stores and then, upon return to the home village, forgotten about for several years. For them, the changes of the 1960s and 1970s significantly expanded the range of contexts in which they could earn and spend money. For women, who had never dealt with money in any substantial way, the change was even more revolutionary, since it required an adaptation to an idiom for conceptualizing the value of goods and labor with which they had been almost totally unfamiliar.

The potential effects of this shift on social life are clearly profound, and Saramakas are expressing an awareness of them. A man who, ten years ago, would have divided the spoils of a day of solitary hunting with his wives and relatives now is tempted by the possibility of selling the meat instead (for example, to missionaries or to a fellow Saramaka who has no time to hunt because he is running a store) and using the money for personal needs. Women accustomed to sharing with their sisters and older kinswomen now know that their rice, manioc cakes, and ground peanuts are marketable commodities and that the money they produce can be converted directly into personal luxuries at local stores. People who are too old to work and women who are not married have begun to lament the increased self-interest with which goods are used and are attempting to adjust to the inevitable decline in their standard of living resulting from the new trend.

Saramaka Reciprocity

While the concept of money has traditionally been unimportant in Saramaka village life, the notion of "paying" has not. The terms *paká* and *paimá*, "to pay" and "payment," are heard frequently in conversations, and the kinds of situations in which they are relevant range from hunting and housekeeping to marriage and adultery, and include the whole range of ritual life.

The ways in which payments are used and the rhetoric with which they are discussed indicate that, in addition to functioning in a strict economic sense, the concept of paying carries strong symbolic meaning for Saramakas, and eighteenth-century missionary reports suggest that this has been true throughout Saramaka history. When one person performs a ritual service for another, such as preparing an herbal treatment for an illness, a symbolic "payment" is required to legitimize the favor. This mode of payment, known as "shouting *madjómina*," typically consists of the formal presentation of three small green sticks, accompanied by a dramatic verbal exchange in which they are elevated rhetorically to the status of a major economic transfer. Other token gifts may also contribute to the transaction. One person calls out a loud *"Madjómina!!"* The other replies *"Kaa!* Payment on the ground!" and lays down one of the sticks. The procedure is repeated twice more until all three sticks have been put down. Interspersed comments brashly identify each stick as, for example, "a hundred cloths" or "twenty manioc cakes," and other payments are similarly inflated. A person offering a small vial of rum may declare, for example, "Take this heavy jug of liquor!" Saramakas consider such a presentation necessary to satisfy the ancestors from whom the ritual knowledge was inherited, and believe that without a convincing "payment," the power of the medicine would be lost. This logic extends to other situations as well. People who are dissatisfied with medical treatment provided at the local missionary clinic, for example, sometimes travel to Paramaribo (where they are also eligible for free treatment at mission hospitals) and seek out a doctor who charges a fee for his services. Although they cannot easily afford to pay, Saramakas generally view compensation for treatment as a way of increasing the probability of a successful cure.

Related to the concept of *madjómina* is the custom of paying a person's soul (*akáa*). Saramakas sometimes "pay" the soul of a man who has returned from the coast with large amounts of goods, for example, by anointing him with an imported sweet drink during a special ritual and asking his soul for continued support. And even when a man distinguishes himself by buying a prestige item that he keeps for his own use, the notion of paying is appropriate. When one man told a kinswoman that he had purchased an outboard motor, for example, she sang a brief spontaneous song about it and then exclaimed, "What will I find to pay you? I'll have to *nyá papái* [be shamed by a failure to reciprocate properly³]."

The concept of paying is used in a wide variety of other contexts as well. If a girl is found to be a virgin on her wedding night, she is "paid" with gifts, such as a gold necklace, a hammock sheet, or some cooking pots, by both the husband and her lineal kin.⁴ A man whose wife scrapes clean the ground around his house may reciprocate with an item from his storage trunks, such as a piece of cloth or an enamel bowl—an action referred to either as giving thanks or paying. If a woman commits adultery ("takes a [new] husband in her [former] husband's house"), her lineage may demand a "payment" from the new husband in order to compensate the former husband for his loss. And there are some men who (like the Aluku Maroons [Hurault

1961:151]) have a practice of "paying" their wives with small gifts whenever they enter a new marriage, to compensate them for the burden of the additional co-wife. Indeed, any reciprocation of a gift or service may be referred to in Saramaccan as a "payment." In most cases, the return gifts involve only token amounts of goods, but they serve a crucial function in symbolically balancing the exchange by making it a two-way transaction.

The negative counterpart of payment is revenge, and the place of this concept in Saramaka life further attests to the importance of "paying" in Saramaka understandings. The concepts of avenging spirits (*kúnu*) and "planting sweet potatoes" (*paandí batáta*) represent the two most developed manifestations of the Saramaka notion of revenge. In the institution of *kúnu*, spirits who are thought to have been offended by living individuals pay back the injustice against them through an eternal succession of aggressive acts aimed at the wrongdoer's matrilineal kin and descendants. The theory behind "planting sweet potatoes" is identical. Just as sweet potatoes, once planted, tend to sprout again long after they have been forgotten, it is believed that a person's hostile actions toward someone else (such as adultery or slander) will inevitably be "paid back" in some way, whether intentionally or not, in the future. And countless smaller aspects of Saramaka life are phrased in a similar idiom; a standard retort to an insult is "You'll have to pay me!"[5]

Gift Presentations

In Saramaka, the importance of reciprocity and the strong complementarity of men's and women's contributions to material life combine to give special importance to those exchanges that occur between men and women. There do, of course, exist situations in which a man gives to a man, or a woman to a woman. Ritual specialists of both sexes receive payments for their services; inheritances involve both male and female relatives of the dead person; women sometimes share food supplies with a kinswoman; formal friendships between same-sex pairs are cemented through occasional gifts; and certain kinds of compensatory payments, such as those for adultery, are distributed by the receiving kin group to both male and female members. But the great bulk of goods that change hands are passed across male-female lines, and all of the major institutionalized occasions for the presentation of goods are centered on exchanges between husbands and wives.[6]

Within male-female exchanges of goods, men are providers more than women, and the nature of the goods proffered differs by sex as well. Men supply women with virtually all imported goods (cloth, cookware, kerosene, soap, salt, hammocks, sewing supplies, lanterns, commercial jewelry, and other items), the bulk of the fish and game in their diet, most of their basketry, and all objects fashioned from wood (houses, canoes, mortars, winnowing trays, combs, and so forth). Women supply men with prepared foods and sew most of their clothing.[7]

In Saramaka ideology, the primary social context in which all these goods are supplied is marriage. Goods do flow between children and parents, between brothers and sisters, and between affines—because not everyone has a spouse at all times, because spouses are not always available, and because people also use goods as symbolic expressions of solidarity with nonspouses. But these are, both in amounts and in Saramaka perceptions of them, only supplementary to the exchanges which continually affirm and reaffirm conjugal bonds. And the provision of labor (horticultural tasks, housekeeping, and so forth) follows the same pattern.

There are, in the course of almost all marriages, three particularly important presentations between husband and wife, as well as a series of opportunities for ongoing exchanges of more modest proportions. The initiation of a marriage involves a visit by the man to the woman's village, for which he loads gifts into a special Indian basket (for a woman who has never had a husband before) or an imported valise (for a woman who has previously been married). This event is referred to as "loading the [marriage] basket" (*lái pakáa*).[8] Shortly thereafter, the woman reciprocates with her first visit as a wife to the man's village, taking with her carefully prepared baskets of gifts. The terms for this visit also focus attention on the presentation of goods—"loading the [standard woman's] basket" or "breaking open the [standard woman's] basket" (*lái mánda, boóko mánda*). Third, the celebration of a man's return from an extended work trip to the coast represents an important renewal of the marriage after a period of separation. This event is known as "pulling the goods to the ground" (*púu dí gúdu a goón*).

In addition, as should already be clear, smaller gift exchanges intermittently punctuate conjugal relationships. Even before a marriage is entered, lovers offer each other material tokens of their affection. For example, the man may present a carved comb, a small cooking pot, or one of his own capes, and the woman may give him an embroidered neckerchief. A man betrothed to an "apron girl" is expected to offer periodic gifts to her and her relatives, and she reciprocates by bringing cooked delicacies when she pays him a visit. A man working on the coast sends gifts back to his wives in Saramaka, and the women go to some pains to find couriers for their gifts to him as well. Presents are exchanged between spouses on the occasion of their baby's ceremonial introduction to the community. Other presentations are made just prior to a man's departure for a coastal work trip. And, of course, food—whether the man's fish and game or the woman's cooked meals—represents a continuous ongoing exchange. The following paragraphs are intended to give some sense of the scale of exchanges that are made in the context of marriage.

Betrothal

After the man's kinsmen have conducted formal discussions with members of the girl's family and resolved potential objections to the match, he presents several examples of his wood carving (typically, a comb, a food stirrer, and a paddle), some jewelry (such as a pair of earrings), one of his capes (often one he has made himself) for her to wear if she wishes, and a cape and breechcloth for her to keep in storage, as a symbol of their relationship. For example, one presentation that was made to a prepubescent girl in 1968 consisted of a carved comb, two skirt-cloths, a pair of barrettes, a pair of earrings, a tin of talcum powder, a jar of pomade, and an enamel dish, as well as a cape and breechcloth belonging to the man. The girl's lineage holds these presents until the marriage takes place, since they would have to be given back to the man in the event that the agreement was broken before the marriage was formalized. In the weeks following this presentation, the man makes a special hunting trip for game to offer to his future in-laws, and the girl will later be brought by her kinswomen to the man's village to present a meal and special culinary delicacies. After this, very little is exchanged until the marriage itself. For example, the girl might embroider a neckerchief or dance apron and crochet a pair of calfbands, and the man might offer an occasional small wood carving or help in clearing a garden site for her horticultural camp.

Marriage: The Man's Presentation

Ideals about what gifts a man should give at marriage are usually phrased in terms of a woman's first marriage; those for subsequent unions are envisioned as scaled-down versions of the same list. As one man commented, "taking [marrying] apron girls is the greatest joy for us [male] Saramakas; once a woman has had a husband, it's not quite the same." The following list, compiled on the basis of six different examples from the field, represents the contents of a properly pre-pared marriage basket: two hammocks, two hammock sheets, one "mosquito net,"[9] one hammock tie, five skirt-length cloths, a package of bar soap, a tin lantern, three liters of kerosene, some matches, several metal spoons and a fork or two, a small aluminum pot (used to ladle drinking water), a few enamel plates, a package of needles, and several pieces of the man's own clothing. In addition, a penny and a straight pin must be laid on top of a piece of paper in the bottom of the basket. Saramakas are very careful to observe this requirement as protection, they say, against the woman later accusing the husband of "never having given her so much as a pin/penny." The man does not present the basket in person, but leaves it in his canoe and, together with the brothers who have accompanied him, is served a meal in the house of one of the bride's kinsmen. Meanwhile, her sisters bring the basket ashore and unpack its contents in the house where the couple will be sleeping.

Marriage: The Woman's Presentation

The goods presented by a woman on the occasion of her first visit as an affine to the husband's village do not tend to vary according to whether it is a first or a subsequent marriage. And while, as we have seen, the man seals a new marriage by offering gifts to his wife, the woman's offerings—which are equally important in legitimizing the marriage—consist mainly of supplies for her own future housekeep-ing, plus gifts of food that are consumed that day. Although this important presentation is referred to in terms of a single woman's basket, it is usually voluminous enough so that it must be divided among two such baskets and a large plastic washtub. In addition, the woman brings the marriage basket that her husband has recently given her (containing a hammock, some clothes, and other personal belongings), some winnowed rice (usually in a separate bucket), and a supply of firewood for cooking. An inventory of the food and house-hold supplies brought by one twenty-year-old woman who married a

Dangogo man in 1968 may serve as a representative example of these presentations. In her baskets were three stirring sticks, six calabash ladles, twelve calabash bowls of assorted forms, six metal spoons, one knife, one aluminum pot (to ladle drinking water), one rice stalk broom for the house, one twig broom for the yard, three enamel plates, five calabash containers filled with winnowed rice, two bottles of palm oil, several smoked fish, some okra, and six handsome manioc cakes. In the dishpan were six bowls and pots, each containing a different festive food such as peanut rice, cooked meats, and confections made with peanuts, bananas, coconut, and rice flour. Note that a number of the items in such a list (for example, much of the cookware) represent recent gifts from the husband's marriage basket. Other "basket openings" that I have witnessed included similar supplies, as well as carved wooden food stirrers, prepared hot pepper sauce, and other cooked foods such as root crops, plantains, and coconuts. For this visit, the woman is accompanied by a few of her female relatives (often sisters), and all of them are profusely thanked and "paid" with small gifts by the new husband. Each time I have seen this presentation, the participants have made a special point of the fact that the bride's sisters-in-law, and never a mother-in-law, must have the honor of unloading the treasures. Their steady flow of effusive and very exaggerated compliments on the skill reflected in each carved calabash, patterned manioc cake, and pot of festive food is important in symbolizing their solidarity with the bride. Older female relatives of the man are playfully introduced as her new co-wives. Others salute her with an archaic greeting (*Wêndjè, ódi*) intended to mark the momentousness of the occasion. Women from the man's family may jokingly pretend to have come with the bride and ask to be "paid" for their participation. And compliments to the woman and her companions fill the house. "These people certainly didn't come here in a sloppy way!" "Did you ever see such a houseful of fine things?" "This is something that must be unpacked in full daylight [so the details can be fully appreciated]." "How can she bake manioc without a fire [that is, achieve such perfectly even cooking, with no dark spots where the cake has been burned]?"

Return from a Coastal Trip

The returns of a man from the coast are usually the biggest celebrations of a marriage, and in a real sense symbolize the Saramaka conception of conjugal reciprocity more than any other single event. This is a time of villagewide rejoicing for many reasons. The presentation of massive amounts of goods, which is always conducted in the man's village, means that the man has succeeded on the coast and that the woman has remained faithful during his absence. It means that the community is gaining an important member, who can now contribute to the tasks of clearing garden sites, building canoes and houses, conducting rituals, and hunting and fishing. And it means that the material life of his wife or wives is suddenly significantly enriched, and that others will also receive presents of cloth, cookware, and other goods. This is the time when women break into the joyous and sexually suggestive *bandámmba* dance (see R. and S. Price 1977), and it is generally a moment of loud joking, some drinking, libations of thanks to ancestors and gods, and singing and dancing both at the presentation of gifts in the man's village and upon the woman's return to hers. A Saramaka woman's idealized account that I recorded in 1978 may give some sense of the excitement associated with this event:

> The woman works on art [*têmbe*] while her husband is away on the coast. She does everything; she gathers palm nuts to make oil for him, makes calfbands, sews things, and on and on until her husband finally returns. The husband and wife will sleep together for three nights [before] he gives her the coastal goods.
>
> [On the third day] he loads up a trunk, maybe a hundred cloths, maybe seventy or sixty or fifty or thirty. He and his kinsmen will load up the trunk till it's full, and put it aside. Then they pull over the soap crate and the kerosene drum—just slide it right on over. Then they take buckets, machetes, cooking tripods, and set them there. Finally they take all those enamel and metal things from the coast—dishes, pots, spoons, knives, chamber pots—and they put those there too. They get them all together. Then everyone sleeps until morning.
>
> Then the man calls the woman and he says, "Well, wife, come look at some presents your sisters-in-law have for you." And his sisters arrive at his house. They pick up the trunk—*kidé kidé kidé* [the rhythm of their walking with a heavy load on their heads]—and carry it to the woman's house. They come back and get the kerosene drum—*kidé kidé kidé*—over to the woman's house. Now they get all the goods and load them up in the woman's house. [Here the speaker pantomimed the wife, coyly looking at the floor, fingering the hem of her skirt, and squirming, embarrassed, on her stool.] Well, they'll load up things until they're completely finished.
>
> Then they'll say "Well, sister-in-law . . . well, woman, don't you see? Here's a little something for you, that we're giving you here, since your husband's gone and come back." (Only the sisters-in-law are present; the husband is back in his own house.) The sisters-in-law will address the

woman, "Woman!" She answers shyly, "Yes?" "Well, woman, the things here are really nothing. But here's just a little something for you. Here's a little salt for you, so you can boil some taro leaves for us to eat. We've brought some goods to give you." Then everyone really celebrates in that house!

Then the woman says "Listen to me!" and she jumps up. She'll load [into an enamel dishpan] some calfbands. She'll load some narrow-strip cloths. She'll load some cross-stitch cloths. She tells the others "Take these to the man for me." And they'll set everything on their heads and carry it off to the man. The woman will stay in her own house, rejoicing over her presents while all the others go off to the man's house. Then the man will say, "Well, here's something for you to take over to the woman." This last present can be anything from the coast—any kind of dishware, maybe an aluminum water jug. . . . They bring it over and say "Woman, don't you see? Here's something that your husband sent over for you." The wife will jump right up—*vúúúú!* She'll grab the one thing that she hasn't yet given him and, right there, she'll give it to her husband's lineage. She'll always have one thing held back, to give him separately. It could be some cross-stitch or an embroidered neckerchief, or whatever. "Take this thing here; go drape the man with it for me" [a way of thanking his soul].

After her gift is presented, shouts will ring out *wooooo!!* "My goodness! The woman has really pulled the goods to the ground!" That means that she hasn't *nyá papái* [been shamed by having too little to reciprocate his gifts]. That's what's known as "pulling the goods to the ground."

The volume of goods presented is extremely variable, depending on the length of the man's time on the coast, his skill and luck with both jobs and living expenses there, the number of wives involved, and the current market value of imported goods on the coast. With this important caution, I present an inventory of the goods that a sixty-year-old man brought back in 1965 after a seven-year stay in French Guiana, as an example of the kinds of goods involved. Note that it is usual for Saramaka men to give out less than half of the goods they buy after a long work trip, keeping the rest for future needs over the next several years—occasional presents to their wives, a marriage basket or valise for a new wife, payments for ritual services, and so forth. Note also that because the man reconstructed this list three years after he had assembled the goods, it is somewhat incomplete. Although he remembered two thousand guilders as the amount he spent at the end, the items listed, together with transportation costs, account for only about fifteen hundred guilders. (At the time these purchases were made, a Suriname guilder was worth approximately fifty-six cents in United States currency).

Items Purchased	Total Value in Suriname Guilders	Amount Given to Each of Two Wives
10 crates bar soap	90	1 crate
1 barrel kerosene	44	1 demijohn
3 barrels salt	28	1 barrel
sugar (quantity not indicated)	10	1 bowlful[10]
4 heavy rice pots	43	1 pot
2 large aluminum pots	18	1 pot
6 medium-size pots	20	1 pot
2 washtubs	4	1 tub
6 buckets	24	2 buckets
12 enamel basins	12	3 basins
12 china bowls	10	5 bowls
2 aluminum jugs	12	1 jug
2 dozen metal spoons	7	1 dozen spoons
6 small knives	3	2 knives
30 lengths of French cotton (a type of plaid used largely for men's clothing in Saramaka)	43	3 lengths
200 lengths of striped cotton bought in Paramaribo (used mainly for women's skirts)	200	40 lengths
8 hammocks	160	2 hammocks
12 waistkerchief cloths	6	3 cloths
12 hammock sheets	48	2 sheets
12 balls cotton yarn	12	3 balls
6 machetes	10	1 machete
5 women's tin lanterns	5	2 lanterns
2 cartons matches	1.50	2 boxes
6 aluminum pots (used as water ladles)	9	1 pot
3 "mosquito nets" (see note 9)	45	1 "net"
needles and thread	1.50	unspecified
20 liters rum	60	—
6 bottles súti sópi (a syrupy drink for rituals)	4	—
12 bottles beer (for ritual washings)	6	—
1 shotgun	150	—
5 packages shotgun shells	45	—
1 tin gunpowder	5	—
5 sacks gunshot	25	—
cartridge primers	5	—
1 flashlight	2	—
6 batteries	1.50	—
1 Primus stove	12	—
1 liter alcohol	0.50	—
2 men's lanterns	5	—
2 axes	16	—
3 trunks	69	—
1 tarpaulin for canoe	1.50	—
1 raincoat	3.50	—
2 hats	10	—
1 alarm clock[11]	10	—

As "thanks" for these gifts, one wife gave the man three patch-work capes, one breechcloth, two embroidered neckerchiefs, and one bottle of palm oil, and the other presented him with three patchwork capes, two embroidered capes, and two embroidered neckerchiefs.

Incidental Gift Giving

There are also times when a spouse offers special gifts simply as an expression of affection and conjugal commitment, and these are always explicitly reciprocated. For example, one presentation made by a woman to her husband in 1967 included an undecorated breechcloth, a special narrow-strip breechcloth, an embroidered hammock bag, a bottle of palm oil, a narrow-strip cape, and several smaller presents. It was made clear, both when the gifts were given and when they were commented on (at length) in later gossip sessions, that these were in response to specific conjugal presents from the husband over the previous several months—a wooden rice pestle, four carved trays, five skirt-cloths, and four basketry sieves (one for rice flour, one for manioc flour, one for baked manioc, and one to hang in her house for decoration).

Adultery Payments

When a man simply divorces a wife, or in the rare case when a woman divorces her husband without having another man waiting to marry her, there is no material compensation. When a union is terminated because of the woman's sexual infidelity, however, there may be a substantial payment—defined by the woman's lineage, supplied by the woman's lover, accepted by the wronged husband, and eventually shared with members of the wronged husband's lineage. The size of such a payment is geared to the age of the woman involved. In the 1960s, while a woman in her fifties merited a payment on the order of fifty skirt-cloths, thirty liters of rum, two hammock sheets, two hammocks, and one "mosquito net," Saramakas reasoned that this amount would be "too heavy for the soul" of a younger girl. Adultery with a twenty-year-old would have been appropriately compensated by twenty skirt-cloths, one hammock, one hammock sheet, one hammock cover, and six liters of rum. Earlier in this century, when imported goods were scarcer, adultery payments were considerably smaller. A representative case in the 1940s, for example, involved only twelve skirt-cloths, one hammock, one hammock sheet, and four liters of rum. Regardless of their size, however, adultery payments have always been unambiguously distinguished from other conjugal presentations by their lack of artistically decorated objects.

Mourning

When a married man or woman dies, the spouses enter a period of mourning that is marked by a dramatic change in their material life. They sit on the ground rather than on a carved wooden stool. They wear unlaundered rags rather than clean clothes. They may not wear any jewelry, and their hair is cropped close to the head. Some possessions, such as canoes or a man's gun, machete, and axe, are taken for the duration of the mourning period by the spouse's lineage. The contributions of people who attend the funeral rites are responsible for a large-scale redistribution of material goods. A wide range of people supply food (to be consumed during the period preceding burial) and goods (to be set in the coffin or distributed among people in attendance, as thanks for their support). The dead person's own possessions are partly set into the coffin and partly distributed among mourners. A special role is played by conjugal presents that have been offered in the past. Careful attention is given to the inclusion in the coffin of some piece of clothing that had belonged to each of the person's spouses, past and present. The personal clothing that is exchanged at the beginning of a marriage is explicitly understood not only as a token of affection, but also as proper fulfillment of this future obligation. Finally, one conjugal gift is reserved to mark the surviving spouse's emergence from mourning. After a husband has fulfilled his mourning obligations and gone to Paramaribo to be ritually released from his period of sexual continence through intercourse with a city prostitute, he returns to his dead wife's kin, who dress him in the cape and breechcloth that he had packed in his marriage basket or valise when he first entered the marriage.[12]

Husbands, Wives, and the Value of Things

Several interrelated features of Saramakas' social life and material exchange are directly relevant to an understanding of the arts. First, husbands are scarcer than wives. Second, women are significantly more dependent on their husbands than men are on their wives. Third, women attach more symbolic value to both the giving and the receiving of gifts than men do. I will elaborate on each of these points in turn, for they will be important in building an understanding of the ways in which men's arts and women's arts are differently valued in Saramaka.

The Relative Scarcity of Husbands, Compared to Wives

Even though many Saramaka men have two or three or even four wives, there are, at any one time, many more women without a husband than men without a wife. Furthermore, while for men being unmarried is virtually always a temporary state that can be altered more or less when they choose, women's opportunities for remarriage decline sharply with age, so that women who are widowed or divorced in their forties face a very real prospect of remaining permanently without a husband, and women past menopause virtually never remarry. This asymmetry in the availability of spouses is produced by several features of the social system. The most important is that the long-term emigration of men to the coast reduces by a full 50 percent the pool of potential husbands available at any one time. Furthermore, there is a significantly lower marriage age for women than for men (with most women entering their first marriage at age thirteen to sixteen and men in their mid-twenties). Finally, the strong tendency for all young women (in their teens and twenties) to be married further intensifies the scarcity of husbands for women during the rest of their adult life, so that, as we saw in chapter 3, being without a spouse is a state that is forced on well over half of Saramaka women during their later years.

The Greater Material Dependence of Women Than Men on Their Spouses

While we have observed several institutionalized situations in which men make massive presentations of goods (both at the initiation of a marriage and upon return from each coastal trip), we have also noted that women's gifts are considerably more modest in scale—at the most consisting, for example, of four or five pieces of clothing (when they reciprocate a husband's coastal goods) or an array of festive dishes that will be distributed widely and consumed within a day or two (when they make their first formal visit to the husband's village). In fact, much of what a woman prepares as fulfillment of conjugal responsibilities is never used by the husband at all. It is extremely common for men to accept carefully embroidered clothing or handsomely crocheted calfbands and then never have occasion to wear them. Likewise, the basket opening at a woman's first visit to her husband's village serves to reflect on her aptitude in womanly skills (food processing, calabash carving, decorative sewing, and domestic organization in general), without producing any substantial gifts for the husband.

Because of the different nature and scale of their respective contributions, a man's conjugal gifts materially affect the well-being of individual women, but a woman's conjugal gifts make very little difference in the material well-being of individual men. Let us look at how this comes about. In Saramaka ideals, a woman is dependent for a large range of goods and services on one man—her husband—who should provide her with a house, canoe, and household furnishings (both imported and locally made), as well as the bulk of fish and game in her diet and the male labor needed in garden clearing. When she has no husband or when her husband is away for long periods, she is put in the position of "begging" a kinsman to help out. But a man who builds a house for his kinswoman is not expected to lavish the careful workmanship on it that her husband would have provided (fig. 9). He generally gives fish and game to his kinswoman only when there is some left over from what he has given his own wives. And his responsibilities in clearing gardens for his own wives often mean that his unmarried kinswomen have to make do with reworking an old garden rather than planting a new one.

Furthermore, women's ownership of imported goods, perhaps the most variable aspect of women's possessions, is closely correlated with marital status.[13] A woman without a husband is provided with cloth, cookware, kerosene, and so forth by her kinsmen, but at a sharply reduced level from that she would have enjoyed if she had a husband. Locally made products are treated similarly. A husband may present wooden objects (combs, kitchen utensils, trays, paddles, and so forth) as gifts of affection, whether or not they are really needed, and he takes pride in their design and decorative embellishment. But for an unmarried kinswoman, these objects are crafted only when there is a pressing need, and they are not given the artistic treatment that would go into a conjugal gift. In sum, then, an unmarried woman "gets along" with the help of kinsmen, but the level of her

Fig. 9. Women's houses in Dangogo. One (*top*) is decoratively embellished by a husband's wood carving; the other (*bottom*) was built while the owner's husband was away on the coast.

material life is significantly lower than that of married women—both
in terms of bare subsistence and in terms of the aesthetic component
of her household.

In contrast, the kinds of dependence that men have on women do
not produce a similar kind of vulnerability. The most important material contributions that women make to men are meals and clothing,
but neither one represents a particularly variable aspect of men's
lives. The most obvious reason for this has already been mentioned—
that men are only rarely without a wife. Not only are men generally
married for most of their lives, but because of widespread polygyny, a
man is frequently in the position of being provided for by two or
three women at a time, all of whom are consciously competing for his
favor. Many men have valises and trunks filled with beautifully designed clothing that they have never worn. In terms of food, the
practice of communal meals for the men of a neighborhood (to which
visitors are welcome as well) means that meals are always available to
men, whether or not their own wives are providing them.[14] Thus, the
fact that men are married for more of their lives than women, that
they often have multiple wives, and that the most fundamental contribution that women make to their lives—meals—is a shared resource,
all combine to create a situation in which individual men cannot be
significantly deprived of female contributions to their lives to the
same extent that women can be deprived of male contributions.

The Greater Value of Conjugal Exchanges
for Women Than for Men

We have already noted that husbands are in shorter supply than wives
and that husbands exercise greater influence on material well-being
than do wives. These two features combine to create different attitudes among men and women toward the fulfillment of conjugal
responsibilities. There is no doubt that Saramaka women are more
insecure than Saramaka men about pleasing their spouses, in terms of
both the proper fulfillment of their own obligations and the adequate
reciprocation of their spouses' offerings. It is perhaps significant that
the term for the shame of having reciprocated a gift poorly (nyá papái)
is used frequently in discussing women, but that it is not usually
applied to men. Even the etiquette of conjugal exchanges (as well as
cross-sex exchanges more generally) reflects different attitudes toward the material contributions of men and women. Women are expected to offer more effusive expressions of gratitude, to display their

gifts to a wide range of other people, and to indulge in behavior similar to that of American women on television game shows who win cars or washing machines or trips to Hawaii. Saramaka men also express thanks, but in a much more subdued style. And the main contribution women make to men's life—prepared food—is treated, not as a gift to be acknowledged, but as the simple fulfillment of a woman's duties. Women focus attention on meal preparation and service because it is a requirement of marriage, and because marriage is a valuable state that cannot be taken for granted. Men expect tasty food and attractive meal service, and they know that if one woman does not provide it, another one will.

The Artistic Dimension

From a "functional" perspective, we could argue that the provision of goods and services by one individual for another operates, at least potentially, in three ways. First and most obviously, it can supply persons with materials or labor to which they do not have direct access. Second, it can provide an idiom by which a person (the giver) expresses affective feelings and social commitments toward another (the recipient). Third, it can furnish materials that have special symbolic potential for the recipient. That is, gift giving can be viewed as an economic transfer, as an expressive act on the part of the giver, or as the provision of socially useful symbols for the recipient. In Saramaka, men's gifts and women's gifts—and especially those that involve artistic efforts—operate differently in terms of these three dimensions, and this fact has had a direct influence on the perceived value of men's arts and women's arts. Because of the respective statuses of men and women within the society, men's gifts to women are treated as important symbols of specific conjugal relationships, but women's gifts to men are not generally used in this way.

The artistic embellishment of a gift is an important clue to its intended meaning. When an unmarried Saramaka woman asks a brother to make a canoe for her because she has none, he carves one with the proper type of wood and is careful to make it the correct dimensions, but he does not spend much time on the decorative touches. In this case, the "economic" value of the gift far outweighs its personal symbolic value. At the other extreme, when a man makes a food stirrer for a new wife, embellishing the entire surface with elaborate openwork carving (occasionally so extensively that it cannot be used for cooking—see S. and R. Price 1980a: figs. 123–25), the expressive value of the gift overrides its economic usefulness. Most gifts, of course, fall somewhere in between.

It may be legitimate to view the artistic dimension of an object as a particularly rich opportunity for signaling the expressive intent behind it. Saramakas go even further than to say that artistic design defines a gift as expressive of social ties. To them, the use of a gift to express social ties also may define it as "art" (têmbe). Thus, a person enumerating a list of Saramaka women's arts may include the processing of palm nuts for cooking oil in situations in which the oil is intended as part of a conjugal presentation, and unadorned objects, such as a rice mortar and pestle, may be referred to as "art" when they are made by a man for his wife. Similarly, the evaluation of artistic excellence is closely tied to social factors. For example, two women commenting for me on the quality and beauty of a large number of calabashes were visibly swayed in their assessments of certain examples once they realized that they had been made by a younger sister-in-law of theirs and presented in her recent "basket opening" ceremony.

A comparison of the social uses of wood carvings and decorated textiles may help to clarify the ways in which attitudes about art and attitudes about relations between the sexes are intertwined. Because each of these arts is produced by members of one sex mainly for presentation to members of the other, the ways in which they are conceptualized, discussed, and used lend themselves to direct comparison.

Just as husbands are scarcer than wives in Saramaka, wood carvings are scarcer than decorative textiles, and this alone confers on wood carvings a special kind of value. Inventories of a number of women's possessions indicate that while women may have two or three combs and up to five or six stools, they tend to own only one or two examples of most kinds of decoratively carved objects—paddles, food stirrers, peanut-grinding boards, and so forth.[15] These objects are displayed in the woman's house (in contrast to textiles, which are stored in trunks), and women are always able to supply a detailed account of who made each one and when it was presented. Wood carvings, then, represent to women tangible and very visible symbols of specific personal relationships (fig. 10).

Textiles are a very different matter. Because most men have two

Fig. 10. The carving on this wooden tray includes the initials of the man who made it and the wife for whom it was a gift.

or three wives at a time (as well as a large number of lovers, who also offer gifts of affection), their storage trunks are generally filled with hundreds of capes, breechcloths, dance aprons, calfbands, and neckerchiefs. I became aware of the scale of men's textile holdings in two ways. First, it is customary for a man who has returned from a several-year stay on the coast to air the contents of his trunks outdoors, in order to remove mold and chase away cockroaches. At such house-cleaning operations, I have often counted several hundred textiles. And in the 1970s, when I began to investigate textile arts, I asked a number of men whether I could inventory their clothing systematically. This, too, produced an astonishing volume of pieces. When I discussed these textiles with their owners, it became clear that only very few of them retained specific romantic meanings. Men often did not know which wife or lover had sewn a particular textile, but tended to see their collections as largely undifferentiated accumulations of gifts from women. Indeed, the only portion of a man's personal textile collection that is certain to evoke memories of specific women is a small, distinctly private, and rarely contemplated set of memorabilia.

Somewhere in each man's trunks is a tied kerchief containing the adolescent aprons that he has obtained, either on wedding nights with never-married girls or as gifts from adolescent lovers. For example, one ninety-year-old man who kindly spent three days opening his trunks for my inspection came upon such a kerchief in the course of the project. Excusing himself with obvious delight and commenting that he hadn't seen this bundle in over twenty-five years, he turned his back to me (and to one of his three wives, who was also present) and unfolded each cloth in turn, reminiscing silently and announcing proudly at the end, in the language that he associated with his youth as a wage laborer in French Guiana, "*Quinze!*[15]."

Calabashes—the third major artistic medium for Maroons—are also intended primarily for use in a conjugal context, but unlike wood carvings and textiles, they are never conjugal gifts. Rather, they serve as an important kind of aesthetic display. Like embroidered linens in an Andalusian dowry or well-polished silver at a formal dinner party in the United States, decorated calabashes are understood primarily to reflect the care and good taste of the woman who sets them out, and as such they form part of the core Saramaka conception of a woman's role in marriage. The display of calabashes is also, as we have seen, an important aspect of the presentation that marks a woman's first visit to a new husband's village, and some women also decorate the interiors of their houses in their husband's village with extensive arrays of carefully selected calabashes (see S. and R. Price 1980*a:* figs. 23–24).

In short, wood, textiles, and calabashes—the three main materials of artistic expression in Saramaka—play complementary roles in social life. Wood carvings are highly valued by women, and each carved object is understood as an important symbol of the relationship between the man who created it and the woman to whom he gave it. Textiles offer an idiom for women to express their love for a man, but they do not tend to be imbued with specific romantic associations by men. Carved calabashes communicate the care with which a woman fulfills her conjugal duties without ever being used as a conjugal gift. Chapters 5 and 6 present more detailed examinations of the two arts that are produced by women, tracing their development through time and exploring the ways in which each one contributes to Saramaka life.

Chapter Five

Carved Fruits

For Saramakas, calabashes are a women's thing. The trees are owned by women, the fruits are processed by women, and the finished products (mainly bowls, ladles, and other dishware) belong to women. Women talk about calabashes frequently, men mention them only rarely. Even covered calabash containers, which are decorated by men, are envisioned strictly as women's possessions. These are grown and turned into containers by women, given to men for the exterior decoration, and then returned again to women for household use.

The tree that provides calabashes (*Crescentia cujete* L.) is about the size of a small apple tree (fig. 11). The fruits vary in size from five to twenty-five centimeters in diameter, and in shape from round to oval, occasionally with a slight bulge at the stem end.

Forms and Uses

Saramakas distinguish at least seven varieties of the calabash tree (*kúya*), and utilize the fruits of each for somewhat different purposes. Large rice-washing bowls are made from one variety (*gaán kúya*) that produces large calabashes with thick shells. Most spoons and ladles are fashioned from the smaller fruit of either *kuyêè* or *Pempe kúya* trees. A variety known as *koómbu kiíki* is used whenever possible for covered containers. Drinking bowls and hand-washing bowls are usually made from the fruit of *bakáa kúya* or *mátu kúya* trees. And calabashes from the *bíngo kúya*, which protrude slightly at the stem, are used for small drinking cups. Ritual uses of calabashes tend also to be specialized. For example, the bowl that holds water for washing a body prior to burial must be made from the fruit of the *gaán kúya* tree. When a woman needs calabashes from a variety that she herself does not own, she asks someone else for them and later "pays" her—either with several calabashes from one of her own trees or, more commonly, with a few of the finished bowls. Women prepare a dozen or

Fig. 11.   A calabash tree (*Crescentia cujete* L.)

more calabashes at a time (producing, for example, two dozen bowls and several ladles), and usually distribute some of them to friends and kinswomen as repayment for a variety of previous favors.

Calabash technology begins with selection of the materials. Fruit that appears to be ready is knocked with a kitchen knife; women explain that if it is ripe, it answers a sharp "*ká! ká! ká!*,"and if not it sounds a dull "*pòpòpò*." Several pieces are thus selected and broken from their stems. The next day these are sawed in half with a knife and the pulp removed with either a metal spoon or the fingers. They are immersed in a large vat of boiling water for something under half an hour, after which the remaining mushy pulp is scraped out with a spoon at the river's edge. (Calabashes destined to become rattles are boiled whole, after which a stick inserted through a small opening is manipulated to loosen the pulp.)

At this point, some shells may be designated as closed containers and given to a man to be carved, but the great majority will be decorated by the woman herself. When she is ready to work on her calabashes, she sits on the ground or a low stool with legs outstretched. Her first job is to shape the bowl or utensil, which she does by breaking off bits along the side with her hands and teeth and smoothing the edge with a knife. She next prepares a small piece of glass from a bottle by striking it carefully with the handle of her knife until it breaks in the desired shape, and begins to plan out the design, scratching it in lightly with the piece of glass.[1] Many women begin their bowls by drawing the interior border, an even band that runs along the edge of the bowl. Then they mark in the central design itself, thoughtfully rotating the shell in their hands again and again as they place, for example, a central lozenge and its curved appendages in the appropriate positions. The entire design is gone over with the broken glass; the interior space of each band is scraped out, with the point of the glass drawn firmly along each of its outer edges to create a sharp, clear line. An even band is scraped out along the exterior edge of the bowl, and the carving is finished. The decorated shells are left soaking in water for about a week to soften them, rubbed smooth with an abrasive leaf and with fine sand, and dried in the sun. Finally, they are rubbed with lime halves, rinsed, and dried again.

Saramaka terminology distinguishes three main types of houseware that are made from calabash shells: (1) *apakí*—two-piece containers made from a single fruit cut apart at the equator, (2) *kúya*—bowls made from half of a fruit, cut through the stem perpendicular to the equator, and (3) *kuyêè*—spoons, ladles, and rice-mounding utensils, made from fruit that has been cut through the stem perpendicular to the equator. Within each category, distinctions are made according to both form and function.

Apakí (fig. 12)

Gwamba apakí, which are large and undecorated, are used to store salted meat or fish. *Maíki apakí* are medium-sized containers that are handsomely carved on the exterior by men and used primarily to carry winnowed rice to a husband's village. Small containers are usually undecorated and include *sátu apakí* which are for storing salt, and *biôngo apakí,* which hold ritual ingredients such as herbs or kaolin and are often equipped with a fiber handle. Covered calabash containers may also serve as lunch boxes for men away from home for the day; a covered enamel bowl with the man's food is put inside the container, together with a calabash drinking bowl and a spoon, and the whole is tied together in a cloth.

Kúya (fig. 13)

Bebé wáta kúya (water-drinking bowls) are round, medium-sized, and handsomely decorated and are served at men's meals. Wási máu kúya (hand-washing bowls) are also handsomely decorated and served at men's meals, but their form is shallower and slightly elongated. Wási alísi kúya (rice-washing bowls) are very sparsely decorated and are used to wash rice prior to cooking. Finally, wási uwíi kúya (ritual washing bowls) are large and undecorated, and tiny calabash cups may be decorated with simple markings and used to give water to infants.

Kuyêè (fig. 14)

This category includes tiny pikí kuyêè (small spoons) used for eating, medium-size lalú kuyêè (okra ladles) used in daily cooking, larger gaán kuyêè (large ladles) used in cooking for community events, and shallow, oval angú kuyêè (rice mounders) used to shape rice when it is served at men's meals.

Although the great majority of calabashes are made into one of these three forms, some are used for rattles, others have (until recently) provided rings on which dishes may be set at meals, and others are used for a variety of specialized ritual purposes. During a difficult birth, for example, a calabash of the gaán kúya variety may be picked from the tree and pounded with a pestle on the floor. Once the baby is born, the mashed pulp is rubbed all over it, and every piece of the shell is pounded until it is totally destroyed. During one stage of Saramaka funeral rituals, calabashes are smashed in a similar manner. Calabashes are also used in the treatment of a chest pain that Saramakas understand as a symptom of a "fallen heart." A small disc cut from a ripe calabash is scraped clean and dried in the sun; later, when it is needed, a little rum is poured into it with a bit of dried corn silk and lit with a match, and the hot disc is pressed onto the chest, where it remains for as long as a day. One of the most frequent ritual uses of calabashes is for ablutions, and in many instances the site of the washing is converted into a small shrine by installing the calabash bowl in a forked stick set into the ground. Finally, calabash bowls are used in the treatment of illnesses that are diagnosed, by divination, as a loss of the person's soul. Severe shock is thought capable of driving a

Fig. 12. Calabash containers (*apakî*). *Left to right:* two for rice and two for salt

Fig. 13. Calabash bowls (*kúya*). *Left to right:* for drinking water, for washing hands, and for washing rice

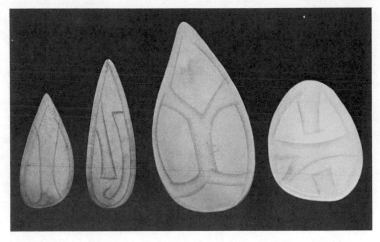

Fig. 14. Calabash utensils called *kuyêè*. *Left to right:* a spoon, two ladles, and a rice mounder

soul out of a person's body and into the river, and the remedial ritual centers on retrieving it and bringing it back in a special head-carried calabash.

Early Roots

The Western world's discovery of calabashes coincides with its discovery of the Americas, for Columbus noted their use to bail out Indian canoes on October 13, 1492, his second day in the New World. Other early observers in the New World described the calabash tree in more detail and made clear that the contribution of its fruit to Indian cultures was pervasive and multifaceted. Breton reported that the calabash was "the most useful of all trees" to early seventeenth-century Caribs in Guadeloupe, supplying water containers, oil containers, plates, cups, and spoons, and that the painted designs on these objects were "very pretty" (*fort gentils*—1647:46). And Rochefort, writing only a few years later, noted that Indians in the Caribbean islands

> polish the bark [of calabashes], and give it so delightful an enamel with *Roucou, Indico*, and several other pleasant colours, that the most nice may eat and drink out of the vessels they make thereof: Nay some are so curious, as to think them worthy a place among the Rarities of their Closets. [1665:49]

Early reports on the Guianas clarify that the calabash tree was an important feature of material life there as well, and that the Indians processed the fruit by cutting, boiling, and scraping out the pulp in just the same way that Maroons do it today (Fermin 1769, 1:192–94).

The decoration of Indian calabash bowls often consisted of extremely delicate, intricate designs executed in natural dyes of many shades. One nineteenth-century traveler in the Guianas was impressed by Arawak calabashes, "the outside of which is stained in beautiful patterns, generally black on a whitish ground" (St. Clair 1834:329–30). And others described in some detail the care with which calabashes were embellished by Indians in the rain forest just south of the Guianas. One reported that they were

> sometimes very tastefully painted. The rich black ground-colour is produced by a dye made from the bark of a tree called Comateü, the gummy nature of which imparts a fine polish. The yellow tints are made with the Tabatinga clay; the red with the seeds of the Urucú, or anatto plant; and the blue with indigo, which is planted round the huts. [Bates 1873:116]

And another commented on Indian calabashes that were

> polished brown on the outside and lacquered black on the inside; while
> the edge or the whole exterior is ornamented with incised patterns. The
> lacquering is done in a curious way. The calabash, after being well
> smoothed on the inner surface and washed with a decoction of carayuru
> (Bignonia) leaves is turned upside down over some cassava leaves sprin-
> kled with human urine, where it remains until such time as the inside
> becomes black and shiny. [Koch-Grünberg 1910, 2:232, translated in
> Roth 1924:302]

Eighteenth- and nineteenth-century collections of Indian calabashes
from this region confirm the written reports (for examples, see Zerries 1980; S. and R. Price 1980*a:* fig. 216).

Looking to Africa for models that could have influenced early
Maroon calabash decoration, we begin by noting the likelihood that,
like Columbus, the Africans imported to Suriname as slaves had never seen the fruit of the calabash tree before they arrived in the New
World.[2] Although the tree is cultivated in Africa today, its introduction appears to have been fairly recent and its distribution relatively
sparse. Most of the fruits referred to as "calabashes" in Africa are
gourds from a vine that is botanically unrelated to the calabash tree.
This "bottle gourd" plant (*Lagenaria siceraria* [Mol.] Standl.) produces
some fruits that resemble calabashes in size, shape, and outer texture,
but others that are many times larger; and many of its fruits have long
narrow necks at the stem end. A seventeenth-century traveler in Africa described these fruits in the following terms.

> Now because I speak of gourdes, which are growing things, it is fit I tell
> you, they doe grow, and resemble just that wee call our Pumpion,
> and . . . being of all manner of different sorts; from no bigger than an
> egge, to those that will hold a bushell. [Jobson 1623:168]

Although the gourds that Suriname slaves were familiar with
from Africa served many of the same purposes as the calabashes they
encountered in the New World, the physical properties and artistic
potentials of the two were quite different. Most importantly from an
aesthetic perspective, the inner surfaces of gourds were porous and
corklike, in contrast to those of calabashes which were hard and
smooth. While gourds lent themselves most readily to decorative carving on the exterior surface, calabashes could also be carved on the
inside.

Faced with memories of carved gourds from Africa and exposure to painted calabashes in Suriname, early Afro-Surinamers developed their own distinctive art—utilizing the American calabash, processing it according to the Indian method, and embellishing it with external African-style carvings. Only much later did their descendants begin exploring the artistic potential of interior decoration and painted designs, as well as a whole range of other techniques such as piercing, varnishing, and collagelike appliqués.

It is worth noting that the bottle gourd plant slaves had known in Africa was also cultivated in Suriname, but that it was never developed as an artistic medium there. Maroons have used such gourds throughout their history, but always in ways that are clearly distinct from calabashes. The two are processed by different methods and used for complementary purposes, and gourds are never decoratively embellished (see S. Price 1982).

Current Saramaka terminology reflects the complex cultural history of Afro-Suriname calabashes. The calabash tree is referred to by an Indian term (Sar. *kúya,* Tupi *kuia*).[3] Covered calabash containers, which resemble African "calabash" (bottle gourd) containers in both their overall form and their exterior decoration, are called *apakí,* which—like the Jamaican word *packy*—would seem to derive either from Ga *akpaki* or from Twi *apákyi* (Dalziel 1955:53–64; Cassidy and Le Page 1967:s.v. *packy*). And the Saramaka word for calabash spoons, which may have developed in imitation of European spoons used on plantations, apparently came from Portuguese, the masters' language on many of the plantations where Saramakas had been slaves (Sar. *kuyêè,* Portuguese *colher*—see Schumann 1778:s.v. *kujeri*).

By the eighteenth century, the calabash tree was supplying the "ordinary dishware and kitchen equipment of the [plantation] Negroes as much as of the natives" (Fermin 1769, 1:192–94). A mid-eighteenth-century report provides an early glimpse of Afro-Suriname calabash art.

> There are some Negroes who engrave on the convexity of this fruit compartments and grotesques in their own style, which they then fill in with hatching in chalk; which produces quite a pretty effect; and although they employ neither straight-edge nor compasses, these designs do not fail to be quite exact and quite agreeable. [Fermin 1769, 1:194; see also Stedman 1796, 2:120]

This description of geometric shapes filled with textured areas is confirmed by the earliest extant example of Afro-Suriname calabash

carving, an early nineteenth-century calabash rattle in the Rijksmuseum voor Volkenkunde in Leiden that is carved with rosaces,
geometric border designs, and a bird, and textured with incised flecks
(see S. and R. Price 1980*a:* fig. 219).

During the second half of the nineteenth century, an increase in
ethnographic reports and collections allows us to distinguish for the
first time the arts of the Maroons from those of coastal Afro-
Surinamers. This seems to have been a period of wide-ranging experimentation with the artistic potentials of the calabash shell. Afro-
Surinamers in the coastal region tried out techniques involving dyes,
commercial paints, varnishes, bas-relief carving, and complex piercing. They sometimes produced calabash bowls with moveable handles
or delicate pedestals. And they incorporated in their more represen-
tational designs everything from lions, cherubs, hearts, garlands of
flowers, and scenes of daily life to florid inscriptions and proverbs
written in Dutch. In the interior of the colony, nineteenth-century
Maroons confined their calabash decoration to nonrepresentational
motifs, developed radically different styles and techniques of calabash
decoration for men and women, and began for the first time to ex-
ploit the shell's inner surface. This experimentation fit into a much
more general period of artistic efflorescence and experimentation, in
which Maroons assigned the arts of wood carving, decorative sewing,
and cicatrization an increasingly central place in their daily life.

From Chisels to Broken Glass

Until the mid-nineteenth century, Afro-Suriname calabashes (including those made by Maroons) were decorated on the exterior surfaces
with commercially manufactured tools such as knives, compasses,
gouges, and chisels. These were men's designs, executed with men's
tools. Today this tradition continues in Saramaka through the decoration of covered containers, which is exclusively a men's art.

During the second half of the nineteenth century, however, an
entirely new calabash art came into existence. It appeared on the
insides rather than the outsides of the shells. It was executed with
pieces of broken glass rather than commercial tools. Its designs were
relatively clean, fluid, and unified, rather than complex, textured,
and composite. And it was the work of women rather than men.

This development formed part of broader changes that were oc-
curring in Saramaka life at that time. First, men were beginning to

spend long stretches of time earning money through logging, river transport, and wage labor. As a result, the ratio of women to men in Saramaka villages greatly increased (see R. Price 1970*a*). Second, men began devoting their artistic energy to wood carving. This medium represented an infinitely richer opportunity for creativity than calabashes. It allowed much greater experimentation (in piercing, bas-relief, tack work, branding, inlays, linked chains, and interlocking pieces) and could be applied to a wide range of forms, from canoes and house facades to combs and food stirrers.[4] In short, there were fewer men in the villages of the Pikilio, and these men were turning their attention away from calabash decoration toward a new and exciting artistic field.

It was in this setting that the crude and somewhat timid beginnings of women's calabash carving were executed on objects and surfaces that were not decoratively treated by men. Ladles—which are often made from broken pieces of calabash shells and are used for women's cooking rather than for men's meals or women's marriage basket presentations—appear with some frequency in ethnographic collections from this period, and many of these exhibit simple gouged-out markings (fig. 15). Similar markings also began to be incised on the insides of male-decorated containers (figs. 16–19). The

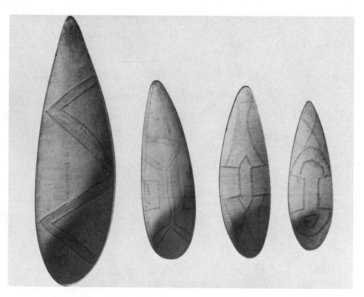

Fig. 15.   Nineteenth-century calabash ladles

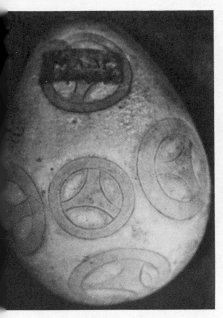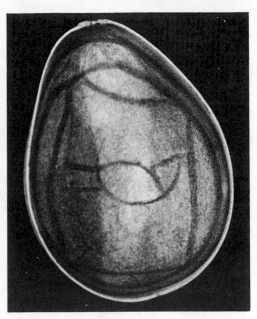

Fig. 16. A nineteenth-century calabash cup carved (*left*) on the outside with a compass and (*right*) on the inside with a piece of glass. The lettering is a museum label.

Fig. 17. A nineteenth-century calabash bowl carved (*left*) on the outside with a wood-carving tool (chisel?) and (*right*) on the inside with a piece of glass

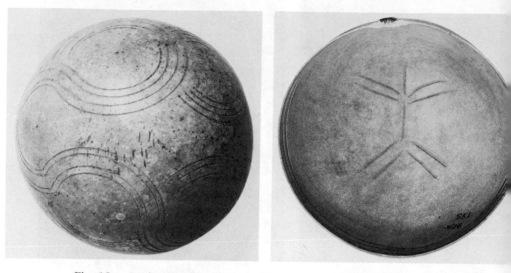

Fig. 18. A nineteenth-century calabash bowl carved (*left*) on the outside with a compass and (*right*) on the inside with a piece of glass

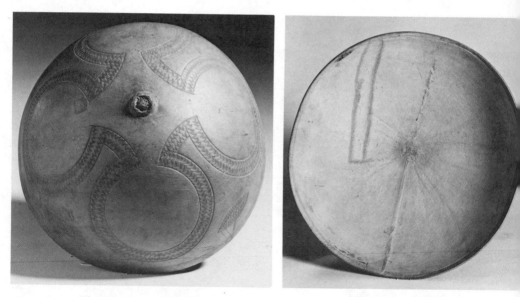

Fig. 19. A man's design (*left*) on the cover of a two-piece calabash container, supplemented by a woman's marking (*right*) on the interior

unevenness in manual control of the carved lines and the lack of a well-formed design style both suggest that something new was being tried out.[5] And the close resemblance of the "shaded" lines to those that are made today with pieces of broken glass strongly suggests that the artists were women. It was several decades before these carvings reflected firm manual control and the designs evidenced a well-defined aesthetic conceptualization. And it was only when the women's design concept and technical control were well established and when male artistry had come to be conceived almost exclusively in terms of wood carving that women's calabash carvings began to appear on bowls and containers intended for men's meals and other formal settings.

This reconstruction, which indicates that women's calabash carving began as a minor supplement to the men's art, makes sense not only in terms of the museum pieces that originally inspired it, but also in the light of fundamental Saramaka attitudes concerning men and women and their respective artistic abilities. Saramaka women frequently express the view that their own artistry is less accomplished than that of men. Although they take pride in their handiwork, they regard any willingness by a man to help in planning out a design—whether in embroidery, cicatrizations, or (rarely) a calabash—as an opportunity for significant improvement. Within the context of this general and pervasive self-image, it hardly seems surprising that women began to carve calabashes when men were shifting their attention to another medium, and that they used their own domestic utensils as the testing ground for the development of the art.

The nature of the tools and raw materials used for interior carvings must also have encouraged the development of this art by women. Unlike the men's calabash art, which required the use of tools purchased in the city, the women's carvings were executed with bits of broken glass from an old bottle, and the finishing touches were accomplished with local products, such as abrasive leaves for smoothing rough surfaces and the juice of limes from the women's own trees. And the calabashes themselves grew right in the villages and horticultural camps.

Tribes, Villages, and Individuals

By the late nineteenth century, Maroon women's calabash carving exhibited a striking unity in both technique and design style. Almost all carvings came to be executed as shallow bas-relief bands, many of which were arranged more or less symmetrically around a center. The inner space of these bands (or sometimes other forms) was scraped out of the shell only very shallowly. The edges were sharp and clear, where the point of the glass was pressed firmly, but the center of the band was less deeply cut. Since the scraped portions of the shell darkened over time, the result was a shaded effect, with the design's "figure" formed by the dark bands, and its "ground" by the lighter untouched portions around the bands. Although the museum documentation for most of these calabashes fails to specify whether they were collected in eastern Maroon (e.g., Djuka) or central Maroon (e.g., Saramaka) villages, the dozen or so cases in which tribal prove-nience *is* indicated make clear that such designs were being produced by women from both regions.

About fifty years ago, however, women's calabash carving from these two regions diverged dramatically. With very few exceptions, modern calabashes can be identified at a glance as either central Ma-roon or eastern Maroon artistry. In central Suriname, Saramaka and Matawai women have continued to carve in the original style, with design elements scraped out of the shell.[6] But women of the eastern tribes (Paramaka, Djuka, and Aluku) have reversed the definition of figure and ground, scraping away the outside (rather than the inside) edges of design elements. In addition, the shape of design elements has become consistently distinguishable in calabash carving from the two areas. Whenever they are not strictly even-sided, the elements of central Maroon designs are concave (as in fig. 20 *left*), but those of eastern Maroon designs are convex (as in fig. 20 *right*). That is, Saramaka/Matawai forms tend to be narrower in their center, while Djuka/Paramaka/Aluku forms are often bulging. Taken together, these two variables—the definition of figure and ground and the characteristic contour of design elements—suggest an actual process by which the eastern and central styles may well have developed. Let us consider the mechanics of this change in terms of the aesthetic interests that would have motivated it.

Saramaka women make clear that although the scraped-out areas of their calabash carvings constitute the bowl's design, they are keenly aware of the background shapes created around this design, and make every effort to control the aesthetic effect of those areas as well.

Women sometimes criticize carved calabashes for having a ground that is unbalanced or that includes shapes they consider ungainly, and the initial planning of a design includes explicit consideration, not only of the design itself, but also of the resultant ground. It seems likely that the mode of decoration developed by women in the eastern tribes originally began with a similar interest in the contours of the background areas, which eventually became so strong that the definition of the design's figure and ground was reversed.

Rare calabash carvings in which figure and ground are ambiguously defined help us to envision how this happened and how such a shift of figure and ground (from scraped to unscraped areas) relates to the distinction between concave and convex design elements. Central Maroon women view a design such as that in figure 21 in terms of the internally scraped areas, which consist largely of even-edged or concave forms. When designs are named it is these forms that are designated. But eastern Maroon women, who had apparently once envisioned calabash designs in the same way, focus their attention on (and assign names to) the complementary areas. And because a design consisting of concave shapes tends to generate a "ground" consisting of convex shapes, the reversal of figure and ground brought with it a newly defined domain of design elements.[7]

Saramakas are interested in regional styles of calabash carving on a village level as well. Certain villages are recognized for producing particularly beautiful calabashes, and these reputations are often strong enough to outlive the particular artists most responsible for them. Upper River women agree that the villages of Pempe and Godo have traditionally produced the best carvings; they are said to "carry the name." But people also point out that many of the most outstanding artists in those villages have died or become too old to carve, and that Asindoopo and its close neighbor, Bendekonde, are taking over the title, largely under the influence of a woman named Keekete and several others who carve in a similar style. Each village is said to have a recognizable style, and while it is not my experience that Saramakas can identify village proveniences as reliably as they think, there is a definite tendency for certain features of style to cluster in each village. I cite four examples. Motifs based on an arrow shape (known as "Indian arrow"—fig. 22) and triangular (rather than oval) rice mounders (fig. 23) are both more common in the village of Pempe than

Fig. 20. *Left:* a central Maroon (Saramaka) calabash bowl with concave design elements and *right:* an eastern Maroon (Paramaka) calabash bowl with convex design elements

Fig. 21. The "ground" of this eastern Maroon (Djuka) calabash carving includes shapes typical of the "figure" in many central Maroon designs.

Fig. 22. Two examples of the "Indian arrow" motif associated with the village of Pempe

Fig. 23.   The triangular rice mounder form associated
with the village of Pempe. The more common forms are
illustrated in figures 14 and 38.

elsewhere. The only villages in the Upper River region where women
execute designs with gouged lines rather than shaded bands (fig. 24)
are those along the upper Gaanlio. Even there, this style is relatively
rare and may represent a more localized specialty. Designs based on a
split oval, sometimes separated by a "stem" (fig. 25), are extremely
common in calabashes made by women from Godo, but I have never
seen these in carvings from any other village. Finally, both the
notched form for hand-washing bowls (known as "motorboat"
bowls—fig. 26) and a popular motif known as "embroidery design"
(fig. 27) are closely associated with the village of Asindoopo, where
they were invented and where they are most frequently made.
     Women's calabash carving is also conceptualized by Saramakas as
an individual specialization, and in this it is quite different from other
Maroon arts. It was frequently pointed out to me that "not everyone"
could produce attractive calabash designs, and that less talented wom-
en were expected to ask friends to design bowls for them. This kind of
assistance sometimes meant that a "good" carver would produce and

Fig. 24. A gouged-line design from a village on the upper Gaanlio

Fig. 25. Two calabash designs associated with the village of Godo

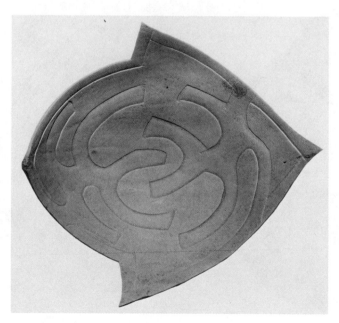

Fig. 26. Two hand-washing bowls cut in the "motorboat" form associated with the village of Asindoopo

decorate calabashes which she would present as finished bowls to her friend. In other cases, the carver would be given shells that had already been boiled, scraped smooth, and trimmed into bowls, and her contribution would involve only the carving of the design. In still other instances, she would simply mark in the faint outlines of a design, which her friend would then use as a guide to execute the actual carving. And finally, women who admired a particular calabash design that was first invented by a well-known carver would sometimes attempt to copy it, without any direct assistance at all from the original artist.

At the same time that "masters" of calabash carving are recognized in these ways and many women protest that they do not know how to carve, it is extremely unusual for a woman not to process and decorate at least some of her own calabashes. Inventories that I have made of women's calabash collections suggest that individuals who see themselves as "noncarvers" in fact decorate the majority of their own

Fig. 27. One version of the "embroidery design" associated with the village of Asindoopo

bowls and utensils. The calabashes that they have solicited from
known carvers *do* generally reflect a different command of the medium, but they also represent a numerical minority of pieces. This
discrepancy between the perceived specialization of the art and the
actual production of it (on variable levels of competence) by nearly all
Saramaka women seems to be part of a more general "etiquette of
deprecation" in this medium. Women who were viewed by others as
expert carvers tended to insist that they had really only begun to learn
the art. Calabashes were also the one item of material culture that
women frequently refused to let me pay for, protesting that they were
not worth anything at all.[8]

Ideals and Motifs

Saramaka women in the villages of the Pikilio have well-defined aesthetic standards for their calabash carvings and talk about them quite
explicitly. Both when they work on calabashes themselves and when
they evaluate finished calabashes made by others, they analyze carvings according to well-agreed-upon principles of design.
First, every calabash is expected to include an inside border and
an outside border. Although the inside border may rarely be omitted
for reasons of design, the absence of an outside border on a calabash
bowl is an almost certain indication that it was made by a woman from
either a Lower River Saramaka village or another Maroon tribe. (The
width of the border is also helpful in identifying the provenience,
since inside borders carved by eastern Maroons are much broader
than those carved by Saramakas.)
Second, the design itself is normally expected to be executed in a
kind of carving that Saramakas call "belly-to-belly" (*bêê-ku-bêê*); that is,
bands are carved with their scraped edges on the inside (e.g., fig. 28).
Some designs include areas that are executed in "back-to-back" (*báka-
ku-báka*) carving (fig. 29), but these were viewed as a departure from
the "normal" mode of design.[9] Not only are back-to-back bands unusual, but they must be exceptionally well planned in order not to be
seen as an artistic error. A few designs executed exclusively in back-to-
back carving are admired for the cleverness with which they allow a
dual definition of figure and ground. One known as "monkey's tail and
turtle's penis," for example, incorporates lines which delineate either
one motif or another, depending on how they are viewed, in an

Fig. 28. Calabash design with "belly-to-belly" carving

Fig. 29. Calabash design with "back-to-back" carving (see also the concentric bands in fig. 13, center)

intentional, Escher-like pun in space (fig. 30). And the carving of a second linear border, back-to-back and just inside the normal one, was generally admired when it occurred with a well-executed carving (fig. 31). Most instances of back-to-back carving, however, look like mistakes to Saramakas and are assumed to reflect ineptitude on the part of the artist. For example, Saramakas ridiculed the design in figure 32 for its "confusing" center, and they suggested that the one in figure 33 would have been acceptable if it had avoided the merger of design and border at the upper right, which led to an awkward reversal of figure and ground. Other "nonstandard" elements, such as the addition of angular protrusions (*tjôni*—fig. 34) or, rarely, minor embellishments within the basic bands are also acceptable as long as they are executed with clear control.

A third ideal of design, for Upper River Saramakas, is a rough bilateral symmetry around the calabash's equator; that is, the half toward the stem (*hédi*, "head") and the half toward the opposite end (*gogó*, "rump") should be approximate mirror images. Saramaka women claimed that this requirement was rather difficult for them. They often expressed the view that symmetry represented a male aptitude—a quality that they tried hard to achieve, but that did not come very naturally to them. In the planning stage, when they laid out a design with light scratches, it was in matching the two sides that women most often consulted others, as a check that they were not misreading which elements on the two sides should be equivalent. (See fig. 27 for a particularly successful implementation of this ideal.)

Finally, careful attention is paid to the balance between figure and ground areas (*kuya pendé ganda* and *kuya sinkii*), and several corrective measures are available to a woman who is dissatisfied with a carving in terms of this variable. I have already mentioned the possibility of adding a second border inside the first; alternatively, a border may be extended slightly toward the center of the design. These details are both explained as a way of reducing an excessive empty space around a central design. In addition, the kinds of marks (*nômbu*, "numbers") which are often incised on the exteriors of shells may also be placed on the interior in order to "fill" an area of ground that would otherwise have been considered too large and empty (see fig. 34). Not only should figure and ground be properly balanced, but the evenness of certain ground shapes is considered critical. When design elements

Fig. 30. Three bowls carved with the monkey's tail/turtle's penis design (see figure 40, motifs 4 and 5)

Fig. 31. Calabash bowl on which a second border has been carved "back-to-back" with the first

Fig. 32.   Calabash carving criticized for confused definition of figure and ground at the center

reinforce one another as concentric curves, the ground areas between them should be of uniform width. For example, Saramakas faulted the carving in figure 35 on this variable, but praised that in figure 36. The shape of ground areas is a recognized feature of the subtle variation that exists between the carving styles of different generations. One calabash design, for example, was identified by a forty-year-old as having been carved by an older woman on the grounds that "we don't use such pointed ground shapes much anymore."

The actual implementation of these ideals is influenced by at least two variables—the type of bowl or utensil being decorated and the individual artist's command of the medium.

The design ideals mentioned above are most applicable to drinking bowls and hand-washing bowls, which women decorate more elab-

Fig. 33. Calabash carving criticized for reversal of figure and ground at upper right border

orately and more carefully than other forms. In contrast, rice-washing bowls are (both ideally and in fact) very sparse in their decoration; as one woman remarked, "You don't really decorate them, you just put a mark on them. If the bowl is 'clean' [well scraped, free of surface blemishes], people will already have reason to compliment it." (See fig. 37 for typical rice-washing bowls.) *Kuyêè* (spoons, ladles, and rice mounders) should also be relatively simple. The most common carving for these utensils is some form of a design known as *kokóima*—a set of slightly concave bands extending between the two ends (fig. 38). Although some *kuyêè* are decorated with more elaborate designs, these are viewed as having been carved "in the fashion of bowl designs" (*kúya fási*).

One of the distinctions between the designs of recognized "car-

Fig. 34.   Calabash carving embellished with angular protrusions

vers" and those of other women is the success with which the various carving ideals are coordinated. Less accomplished carvers often find themselves in the position of having to sacrifice one aesthetic ideal in order to realize another. And evaluative commentary of calabashes was often phrased as a criticism followed by an explanation that the artist's focus on one variable (e.g., balance between figure and ground) must have created a problem in terms of another (e.g., symmetry).

Subtle innovations also contribute to the success, in Saramaka eyes, of many calabash carvings, and designs that reflect new ideas are especially admired. In some cases, these innovations are copied and become generalized features of a particular generation's carving style; figure 39 illustrates three such changes that distinguish Saramaka calabashes of the 1940s and 1950s from those of the 1960s and 1970s. Hand-washing bowls were shaped as ovals during the 1940s and

Fig. 35. Calabash carving criticized for unevenness of "ground" shapes

Fig. 36. Calabash carving praised for evenness of "ground" shapes

1950s, but those carved during the past two decades have generally been pointed. Over the same period of time, both the borders along the edges of bowls and the "belly-to-belly" bands of the designs themselves have been significantly widened. Most importantly, the increased interest in symmetry, which has gradually transformed Saramaka aesthetics on a fundamental level over the past several decades, has encouraged women to envision all calabash designs as constructions built identically on the two sides of an axis, so that designs such as that pictured on the left in figure 39 have been almost completely discontinued.[10]

Furthermore, calabash carving has always involved some innovation at the level of particular motifs. Here again, women who are seen as "carvers" play a clearly distinguishable role. All women try out new

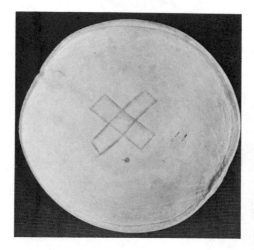
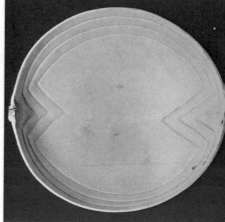

Fig. 37. Two rice-washing bowls, with typically sparse decoration, that were admired by Saramaka women

Fig. 38. *Kokóima*, the most common
design for rice mounders

shapes and patterns, but because of differential skills, the innovations
that are imitated by others and become institutionalized as part of a
village's repertoire are invariably those that are first executed by
women recognized for their special command of the medium. Figure
40 and the accompanying list of named motifs are intended to give
some idea of the kinds of motifs in terms of which Saramakas talk
about calabash designs. Note that many of them are conceptually
related to motifs used in other artistic media, with which they share
names.

The ways in which names for calabash motifs are created and
used are representative of naming in Saramaka arts more generally.
Whether the creation of a new motif is initially inspired by a particular object or named after its likeness to that object only afterward, the
name then serves as a purely descriptive label rather than as an indication of symbolic meaning. Furthermore, the association between
names and designs is fairly loose, and allows for considerable individual variation. Thus, while a given design may be referred to as
"scorpion's tail" by some women and as "Cayenne bottle" by others, it

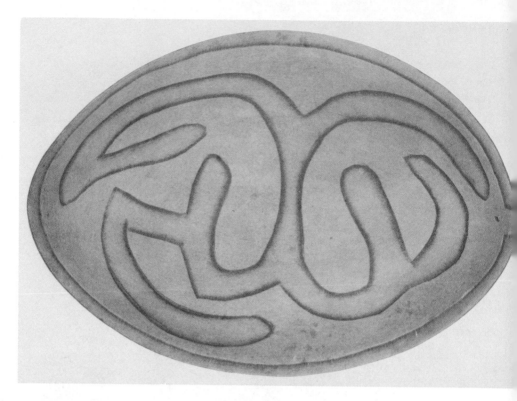

Fig. 39. Hand-washing bowls carved (*top*) in the 1940s or 1950s and (*bottom*) in the 1970s.

may have yet other names in other regions. Even within one village, there is often disagreement, confusion, or indifference about the correct designation for particular designs. In this regard, the naming of Saramaka calabash designs follows the pattern described by Bunzel for painted designs on Pueblo pottery.

> The same element is called in one composition "cloud," in another "flower," in yet another "drumstick." Furthermore, the same composition, with all its parts, will be differently named by the same person at different times. [1929:54]

Fickle Women and Doodling

In one of the very few studies ever written of Maroon calabash art, Philip Dark attempted to analyze the difference between men's exterior carvings and women's interior carvings (1951). Dark described the men's art as "always clearly marked," "always conceived as having to fill a definite surface," exhibiting "apt consideration of the relationship of design to design space," and "always well considered and apt" (1951:58–59). In contrast, he characterized the women's art as "more restricted in flow" and "alien" (to the men's art) and commented that women's designs "may or may not" overflow the design space, "may or may not" be conceived as having to fill a definite surface, and "may or may not" be "apt" in terms of the relationship of design to design space (1951:59).

Wishing to understand the differences that he perceived between men's and women's styles of carving, Dark consulted published ethnographic reports on Maroon life. There he found comments that allowed him to characterize Maroon marriage as a "tenuous" relationship in which "women appear to have the whip hand . . . and divorce is quite an informal matter, a woman being able to break a union on some slight pretext" (1951:59, 57). Putting art styles and marital behavior together, he arrived at the theory that both reflect

> a distinct difference in temperament between the men and women of this culture. The men would appear to be definite in their actions and probably more conservative than the women. The women may perhaps be thought more fickle and more easily susceptible to novelty. Perhaps the decoration of calabashes by the women is their form of doodling. [1951:59][11]

Fig. 40.   Illustrations for some named motifs. Dots indicate scraped-away portions of the design.

Some Named Calabash Motifs (illustrated in fig. 40)

Name and translation	Comments
1. *akuyêè fóu*, "Akuyee's bird"	Named after a rubber duck that a man bought in Paramaribo for his young daughter
2. *íngi piiwá*, "Indian arrow"	A motif closely associated with the village of Pempe (see fig. 22)
3. *báka-ku-báka*, "back-to-back"	Refers to placement of shading (see fig. 29)
4. *makáku lábu*, "monkey's tail"	The spiral motif common in Saramaka wood carving of the early twentieth century (see fig. 30)
5. *logozo pipí*, "turtle's penis"	The form resulting from the joining of monkey-tail spirals (see fig. 30)
6. *koósu maáka*, "embroidery design"	A motif closely associated with the village of Asindoopo, "copied" from an embroidered neckerchief (for variations, see figs. 26 *left*, 27, 34, 36)
7. *lóntu édi*, "around the head"	Used also as a hairbraiding pattern and a manioc cake pattern (see S. and R. Price 1980a: fig. 264)
8. *lakpá* [=*lakwá*, French *la croix*], "cross"	Named after a pendant imported from French Guiana (see fig. 37 *left*)
9. *líba kumútu*, "crescent moon"	Also a cicatrization design (see fig. 26 *right*)
10. *kópu máu*, "house gable"	Also a cicatrization design
11. *íngi kódjo*, "Indian club"	Also a cicatrization design
12. *sán tánda*, "saw tooth"	Also a patchwork pattern of the early twentieth century and a wood carving "filler"
13. *kayána báta*, "Cayenne bottle"	Named after a double-necked oil-and-vinegar bottle brought back from French Guiana. Sometimes called *kúkútu lábu* (scorpion), it is used also as a cicatrization design.
14. *kokóima* [no etymology]	The most common design for ladles, spoons, and rice mounders (see fig. 38)
15. *nyaká kokóima*, "intersecting" *kokóima*	A common variation of *kokóima*

Although he had never met a Maroon of either sex face-to-face, Dark's reading of the contrast between the "personality configurations" (1951:60) of Maroon men and women poses ironic similarities with the ideas of Maroons themselves. Dark's comparative assessment of male and female styles of carving comes to the predictable conclusion that one is art, the other doodling. Maroon sexism, while not reaching quite such an extreme position, also encourages the view that women's calabash carvings are aesthetically inferior to the men's art. We are told by Dark that women's designs are less consistently "well considered and apt" than those of the men. We are told by Saramakas that women's designs exhibit less technical skill than those of the men. We are thus privileged to have two independent assessments of these decorative styles that reinforce one another—one from a museum researcher and another from the artists themselves.

In both cases, however, it might be useful to try to disaggregate the visual properties of the women's art (features of design, technical control, etc.) from the cultural and social settings in which the art is being evaluated—if only in order to be able to reintegrate them in a more perceptive understanding of the ways in which they interact. For the fact that Dark's evaluation of male versus female calabash carvings in a sense corresponds to that of Maroons does not make either one any less a culturally conditioned aesthetic response. And it in no way diminishes the relevance of either one for our understanding of notions of gender, in Europe and the United States as well as in the Suriname rain forest.[12]

Chapters 6 and 7 will continue to trace the relationship between women's social status and artistic life by exploring two other expressive media that are important in their lives—textile arts and song.

Chapter Six

Cloth and Clothing

For many outside visitors to the Maroons, the sight of bare-breasted women provides a crucial confirmation that they have ventured into a truly "primitive world." Shiva Naipaul, for example, recently introduced his foray into the Suriname rain forest through the leering words of his Creole guide, who promised,

> "Soon . . . you will see real Bush Negroes. You see"—he grinned—"you see women wearing nothing on their chests. Soon you see *real* Bush Negroes." [1981:76–79, emphasis his]

Unlike many "exotic" societies, however, Maroons have developed no artistic traditions involving garments made of local fibers, bark cloth, dyes, feathers, or shells. Rather, their clothes are made of low-quality imported trade cotton and are combined in selective ways with factory-made garments such as hats, T-shirts, bras, and plastic belts that have always seemed out of place to purists in search of the Noble Savage.

Disparagement of the Maroons' enjoyment of mixing Western and non-Western clothing dates to the earliest days of their history. An eighteenth-century missionary, for example, described a group of Saramaka men in the following terms.

> Our very proud Commodore whose name was Akra was particularly excellent in the manner in which he dressed. Due to his bartering in Paramaribo, he had gotten a splendid colored nightshirt which had been made at Zitz, and for which he had been charged 50 guilders. He wore it, tied together with a sword, and he had a hat with tresses on it. With this ridiculous attire he ordered his comrades about. I had a difficult time supressing my laughter when I saw him. When our flintlocks were finally loaded, the Negroes, with pride in their splendorous dress, continued the trip in a very uncommon silence. [Staehelin 1913–19, 3.2:197]

In the nineteenth century, a commentator expressed similar sentiments about the clothing of the Aluku Chief, Adam, and suggested that, like his biblical namesake, shame had compelled him to replace the simple figleaf by "a grotesque parody of the military costume," which he wore with "an incredible awkwardness" (Bouyer 1867:302).

In the early twentieth century, this same attitude was restated in an observer's reaction to the uniforms worn by village officials.

> How much more natural, more free of pretentiousness, for us less laughable and, in contrast, more magnificent to view are the other, simple villagers, whose athletic dark-naked bodies, glistening in the sun, resemble bronze statues of herculean primitives. [van Lelyveld 1919/20: 466]

And as recently as 1970, Maroon choice in clothing was related to the imminent decline of the culture and the spread of prostitution among Maroon women.

> They can be seen wearing shirts and shorts of yellow, red, purple or green that come from that atrocious tawdry commerce that rages on the coast of the Guianas as much as in Africa; made with material of the lowest quality, these clothes fall apart quickly in the humid climate, taking on a pathetic look that their bearers seem not to notice. One even sees women decked out in halters, "mission dresses," multicolored brassieres, etc. In recent years, hideous jockey caps were the thing on the Marowyne River, as well as jerseys adorned with ads for outboard motors and other motifs equally ugly, ridiculous and vulgar. . . . One gets the feeling that certain firms must have research centers with experts in the art of uglifying and degrading men. [Hurault 1970:58–59]

For Westerners, then, Maroon dress is neither properly civilized nor properly savage, and it is perhaps partly for this reason that it never received recognition from them as an artistic medium. For Maroons, however, clothing—from pubic aprons to commercial T-shirts—presents a rich opportunity for artistic creativity and aesthetic expression. As we saw in chapter 4, clothing also figures centrally in relations between men and women—"raw" (unsewn) cloth being the most important gift, in both volume and affective meaning, that men give their wives, and sewn clothing being the most important gift that women give their husbands.

Conventions of dress for Saramaka men and women contrast in several important ways. Men's clothing includes many more Western imports—from sunglasses, watches, and felt hats to trousers, T-shirts, and plastic sandals. Men tend to have in their possession larger supplies of never-worn clothing. Men's accessories are, in general, more varied and more ostentatious than those worn by women. And, most importantly, the decorative sewing on men's clothing is consistently more elaborate, more carefully planned out, and more meticulously executed than that on women's garments. This chapter traces the development of Saramaka clothing traditions through time and explores the ways in which such contrasts reflect the relationship between men and women within the society more generally.

Early Accounts

The earliest available descriptions of Maroon clothing are contained in reports, diaries, and a word list written by the German Moravians who lived among the Saramaka during the second half of the eighteenth century. During their years in the tropics, these missionaries wore the top hats, lace collars, stockings, vests, and other items of European dress to which they were accustomed. From this perspective, they viewed Saramakas essentially as naked savages, and generalized cryptically that "they have no clothing except a small covering over the abdomen" (Staehelin 1913–19, 3.2:141). Sketches provided by Brother Riemer, the most ethnographically conscientious of the Moravians, conform to this image, depicting men with only a tiny square of cloth hanging in front from a waist tie (see, for example, S. and R. Price 1980a: fig. 63).

Isolated comments in eighteenth-century missionary diaries as well as entries in a contemporaneous dictionary, however, permit us to infer that Saramakas were, even then, highly fashion-conscious people. In spite of being extremely incomplete, the dictionary (Schumann 1778) distinguishes two named styles of breechcloths (*abadjà, kamissa*), as well as knitted and sewn caps (*brae mussu, kwefa*); it includes two terms each for women's skirts (*krossu, saija*) and finger rings (*aneru, linga*); it mentions the use of adolescent girls' aprons (*kojo*), as well as kerchiefs (*lensu, hangisa*), tassels (*franja*), necklaces (*kónda*), walking sticks (*kokotti, molaù*), and hunting sacks (*sakku*). And it suggests, through three entries—*prolo* ("showing off in dressed-up clothes"), *jangra* ("getting dressed in one's best"), and *sakla* ("old, raggedy clothes")—that eighteenth-century Saramakas showed at least some interest in gradations of elegance. A 1792 diary entry inadvertently confirms these aesthetic sensitivities in complaining that "many [of the people at church] came just to show off their finery" (Staehelin 1913–19, 3.3:44).

The 1778 dictionary also includes many Saramaccan terms for Western clothing and accessories—beads (*pellula*), umbrellas (*parasol*), shirts (*hempi*), jackets (*jakketi*), shoes (*sappatu*), and stockings (*meija*). Other sources of information on this same period suggest that the use of these items was, with the probable exception of shoes and stockings, part of Saramaka (as opposed to just missionary) finery. Tribute lists consistently include various kinds of costume jewelry; umbrellas have long been an essential ingredient of Maroon men's formal dress; and the few detailed descriptions that Moravians wrote about the attire of particular Saramaka men indicate that Saramakas not only made use of Western clothing and accessories, but also wore them with real pride.[1] A 1779–80 account of one headman's uniform, for example, includes mention of a hat with golden tassels and a shirt fastened with cuff links (Staehelin 1913–19, 3.2:217). And the passage cited earlier about men returning upriver after a trip to Paramaribo indicates that such items were not only provided by outsiders (as official recognition of political offices), but also purchased at high prices by Saramaka men themselves.

A few isolated comments in the missionaries' writings make clear that early Saramaka dress—at least for men—was strongly influenced by ritual as well as aesthetic considerations. One old headman, for example, is described as being hung all over with *obia*s (Staehelin 1913–19, 3.3:131). The dictionary includes mention of men's protective iron fighting rings (*mulungà*). One missionary describes his boatmen pouring libations of rum over jaguar teeth and brass blades which they wore around their necks (Staehelin 1913–19, 3.2:232). Another reports:

> Wherever one looks, one finds traces of the most stupid superstition. The streets, the houses, and the people are covered with all kinds of amulets and all types of protective idols. [Staehelin 1913–19, 3.3:208]

Stedman's observations on his eighteenth-century Aluku adversaries suggest that contemporary clothing worn by the eastern Maroons closely resembled that of the Saramaka in combining an attention to aesthetics and ritual protection with an enjoyment of Western imports.[2] His brief description of Aluku warriors in the heat of battle specifies wrist and ankle ornaments, a necklace with supernatural protective powers, a braided hairdo, and a gold-laced hat (Stedman 1796, 2:88–89, 108, pl. 53).

During the nineteenth century, accounts of Maroon clothing became richer, photographs became available, and artifactual collecting was added to the expected activities of visitors to Maroon villages. The resulting documentation both confirms and embellishes the somewhat cryptic eighteenth-century descriptions of Maroon dress in terms of at least three features: (1) the ritually protective function of much jewelry, (2) the importance and status connotations of imported manufactures, and (3) the presence of significant aesthetic distinctions between everyday and formal dress. A. M. Coster, an observer of life along the Marowyne River in the 1850s, describes a woman's daily outfit as a single skirt and strings of beads on neck, wrist, and ankles, with no covering for the upper body, but adds that for celebrations, a "great number" of colored cloths, either cotton or muslin, were worn over the shoulders (1866:27). Men likewise supplemented their dress on special occasions, he notes, with colored cloths over the shoulders, and sometimes added a broad-brimmed hat with a long ribbon hanging over the side. In terms of accessories, Coster describes bracelets made of copper or iron, copper rings worn as many as ten at a time, necklaces made of jaguar and peccary teeth, and legbands hung with animal teeth, feathers, and tassels (1866:27–28). His frontispiece illustrating a group of Maroon men shows, in addition, a shell necklace, loose anklets, arm- and leg-rings, a string of beads worn over one shoulder and under the other arm, and a double sash of cloth crossed over the chest (see S. and R. Price 1980a: fig. 64).

August Kappler, a long-term resident among the Djuka in the mid-nineteenth century, also reported the extensive use of iron and copper anklets, bracelets, and rings. He described ritual jewelry— worn on "knees, ankles, arms and shoulders"—as including glass beads, beetle antennae, tiger teeth, parrot feathers, snails, and wooden figures, and mentioned that hunting dogs were similarly hung with obias (1854:124–25; 1883:141; 1887:257, 263). Hostmann, a physician and amateur naturalist who strongly deplored the "wretchedness" and "poverty" of Djuka material culture (asserting that "their whole supply of clothing may be eaten by termites in a single night"), nonetheless mentioned that both men and women sometimes wore iron bracelets and small imported bells around their necks (1850:279). Finally, van Heeckeren commented that, in addition to a breechcloth, Maroon men's clothing consisted mainly of "an expensive European hat, which generally represented their principal wealth" (1826:71).

During the second half of the nineteenth century, Maroon clothing continued to be dominated by jewelry and other accessories. A wide variety of reports (for example, Bonaparte 1884; Cateau van Rosevelt and van Lansberge 1873; Crevaux 1879; Joest 1893; Spalburg 1899) lend support to a generalization made by Brunetti in 1890: "While, on the one hand, clothing is treated as an accessory, [personal] ornaments play a central role in their existence" (1890:172). Almost all accounts include some mention of the simplicity of clothing on the one hand and, on the other, the pervasive use of necklaces and rings of many sorts, legbands, stacked anklets, multiple bracelets, and so on. The description of K. Martin, a geologist who conducted an 1885 expedition to the Sara Creek and lower Suriname River, is typical (1886:23–25). He reported that men wore breechcloths and, for festive occasions, capes "as gaily colored as possible" that were tied over one shoulder and sometimes reached as far as the knees. Women wore skirts to their knees and tied babies on their backs with a cloth. And children were naked until the age of twelve or fourteen. Martin says nothing more on clothing, but describes jewelry in some detail. Curtain rings were worn on fingers. There were arm-, leg-, and thumb-rings made of brass, iron, and straw. Women wore beaded necklaces and both sexes wore earrings. And there were ritually protective necklaces strung with symmetrical arrangements of jaguar teeth, feathers, red pieces of wood, metal-and-wooden cones, and clappers and Dutch coins (the last two intended as noisemakers to frighten away evil spirits).

During the twentieth century, accessories continued to be an important aspect of Maroon dress, but the greater availability of cloth resulted in a new focus on the clothes themselves. The tailored "nightshirt" mentioned as a novelty in the eighteenth century became common formal dress for Maroon men in the early twentieth century, and was commissioned in a variety of colorfully patterned fabrics. (See, for just two examples, S. and R. Price 1980a: fig. 41; M. and F. Herskovits 1934: pl. facing p. 24.) Furthermore, shoulder capes, which had previously been used only for special occasions and generally consisted of an undecorated piece of cloth, began to be worn more routinely by men and were developed by women into articles of spectacular artistry through both patchwork sewing and embroidery. Among the eastern tribes and in Lower River Saramaka villages, such decorative sewing was sometimes used for women's clothing as well, but Upper River Saramakas preferred to reserve both patchwork and embroidery for men's garments. The development of these textile arts is described in greater detail in later sections of this chapter.

If we review the eighteenth-, nineteenth-, and twentieth-century materials, it is clear that Maroon dress (like other aspects of their culture) has repeatedly drawn on a diversity of cultural models, combining in an original synthesis elements of African, Afro-American, Amerindian, and Euro-American clothing and jewelry.[3] I cite just a few examples. One style of breechcloth that was worn in the eighteenth century can be tentatively attributed to an African origin on the basis of its Saramaccan name, *abadjà,* which is nearly identical to that used for the same garment by Ga speakers on the Gold Coast, *gbadša* (Schumann 1778:s.v. *abadjà*). Women's striped wrap-around skirts and men's everyday breechcloths exhibit parallels with Afro-American dress throughout the hemisphere (for one strikingly similar example from Brazil, see Johnston 1910: pl. 78). The aprons worn throughout Maroon history by adolescent girls were originally modeled on Amerindian womens' aprons and called by a Suriname Indian term (Sar. *koyó,* Ndj. *kway,* Trio *kwayu,* Galibi *kwai*). And the two types of men's caps cited in Schumann's 1778 dictionary reflect the diverse European origins of the slave masters. Knitted caps were known as *brae mussu,* from the Dutch words *breien* (to knit) and *muts* (cap), and sewn cloth caps were called *kwefa,* either from the Portuguese term for cap (*coifa*) or, possibly, the English "coif."

Raw Cloth

Throughout Saramaka history, the bulk of cloth supplies has been imported from coastal Suriname. During the wars of liberation, cloth was one of the many subsistence items brought back from raids on plantations, and government archives contain detailed records on the amounts and kinds of cloth that were provided by the peace treaties and distributed on a regular basis to Saramaka villages for about the first century of their independence. The 1749 peace agreement— which was sabotaged by a rival to the Saramaka chief and resulted in the deaths of the soldiers bearing a first installment of the tribute gifts—specified the delivery, among other goods, of twelve lengths of salempouri cloth (the blue cotton originally imported from India to the West Indies, chiefly for use by slaves), twenty lengths of patterned cotton cloth, one hundred handkerchiefs (which were apparently used as women's aprons [Riemer 1801:332]), and fifty "ordinary" cloth sheets. The various tribute lists associated with the final treaty agreement with the Saramakas (which was successfully concluded in 1762) included thirty pounds of undyed thread, sixty skeins of blue thread and sixty of white, and one hundred bolts of cotton cloth (see R. Price 1983b:48, 217, 237). Most recently, when men began purchasing large quantities of coastal goods to bring back to Saramaka villages (see chap. 4), *kúakúa koósu* ("raw" cloth—that is, cloth that has not been cut, sewn, or softened by washing) has represented the most important portion of these imports, in terms of both monetary and social value.

Ever since the earliest years of their life in the Suriname forest, Saramakas have also cultivated and spun small amounts of cotton (Schumann 1778: s.v. *kekè, mâulu, fassi mâulu;* see also von Sack 1821:128; and Coster 1866:10). Some of this was woven into a coarse, undecorated cloth (Schumann 1778: s.v. *fumm krossu, [matu] krossu;* see also an 1837 archival report on weaving by Alukus cited in Hurault 1960:110), and according to older Saramakas this skill was still plied by a few persons up to the first decade or two of the twentieth century. Hammocks were also woven, by men, but never as more than a supplement to those acquired in trade from Indians or purchased in coastal Suriname. By the mid-twentieth century, hammock weaving had been completely discontinued by Saramakas. Throughout Saramaka history, the bulk of the locally spun cotton has been used in one of three ways. Much of it has been made into the crocheted calfbands (*sepú*) that are worn by men, women, and children (see, for example, the jacket or cover photo of this book). Some has been knitted into ribbons that are used as men's waist ties, ties for hanging hammock coverings, and a variety of miscellaneous decorative purposes. And some has been used for the special knitted calfbands (*bánti*) that are always made for infants before they receive their first pair of crocheted calfbands[4] (see figs. 41 and 42).

In addition to spun cotton and imported thread, early Saramakas processed the fiber of the *Bromelia alta* plant (*singaási*) for both rope and sewing thread (Schumann 1778: s.v. *singrasi*). Later, threads

Fig. 41.   Woman spinning cotton from her garden

Fig. 42.   Woman crocheting calfbands around a bottle

pulled out from scraps of imported cloth were used for sewing. This practice, though much rarer than a few decades ago, can still be observed in Pikilio villages. Spool thread (*masíni maáu*) has never been widely used except for hand-cranked (or, rarely, foot-pedaled) sewing machines, but commercial embroidery thread (used for both hems and decorative embroidery) and the somewhat thicker threads used to crochet legbands have for at least several decades been standard items for men to buy at the end of their wage-earning trips to the coast.

Even during the period when they were receiving tribute shipments from the government, Saramakas were not passive recipients of cloth supplies. From the first, they both expressed their preferences, in terms of colors and types of fabrics, and supplemented government supplies with selective purchases made on the coast. Once men began earning significant amounts of money through logging and wage labor in the mid-nineteenth century, they were in an even better position to influence Saramaka cloth supplies according to their own aesthetic preferences. By the late nineteenth century, when Saramaka earning power and opportunities for direct selection of Western products had dramatically increased over a several-decade period, imported cloths grew to be the focus for the most important exchange relationship in Saramaka society—that between husbands and wives. On the one hand, the amount of cloth that a man brought back from a coastal trip was used as the measure of his success in the outside world and of his devotion to his wives. Reciprocally, within the context of a woman's gifts to her husband, special attention began to be focused on those involving cloth.

In terms of Saramaka dress, this change was visible in two ways. First, it meant a shift in the balance between accessories and clothing, especially for men. The seventeenth- and eighteenth-century men's everyday outfits centering on hats, jewelry of all kinds, and arm- and legbands were gradually supplemented with increased clothing—chiefly shoulder capes and neckerchiefs. Second, women began to treat men's clothing more frequently as a creative artistic medium—through embroidery, appliqué, patchwork, and other decorative touches.

Over the past hundred years, the cloth available to Saramakas for purchase has varied in pattern, price, and quality and, as we will see in later sections, these changes have in many cases had direct influences on aspects of fashion in Saramaka villages.[5] Until several decades into the twentieth century, the bulk of cloth was either a predominantly white cotton with red or blue stripes (and sometimes cross stripes) known as "twelve-cent cloth" (*twálúfu sen koósu*) or a thinner grade of cotton produced in a variety of solid colors. The solid color cloth (mostly in red, white, or navy) continues to be bought by Saramakas, though it is now used exclusively for women's waistkerchiefs and embroidered men's capes and, in the case of white, for a variety of ritual purposes.[6]

Around the time of the First World War, the "twelve-cent cloth" began to be replaced by an inexpensive grade of cotton (*avênge koósu*), printed in a variety of patterns consisting of lengthwise stripes in different widths and colors. These cloths, which were worn as skirts and, until the early 1970s, sewn into narrow-strip textiles, were individualized through an extensive system of cloth names (see chap. 7). In the 1960s, the largest-volume fabric store catering to a Maroon clientele was selling between 200,000 and 250,000 yards of such cloth annually, and its owner was devoting considerable time and energy to the continuous task of creating new patterns of striped cotton—in some cases supplying names for them as well. Over time, cross (weft) stripes gradually came to be added more frequently to the lengthwise (warp) stripes of skirt fabrics, and the durability of the cloth continued to decline, hitting its low in the early 1970s. At the same time that colorful stripes were dominating women's skirts, solid color cloths (*ángísa koósu*) and "calico" cloths (*káikó*) were being used for women's capes. In the 1960s, wage labor opportunities at the missile base in Kourou, French Guiana, also resulted in the popularity of the brightly colored cotton plaids sold throughout the French-speaking Caribbean (called by Saramakas *baái páki*), which were used for men's capes and breechcloths and occasionally for women's capes.

During the early 1970s, a new, more closely woven grade of striped cotton became available (dubbed by Saramakas *dégi míñ*, "little thickies"), and although the thin stuff of the 1960s continued to be sold at a lower price, this heavier cotton quickly became a more common material for women's skirts.[7] Around 1976, coastal stores began stocking a very thin cloth with a pattern of wide stripes which was more finely woven and almost twice the previously standard width; this *alatjá balán* ("It splits [into two full skirts] *balán!*") achieved instant popularity and every woman on the Pikilio tried to see to it that she had at least one skirt made of it, for use on festive occasions. Finally, a heavily textured solid color cloth (*lápu*) was introduced during the 1970s in conjunction with the development of cross-stitch embroidery, and in spite of bitter complaints about its high price, this became the standard material for men's shoulder capes.

Because of fluctuations both in labor opportunities and in the price of trade cotton, the quantity of cloth owned by individual Saramakas has varied dramatically over the past hundred years. Changes in the number of skirt-cloths that men are expected to bring back from the coast to their wives are often cited as a measure of variations in the level of cloth supplies more generally. Around the turn of the century, when the gold rush along the Marowyne River and its tributaries was at its height and "twelve-cent" cloth was being sold in coastal stores, wives were being presented with as many as three hundred skirt-length cloths apiece. By the 1920s and 1930s, the "golden days" of coastal wage labor were over (see de Beet and Thoden van Velzen 1977), and it was more usual for men to return from a year or more on the coast with about ten to twelve skirt-cloths for each wife. By the 1950s and 1960s, construction jobs at the Afobaka hydroelectric project and at the missile base in French Guiana brought a higher level of material wealth to Saramaka villages. Most men who returned to their villages in the late 1960s were distributing between thirty and one hundred cloths to each wife, and I heard excited reports of one (monogamous) man who gave his wife one hundred and thirty. I cannot provide reliable estimates for the 1970s, but do know that expectations were considerably lower than they had been during the previous decade, due largely to sudden inflation in coastal Suriname.

In terms of cloth prices, Saramakas report that skirt-cloths cost 2.50 Suriname guilders (Sf.) during World War II, but that immediately after the war it was possible to buy twenty skirt-cloths and a large hammock for Sf. 8. In the early 1960s, skirt-cloths were sold for Sf. 1.25 apiece. By the late 1960s they cost only Sf. 1, and during the 1970s they cost between Sf. 2 and Sf. 5, depending on the type of fabric. The Saramakas who quoted these prices were not considering the influence of variations in the wages with which they bought the cloth. But even without this adjustment, their observation that cloth prices and cloth supplies have been inversely related over time still tends to be correct.

The Past Hundred Years

During the second half of the nineteenth century, when ethnographic collecting began to provide extensive artifactual documentation on Suriname Maroons, items of clothing were conspicuously absent from the assemblages brought back to Europe. For example, the large collection made on the Marowyne River by Jules Crevaux in the 1870s (now housed at the Musée de l'Homme in Paris) provides rich documentation of Djuka and Aluku material culture, including a wide range of wood carving and calabash decoration, but contains not a single cloth. And most of the collections in Dutch museums that are documented by collector and date (e.g., those made by F. A. Kuhn, K. Martin, and C. A. van Sijpesteijn) include no clothing. The several pieces of nineteenth-century clothing that *were* collected, however, suggest that this gap in the ethnographic record does not reflect a corresponding gap in the actual history of Maroon textile arts. One example is a lined white cotton cap with blue appliqués representing two caymans, which was collected by H. F. C. ten Kate among the Aluku before 1881 (S. and R. Price 1980*a*: fig. 256). The complexity of the figures and the fineness of the stitching and embroidered details (the claws, teeth, and eyes) all attest to the existence at that time of a technically and aesthetically developed art.

One of the earliest mentions of Maroon decorative sewing is a description by L. C. van Panhuys of an embroidered Djuka cloth that he collected for the 1899 exposition in Haarlem.

> On a piece of cotton bought in a store, and destined for use as a skirt or shoulder cape, figures are drawn in charcoal by the men; these figures are embroidered by the women.
> The figures on the accompanying skirt represent: a monkey's tail, a bird's claw with a snake and two "akema's" (figures with an erotic meaning) placed opposite one another. The meaning of the oblique cross is not known definitely to us. [1899:81]

Although I have found no record of the eventual disposition of individual pieces from the 1899 exposition, there is one skirt in storage at the Tropenmuseum that I believe is the cloth van Panhuys collected (see S. and R. Price 1980*a*: fig. 71).[8]

The earliest cloths from Saramaka that I have seen are also embroidered. The neckerchief in figure 43 was made by Chief Agbago's

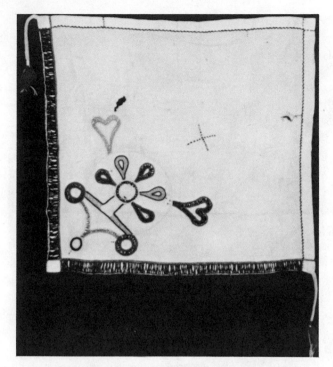

Fig. 43. An embroidered neckerchief

mother—a Dangogo woman named Bo who was born around 1860. The shoulder cape in figure 44 was sewn either by this same person or by Apumba, a woman from Pempe whom Agbago married around 1910.

One other undated but apparently "old" cloth can be tentatively identified as turn-of-the-century Maroon embroidery, on the basis of its technical and stylistic resemblance to these three cloths and the type of fabric that forms its center. The youngest child of Bo, Captain Kala of Dangogo, who was born around 1899, gave me this aged and frail embroidered cape (fig. 45), but was unable to remember who had made it for him. The body is a white cloth embroidered in red, yellow, and white with a bird motif not unlike that on the Tropenmuseum skirt. Two striped materials, which Saramakas identified as patterns from the 1920s or 1930s, provide edge strips along the sides and bottom and a decorative line of fringe underneath the embroi-

Fig. 44. A man's cape with embroidered design and patchwork appliqué on three sides

dery. These are all sewn by machine and, to judge from their better condition, represent a later addition to the embroidered portion.

These several stylistically homogeneous pieces suggest that Saramaka women had, by the turn of the century, developed a technically and aesthetically mature art of embroidery. Curvilinear designs were outlined with linked stitches which sometimes shifted from one color to another; the interior areas were textured with a variety of "filler" stitches; and the dominant colors of the embroidery were black, red, white, and yellow. This embroidery style seems to have been discontinued by Upper River Saramakas during the first two or three decades of this century. The few more recently made examples

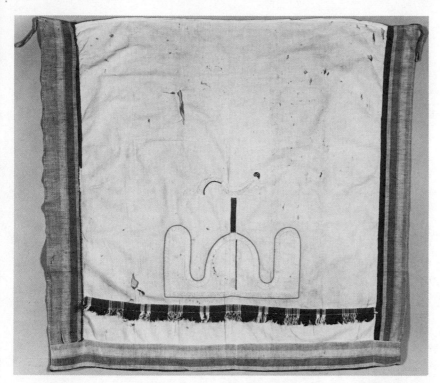

Fig. 45.   A man's cape with embroidered design, horizontal strip of fringed cloth, and border strips on three sides

that I encountered in the field were said by their owners to have been made by former wives from either Lower River villages or the eastern tribes, and women who examined with me the textile holdings of the Suriname Museum identified all cloths in this style as having been made by eastern Maroons rather than Saramakas.

Nineteenth-century women incorporated one barely noticeable feature in their sewing which seems to have arisen from practical considerations but was transformed by their descendants into the basis for the most richly elaborated and visually striking textile arts in Saramaka history. The joining of pieces of cloth to form a composite whole can be found on Saramaka garments of almost every type and decorative style. In some cases, this procedure was clearly intended to expand the size of a particular piece of clothing or to change its relative proportions; in others, it was aesthetically motivated; and in still others, both of these considerations are apparent. The white background of the cape in figure 44, which is sewn in the late nineteenth-century style of embroidery, consists of three pieces of white cloth of different sizes, carefully sewn together to form a rectangle of the correct proportions. (For additional examples of same-color patching, see S. and R. Price 1980a: cover, pls. IX [upper right white square] and X.) Men's neckerchiefs and women's waistkerchiefs have often been similarly pieced together, using odds and ends left over from other sewing projects. Girls' adolescent aprons have almost always been patched from small pieces of cloth. A popular style of man's shoulder cape from the early twentieth century was created by segmenting and resewing a single piece of striped cloth (see S. and R. Price 1980a: fig. 274 for a diagram of its construction). And one of the standard methods for making a breechcloth in the 1960s, when men were expressing a preference for a larger style than in the past, involved the cutting, rearranging, and joining of a length of striped cotton plus two supplementary strips (see fig. 46). Examples of caps, cartridge sacks, hunting sack covers, and hammock sheets also make clear that patching, with variable degrees of attention to the aesthetic dimension, has always been an option for Saramakas working with cloth.

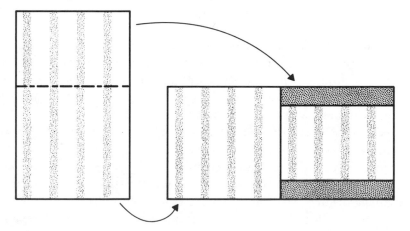

Fig. 46.   A length of trade cotton is cut into two sections and resewn with supplemental pieces of another cloth to form a man's breechcloth. Dashed line indicates cut.

At the very end of the nineteenth century, the practice of cutting and joining pieces of cloth began to be used to create intricate patchwork compositions. Saramakas refer to these as *bè-ku-baáka* (red-and-navy), *pèndê koósu* (patterned/striped/multi-colored clothing), or *píspísi* (bits-and-pieces) sewing. The essential elements were small square, triangular, and rectangular pieces of cloth in solid red, white, and navy, but many examples also include yellow, pink, blue, or green cloth, and some incorporate striped patterns as well (fig. 47).

The individual elements of bits-and-pieces textiles were seamed together by extremely meticulous sewing.[9] On most capes and aprons these seams were tucked under and hemmed, as closely as possible to the seam itself, so that the joining was barely noticeable. On all breechcloths, as well as a few capes, the patchwork was instead sewn onto a larger cloth (usually white with stripes of a single color) with a

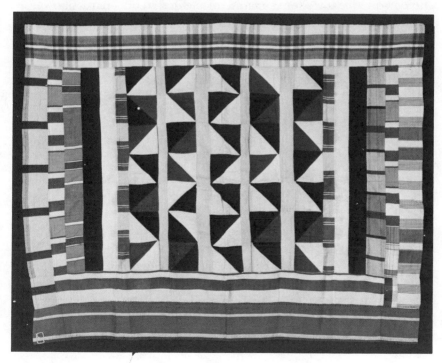

Fig. 47.   A man's shoulder cape sewn with "bits-and-pieces" patchwork

line of colorful embroidery. Many examples include some decorative embroidery, but only as small accents within the more extensive patchwork composition (see lower left corner of fig. 47). The most elaborate bits-and-pieces compositions were always on men's capes, breechcloths, and dance aprons, but men's caps and young girls' aprons were also often decorated with appliquéd border designs of a similar style, and women's formal dress at the time commonly included a "red-at-the-edge skirt" (*bè-a-búka koósu*), made by superimposing a thin strip of red cloth onto the hem and visible front edge of the wrap-around skirt.

As with other artistic media, design names contributed importantly to Saramakas' enjoyment of bits-and-pieces textiles. And as with the names used for other artistic media, there was greater unanimity about the overall pool of names and the overall pool of designs than about the matching of names and designs on particular textiles. In response to my questioning, most Saramakas enumerated roughly the same set of names for bits-and-pieces designs, but when more than one person was asked for the name of the design on a particular piece of clothing, they often gave different responses. For this reason, I do not present an illustrated classification of bits-and-pieces designs, but merely cite several design names to give some indication of how they relate to other naming systems in Saramaka (e.g., those for calabash designs or cloth patterns). Names for bits-and-pieces designs included *gaamá wáka a kombé* (the chief goes to Kombe [a section of Paramaribo]), *kágo búka* (gourd's mouth—a square design said to resemble the square opening in a gourd water vessel), *sán tánda* (saw tooth—a series of triangles), *ayánga* (the name of a fish—a design dominated by rectangles), *adòmítòtò* (butterfly), *agidá kúnya* (pegs of the *agidá* drum), and *agadáwede hánza* (wing of the *agadáwede* [a small bird]).

During the early twentieth century, Saramaka women occasionally decorated men's breechcloths with a kind of appliqué that can be related in form to both the early embroidery style and the bits-and-pieces patchwork compositions (S. and R. Price 1980*a*: pl. VIII*a,b*). The designs, which Saramakas refer to as *akeema* (see the van Panhuys quotation earlier), were curvilinear and outlined with linear embroidery, but the interior areas were appliquéd with the red, navy, or white typical of patchwork cloths rather than filled with embroidered textures.

During the period in which bits-and-pieces textiles were at the

height of their popularity, women were already beginning to experiment with a new kind of composite textile construction, using the
brightly colored striped materials that were becoming available in
coastal stores (fig. 48). The bodies of these cloths provided the wom-
en's own skirts, which were quickly made by trimming the two-ell
length to the correct dimensions and then hemming the three raw
edges. The two strips that had been trimmed from each cloth were
saved, and these were selectively incorporated into the patchwork
compositions, most commonly as borders. (See figs. 53–54 for dia-
grams of the way in which skirts and strips were separated.) Just as
bits-and-pieces designs had made their first appearances as decorative
borders on embroidered cloths (see fig. 44), the next major technique—narrow-strip sewing—began by providing borders for the
bits-and-pieces cloths (fig. 47).

A number of other cloths which cannot be labeled as either pure

Fig. 48.   A man's shoulder cape sewn with narrow-strip patchwork

bits-and-pieces or pure narrow-strip compositions provide an excellent illustration of the creative experimentation that has allowed the gradual replacement of one art style by another in Saramaka. (1) For some cloths designed with square, triangular, and rectangular pieces, women utilized, in place of the traditional solid color cloths, the colorfully striped cottons that eventually provided the basic material for narrow-strip textiles. (2) Other apparently "transitional" cloths create the visual effect of a "pure" narrow-strip textile, but are actually composed of small rectangular pieces of cloth, seamed together to form the long "strips." (3) Some early versions of narrow-strip capes were divided into two or three panels, so that the constituent elements were midway between the small rectangular pieces characteristic of early patchwork and the long strips which came to dominate narrow-strip sewing later on. (4) Finally, on some men's shoulder capes narrow sections of traditional bits-and-pieces patchwork have been alternated with long, narrow strips of colorfully striped cotton. (For illustrations of these four types of patchwork, see S. and R. Price 1980a: figs. 83, 85, 84, and 79, respectively.)

Once the popularity of bits-and-pieces clothing began to fade in the 1920s, women were already composing some cloths exclusively from narrow strips of striped cotton. The term *aseésènte,* one of several terms designating a man's shoulder cape, began to be used to refer to this narrow-strip construction as well, whether it was used for a cape, a baby's bonnet, a hammock sheet, or an adolescent girl's apron. The composition of narrow-strip textiles was a sociable task. Both the initial planning and the actual sewing were done outdoors, usually in the company of several other women, and critical comments about the aesthetic success of proposed compositions were interspersed with gossip and other topics of discussion. Once a satisfactory layout was decided upon, the woman would tack the pieces together by a stitch or two at the upper corners, and the sewing itself would take place during leisure hours over the next few weeks. Until the late 1960s, narrow-strip textiles constituted a central feature of Saramaka material culture, epitomizing a woman's artistic offerings to her husband and representing the unchallenged focus of men's fashion. Because of their long-term importance in Saramaka, I devote a later section of this chapter to the analysis of these compositions.

During the same half-century, the art of embroidery continued, but with new stitches and with changes in the overall patterning.

Designs came to be executed in single more often than double lines (figs. 49–50); the once-common use of black became rare; and the fringes that had been made by unravelling strips of cloth were replaced by overlays of lace, rickrack, ribbon, and eyelet (S. and R. Price 1980*a*: fig. 95). The general terms for embroidering (*nái a goón,* "sewing along the ground") and embroidered textiles (*goón koósu,* "ground cloths") were complemented by more specialized terms for particular decorative stitches, such as *matawái agúya* (Matawai needle), *konôpu* (button), *hêlèn bónu* (herring bone), *teíya* (star), and *agoósa* (no translation).

Women continued to ask men occasionally for help in "marking" embroidery designs, but pencils replaced charcoal for this task and the straightedge and compasses that every man owned for wood carving were used to produce more strictly geometrical designs. As with calabash carving, men's designs for embroidery were consistently valued over women's. As one woman told me, "Embroidered neck-

Fig. 49. Embroidered cloth, made to be tied onto the hunting sack of a man dressed up for a formal occasion

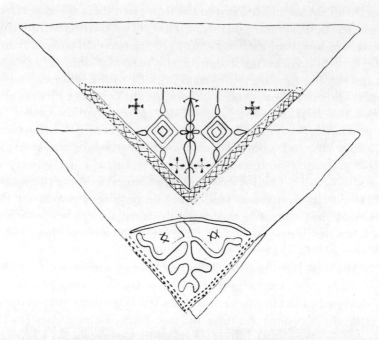

Fig. 50.   Male- and female-designed embroidery. The neckerchief on the top was designed in pencil by a man before being sewn by a woman. The one on the bottom was designed and sewn by a woman.

erchiefs that men design are more handsome than women's because they [the men] design them like a wood carving [i.e., with greater symmetry and geometric precision]." Women were always eager to elicit the help of a man in laying out the design and sometimes even pressed for advice about which lines should be executed in which colors, because of their conviction that men's design skills reflected a higher degree of accomplishment than their own (fig. 50).

The most recent fashion in Saramaka textile arts differs from those that preceded it in the degree to which it has been borrowed from the outside rather than developed through creative experimentation within Saramaka villages. By the late 1960s, young girls from the missionized villages of the Middle and Lower River regions and from the villages relocated by the hydroelectric project had begun to learn the art of cross-stitch embroidery, as part of their elementary school program, and to teach it to the women of their villages. Whenever one of these women came to a Pikilio village to visit her husband, her sisters-in-law would watch carefully as she copied a pattern from a needlework magazine, fascinated by the idea of having to calculate rows and stitches so exactly, and acutely aware of the pride with which the men wore the final product. Young men began at this point to question the aesthetic supremacy of the narrow-strip art, and a few even proclaimed defiantly that they would never condescend to wear such a cape. Instead, men tended to wear the standard alternatives— capes of patterned cloth, embroidered cloth, or cloth decorated with ribbons and eyelet. The Pikilio women continued to apply themselves to narrow-strip cloths and traditional embroidery, convinced that they would never be able to master this new art of their educated affines, but the demise of narrow-strip capes was already clearly on its way.

By 1975, all but the older men had packed their once-cherished narrow-strip capes in the bottom of their trunks, and most women were diligently working to create cross-stitch patterns that properly reflected the fashions set out by the foreign magazines.[10] The narrow-strip capes (like outgoing fashions before them) were subjected to a new, derogatory terminology that reflected current attitudes toward their status, and the strips of cotton cloth were being hastily sewn into women's narrow-strip skirts (which Saramakas, unlike Djukas, had never made before) or, more frequently, simply discarded. Although a new bride was still officially required to sew a narrow-strip cape for her husband, this part of the marriage exchange was beginning to be treated with some flexibility. Realizing that the young girl's husband would probably never wear such a cape, older women could either volunteer to lay out an acceptable pattern for the bride or accept rhetorical promises that the cape would be done "eventually."

By 1978, the cross-stitch art was being executed on every kind of cloth object, from babies' caps to hammock sheets. And by that time it had already gone through a number of stylistic and technical developments. The original exemplars from the mid-1960s, called *púu maáu koósu* (pull-the-thread cloths), were made of fine cotton cloth from which threads were removed at close intervals in order to set up a working grid in the area to be decorated. Toward 1970, a somewhat bulkier cloth, with a built-in grid texture on the same scale, allowed the tedious initial preparation to be bypassed and designs began to cover larger areas. And in the 1970s, women began to use an even heavier cloth with a significantly larger grid, and the patterns have reached their greatest extensiveness (fig. 51; see also S. and R. Price 1980a: figs. 96–99).

Fig. 51.   Man wearing shoulder cape with cross-stitch embroidery typical of the 1970s

The names for cross-stitch designs are both less extensively developed and more dependent on outside sources than the names for other domains of Saramaka artistry (cloth patterns, bits-and-pieces compositions, wood carving motifs, and so on), reflecting the newness of the art and its largely non-Maroon origin. In 1978, most Pikilio women could not list more than two or three names for cross-stitch designs, in spite of the fact that they all devoted considerable time and energy to their production. And because many of the names they did know had been devised by speakers of Dutch or Sranan-tongo, they were generally used by Saramakas as pure labels, without other meaning. For example, of the half-dozen women who listed *negelánti* (apparently a distortion of the Dutch *Nederland*) as one of the design names they knew, none could explain what it meant.

In textile arts, technical and stylistic changes have occurred gradually, sometimes over periods of several decades. The report of Eilerts de Haan's 1908 expedition to Saramaka, for example, documents the overlap at that time of (1) late nineteenth-century curvilinear embroidery, (2) bits-and-pieces patchwork, which was then at its height, and (3) narrow-strip capes, which women were just beginning to sew (fig. 52). And during the 1970s, although narrow-strip capes were no longer sewn and most men spoke of them as a *fésitén* (antiquated) relic of the past, men over the age of about sixty continued to wear them as a standard part of their clothing.

Even a relatively straightforward replacement of one artistic style by another involves a complex reworking of skills, perceptions, and patterns of use by different members of the community. In the case of cross-stitch embroidery, for example, those who wear but do not design the capes (the men) initiated a change which the artists themselves (the women) felt obliged to follow. But the different perspectives of men and women are further complicated by differences of generation, experience with Lower River and coastal societies, temperament, and even manual skills. As a result, the relative merits of competing styles are worked into the larger idiom through which individuals express themselves and their place within the society. The designing of a cape, the giving of a cape, the owning of a cape, the wearing of a cape, the evaluative discussion of a cape, and even the final rejection of a cape all become, in this context, part of the ongoing definition of cultural identity, by individuals and, over time, by the community as a whole.

Fig. 52. Three styles of decorative sewing in the early twentieth century. *Top:* two men's capes with panels of narrow-strip patchwork. *Bottom:* embroidery (*left*) and "bits-and-pieces" patchwork (*right*).

Narrow Strips

For roughly a half-century (1920–70), narrow-strip textiles, particularly in the form of men's capes, constituted a crucial item of Saramaka material culture and one of the central symbols of male/female relations. These capes were created by the parallel placement of strips of colorfully striped imported cotton cloth, arranged and sewn together with great care. The women I knew in Saramaka included some who had witnessed the first experimentation with strip compositions in the early 1900s, others for whom these compositions represented the central artistic activity of their lives, and still others who, reaching adulthood in the 1970s, disparaged strip sewing as a thing of the past. Because their collective experience covered the full history of Saramaka narrow-strip textiles, it has been possible to document this art and to explore its meaning in Saramaka life more fully than either the earlier or the more recent sewing fashions.

Perhaps because of the long-term association of narrow-strip sewing with men's capes, one of the terms designating a man's cape (*aseésènte*) came to be used also as an adjective, referring to the narrow-strip construction itself. *Aseésènte* is still used (like the synonymous alternative, *bandja koósu*) to designate men's capes in general; a *pèndê aseésènte* (striped/patterned/multi-colored *aseésènte*), for example, is a bits-and-pieces cape. But there are also *aseésènte* (narrow-strip) breechcloths, *aseésènte* hammock sheets, *aseésènte* skirts, and so on. That is, the term *aseésènte* has contextually determined referents that are analogous to those for the American English term *blue jean*. Initially designating particular garments (capes in one case, pants in the other), each one came to be associated with the kind of material and sewing which characterized that garment during a period in which it was especially fashionable. Later each one came to designate the material and sewing even when they were disassociated from the garment itself (e.g., *asseésènte* caps and sheets, blue-jean jackets and jumpers). As a result of this double usage, there exist in Saramaccan synonymous terms for narrow-strip capes, with *aseésènte* meaning "cape" in one and "narrow-strip construction" in the other; a *saa saa aseésènte* is a "plain *assésènte* [cape]" and an *aseésènte bandja koósu* is an "*aseésènte* [narrow-strip] cape."

During 1966–68, when my fieldwork goals leaned strongly toward a general absorption of Saramaka life, my understanding of *aseésènte* sewing was based almost purely on informal socializing. Women whom I visited were often engaged in some stage of the production of narrow-strip textiles, and the evaluative comments that I heard were those that they offered spontaneously to me or to each other. By 1968, I understood the social importance of *aseésènte* artistry within a conjugal context, the sociability among women which characterized the planning of these cloths, and the basic stages of the production process. However, while my own attempts to produce *aseésènte* compositions were enthusiastically encouraged by Saramakas, they were technically and aesthetically distinguishable from others in the village. There were clearly other, more subtle cues to be learned.

During the mid-1970s, I became interested in the potentials of formal analysis for the study of art and read a number of attempts to "program" particular graphic domains through techniques developed for computers and a variety of linguistic models. This exploration eventually became the theoretical focus of my Ph.D. dissertation at Johns Hopkins, in a chapter entitled "Artists and Models." Returning to Saramaka during the summers of 1975, 1976, and 1978, I centered my research on this subject around a number of structured settings designed to generate and jeopardize hypotheses concerning the principles used in the creation of *aseésènte* compositions. For this, my basic working knowledge of the activity proved essential in planning acceptable "tests" of the principles involved, and a familiarity with the vocabulary of clothing, sewing, and aesthetic concepts was crucial to the appropriate phrasing of questions.

In 1976 I brought to Saramaka two collections of cloth strips, intended to test certain hypotheses concerning the principles governing *aseésènte* compositions. One set consisted of trimmings left over from cloths that I had previously sewn into skirts for myself. These represented a variety of colorful striped (and sometimes cross-striped) patterns of varying lengths and widths. The second set, bought in the United States, were uniform strips of solid red, blue, white, yellow, and green, on each of which I had placed a masking-tape stripe—either lengthwise or crosswise. The hypothesis to be tested with these props was that *aseésènte* compositions were designed in such a way as to alternate strips that had lengthwise and crosswise stripes. In examining a large number of narrow-strip cloths, I had noticed that such an alternation was generally respected, but there were enough exceptions to justify a test of the principle.[11] I kept the skirt trimmings handy so that whenever women visited I could enlist their advice in laying out an attractive man's cape. Their layouts were recorded after the visit with color Polaroid film, and these were subsequently presented to other men and women for critical commentary. In contrast, the solid color strips were intended as a less "natural" but more controlled means of testing my stripe-alternation hypothesis, by limiting the variables strictly to color and direction of stripe.

The results were not what I had predicted. Women were enthusiastic about planning "real" *aseésènte* capes, but distinctly uncomfortable with the more artificial experiment. With the solid color strips, some women produced arrangements using only lengthwise-striped pieces; most simply declined to participate, on the grounds that they did not know the proper rules for arranging that kind of cloth. The comments made during the planning of "real" capes eventually pinpointed the problem, and a quite different explanation of the regularities emerged. The pattern that I had interpreted as a nearly consistent alternation of lengthwise and crosswise stripes became recognizable as a (virtually) completely consistent (and consciously produced) alternation of strips cut from the warp and the weft of the fabric. To the women themselves, it was less an aesthetic principle than a technical one (affecting the way the cloth would hang when it was worn)—though it tended also to produce a distinctive aesthetic effect which Saramakas evidently found pleasing.

The naturalness of the setting in which women planned out "real" narrow-strip capes for me was important in clarifying their principles. There were usually two or three women present, and the vocabulary they used in talking out their ideas together provided direct clues to the variables that structured their narrow-strip compositions. In terms of the stripe-alternation hypothesis, for example, I noted that women did not discuss their choices in terms of the direction of stripes, but referred rather to *hédi* (heads) and *bandja* (sides). These terms turned out to designate the position that the piece had occupied on the original skirt-cloth; "heads" were pieces cut across the width (the weft) and "sides" were from along the length (the warp).

It eventually became possible to clarify the relationship between my original stripe-alternation hypothesis, which had been based on an out-of-context examination of narrow-strip cloths, and the warp-weft alternation principle, which emerged in the field. As indicated in figures 53–54, the dominant stripe of Saramaka skirt-cloths runs

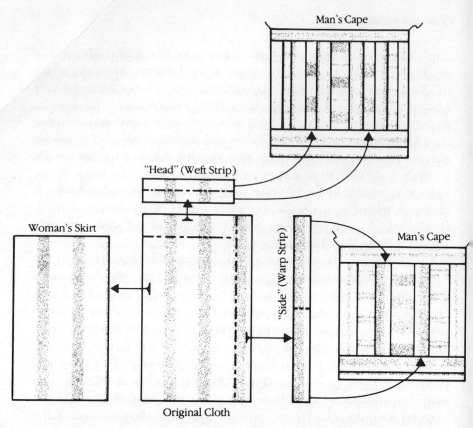

Man's Cape

"Head" (Weft Strip)

Woman's Skirt

"Side" (Warp Strip)

Man's Cape

Original Cloth

Fig. 53. Strips trimmed from the edges of a skirt-cloth are used in the construction of narrow-strip capes for men. Dashed lines indicate cuts.

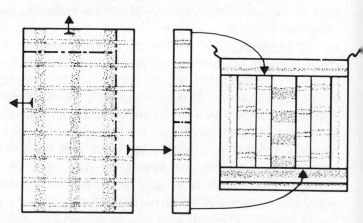

Fig. 54. An alternation of warp and weft strips does not always produce an alternation of lengthwise and crosswise stripes. See also figure 55.

along the lengthwise grain of the fabric (the warp), though there is often also a weaker secondary stripe along the weft. When the edges of these cloths are trimmed to make skirts, the dominant stripe falls *along* the warp pieces and *across* the weft pieces. *In general,* then, when women alternate warp and weft pieces in their composite textiles, they tend also to produce an alternation of lengthwise and crosswise stripes. However, in some cloth patterns, the dominant stripe occurs at fairly wide intervals, and a piece trimmed from the warp of the cloth may miss it. In such a case only the weaker secondary stripe is included, and this cuts across the piece rather than running along it. (It should be clear from figs. 53–54 that pieces cut along the weft always include the dominant stripe.)

Returning to the cloths that had not conformed perfectly to the original stripe-alternation hypothesis, I realized that they were all of one type; they were capes in which pieces with crosswise (never lengthwise) stripes were juxtaposed. Furthermore, these adjacent pieces of cross-striped materials occurred in sets of three (never two). On closer examination, the middle piece of the three turned out, in nearly every case, to have been taken from the warp. This piece was characterized by crosswise stripes only because it had fallen to one side of the dominant lengthwise stripe that ran along the warp of the original cloth. In several cases, a thread or two of the dominant stripe was visible at the seam edge, attesting to the fact that the piece had been taken from along the warp of the cloth. Figure 55 illustrates a cape of this type; the second strip from each edge is a warp piece with crosswise stripes.

In addition to the alternation of head and side pieces, several other principles of *aseésènte* cape construction became clear through repeated observation of the production process and attention to the accompanying commentary. First, women always began a layout by choosing the center strip with great care. They explained that this was the "spine" (*báka míndi*) of the composition. They all insisted that it should if possible be a head piece, and ideally the widest strip in the composition. Planning then progressed simultaneously to both sides, through the placement of matching (ideally identical) pieces at the right and left extremes. Here, color contrast was the guiding principle; women explained that the colors should "shine" or "burn" (*sèndê*), and that the color of one piece should "lift up" (*ópo*) the one next to it—that is, provide strong contrast. In addition to head and

Fig. 55.   A narrow-strip cape in which the alternation of warp and weft strips has not produced an alternation of lengthwise and crosswise stripes. (For another example, see S. and R. Price 1980*a:* fig. 116.)

side pieces taken from striped skirt-cloths, there were sometimes solid color pieces trimmed from women's waistkerchiefs or from cloths used for men's embroidered capes. Within the general pattern of warp/weft alternation, these were treated either as warp pieces (placed between two weft pieces—see fig. 48) or as "neutral" additions (inserted as extra elements within the otherwise regular alternation of warp and weft pieces). In considering their options for different arrangements, women remarked that certain grades of cotton should never co-occur on the same cape because of differential shrinkage; pieces of thin *avênge* cloth, for example, were not used in capes that contained pieces of the heavier *dégi miíi,* because the latter shrank considerably when washed. They also made explicit that no one color should be allowed to dominate the cape.[12]

Once the body of the cape was laid out, the woman would choose the lower border—one to three side (warp) pieces (depending on the intended wearer's height), which were selected for the brilliance of their colors and for sharp contrast with each other and with the rest of the cape. The bottom strip, termed the *sepú búka* ([at the] mouth of the calfband), was considered particularly important from an aesthetic point of view, since it would call attention to the wearer's calves (and calfbands)—a central focus, to Saramakas, for personal physical beauty. Finally, another side piece was laid along the opposite side of the cape, with the selvage (finished edge of the weave) at the top. Women often used the pieces they considered least attractive (frequently light yellow or white strips) for this part of the cape, since, they explained, it did not accent a particularly important part of the body.

Once the composition was planned and the pieces tacked together in the proper order, the arrangement would no longer be altered. The seams would be sewn over the course of the next week or two; the raw edges on the wrong side would be tucked tightly under with the needle and sewn with tiny stitches; the side and bottom edges would be hemmed (sometimes with a line of decorative embroidery—see fig. 55); and ties would be affixed to the upper corners. The final task was to wash the completed cape at the river, dry it in the sun, and fold it, wrong side out, into a small neat packet.

The compositional principles of these narrow-strip capes, then, included:

1. bilateral symmetry around a central spine,
2. sharp color contrast between adjacent strips,
3. avoidance of the domination of the composition by any one color,
4. alternation of side (warp) and head (weft) strips (with solid color strips occasionally inserted as additions to the pattern or as substitutions for side pieces),
5. exclusive use of side (warp) pieces for the upper and lower borders,
6. differential aesthetic attention to the various portions of the cape, with the spine and lower border pieces considered the most important and the upper border the least, and
7. avoidance of combining pieces taken from different grades of cotton.

These principles combine abstract aesthetic ideals, specific attitudes toward different parts of the human body, technical concerns regarding physical properties of the materials, and attention to the individual build of the intended owner—in a mix that I believe could not have emerged without direct observation of the production process and extensive discussion, in Saramaccan, with the women who

planned and sewed the capes. Indeed, the very delineation of a domain within which relevant principles could be correctly applied was a
Saramaka contribution. There would have been no indication, had I
worked only with museum collections and the literature, which
narrow-strip capes were from the same general region or time period,
and therefore no way of defining a corpus within which I could rea-
sonably expect compositional regularities.

Aesthetics and Time

It should be clear from the discussion of these *aseésènte* layouts that
the composition of a cape in this form was governed by principles that
were both generally observed and consciously recognized. Although
there was minor variation in the relative importance of the different
principles, there was no disagreement about the ideals themselves and
most capes adhered to the articulated "rules."

Saramakas' insights regarding the principles of *early* narrow-strip
capes were a different matter. During my 1975–78 visits, I had in the
field a large supply of photographs illustrating *aseésènte* compositions
from museum collections and earlier fieldtrips; I also borrowed, purchased, or was given a number of actual capes. Those identified as
"early" (roughly pre-1950) *aseésènte* capes frequently failed to conform to the principles that were visible in the more modern examples,
and this failure was the source of considerable confusion for the
Saramakas who commented on them. When the same people who had
been so articulate and consistent about the "rules" of modern *aseésènte*
capes were asked to discuss older pieces from a similar perspective,
they were unable to provide a satisfactory analysis.

Most began by attempting to identify a central spine, but voiced
frustration that the bilateral symmetry it defined was not carried
through the whole composition. Some suggested that the seamstress
must have run out of strips and had to make do with whatever she
had on hand. Older women who had sewn such textiles themselves (in
some cases even commenting on cloths of their own making) explained that the proper rules for *aseésènte* capes had not been well
known at the time; it was only women of later generations who figured out how they were really supposed to be designed. Another
woman asserted that "women in those days didn't take the time to
plan things." Even when, as a last resort, I pointed out certain reg-

ularities of patterning which I had perceived in examples of these cloths, I convinced no one. In terms of compositional analysis, everyone expressed confusion. Evaluatively, they all commented on the cloths' failure to meet modern standards of unified symmetry and head/side alternation. Women who had made these cloths themselves were unanimous in humbly commending the stylistic progress that had been made since the time of their youth. As one remarked, "these women who have come along after us are more artistic than we were."

Two factors seem to have contributed to Saramakas' differential readiness to analyze "early" and "modern" *aseésènte* compositions. First, there has been an actual increase, over time, in the regularity of the compositions. Second, the process of rejecting one artistic style in favor of another seems to have been lubricated by the gradual denial of any "sense" or "logic" to the earlier style.

In terms of any readily observable variable (symmetry, warp/weft alternation, horizontal/vertical stripe alternation, horizontal/vertical placement of strips, and so on), there has clearly been increased standardization in *aseésènte* compositions over the past fifty years. Compared with narrow-strip textiles of the 1960s, the early cloths were designed with great individual freedom. Some are divided into two or three panels of parallel strips. Some are dominated by vertically and others by horizontally positioned strips. The relative proportions of strips taken from the warp and weft vary dramatically from one composition to another. Many contain more than one recognizable center for bilateral symmetry and allow the several sets of symmetrical arrangements to intersect with one another in complex ways. Others invert the right and left segments of otherwise symmetrical arrangements. And still others have no discernible symmetry at all. In this sense, Saramaka narrow-strip textiles seem to have moved in the same direction as narrow-strip textiles in West Africa—their most obvious formal parallels. Venice Lamb reports that

> an examination of a large number of Asante cloths of various ages leads one to the conclusion that regularity and order in patterning have tended to increase with time, and it can be argued that Asante patterns today are far more stereotyped than they were even fifty years ago. [1975:134]

Descriptions of this kind of actual stylistic change, based primarily on examination of datable artifacts, have not been frequent in the anthropological literature. But even more rare is the exploration of

~~the attitudes and perceptions that accompany such change, simultaneously contributing to it and resulting from it. Saramakas' comments on outdated sewing techniques, designs, and overall style pointed to the importance of reconstructing the subtle *conceptual* developments that surround more tangible artifactual developments, and of trying to understand their role in the complex process of~~ cultural change.

In contrast to the study of current evaluative frameworks, which can be based on relatively spontaneous commentary, the exploration of their equivalents from the past requires a somewhat more "forced" elicitation of ideas. Saramaka women readily understood that I would want their advice in laying out an attractive modern *aseésènte* cape (though in the 1970s, they often suggested that a cross-stitch cape would be more appropriate to make), but all were at least initially bewildered by my serious interest in totally outdated styles. Saramakas who were asked to discuss obsolete art forms wanted to understand my motives for acquiring this apparently useless knowledge, and their inferences on the matter were potential influences on the kinds of remarks they provided. For example, it was hard for people not to be somewhat more positive about the merits of a particular style once they realized that I was seriously interested in it. This consideration varied from one person to the next and was in all cases an extremely subtle matter, but it was clearly a factor that needed to be taken into account in the conducting of my field research.

I dealt with the problem in several ways. First, I attempted to initiate discussions that would most nearly replicate conversations that could have occurred among Saramakas themselves. This meant embedding all specific questions within more general discussions of the past—encouraging older Saramakas to reminisce about the personalities and events of their youth, about songs and dances that were popular then, and about their own personal lives at the time when men and women were producing (and talking about) the "old style" arts. Second, impromptu conversations with individuals from different villages who were unfamiliar with my interests were frequently useful in checking potential distortions in the information given to me by more regular discussants. And finally, there were some kinds of evidence for changing attitudes that were independent of Saramakas' retrospective evaluations. During my last field trip, for example, I discovered the existence of a number of terms for particular clothing/sewing styles that had been limited to certain periods of their history. The strong evaluative component of these terms not only underscored the sensitivity of Saramakas to fashion trends, but also provided clear indicators of the changing status of particular styles over time.

As old techniques and designs are abandoned, there is an equally important phasing out of the conceptual frameworks within which artifacts in the old style had been made and appreciated. The understanding of past arts does not, moreover, die a completely "natural death" through population turnover. Rather, the conceptualizations that guided both the production and the appreciation of earlier arts are systematically discouraged through the development of disparaging attitudes that tend to deny the earlier art any sense of order. The classification of bits-and-pieces designs, which Saramakas make clear was once a part of general cultural knowledge, has been largely lost, even by the women who composed them and the men who wore them. More remarkable, because of the recency of the change, is the confusion women express over the principles behind early *aseésènte* compositions. The anachronistic attempt to squeeze them into the mold of modern narrow-strip capes by designating a spine and looking for bilateral symmetry around it was quite general. When this proved unsuccessful, most people would dismiss the cloth as a random arrangement of strips. The complex structure of a cloth such as the hammock sheet illustrated in S. and R. Price 1980*a* (pl. XII) was not perceived. In Saramakas' analysis of this hammock sheet there was no acknowledgment, for example, of the inverted symmetry in the placement of the predominantly yellow strips on the top and the bottom of the center panel, of the off-center section of symmetrically arranged strips in the right-hand panel, or of the balance between the upper right and the lower left corners of the composition. Rather, this whole cloth was seen as a random (if impressively colorful) collection of strips. Several people remarked that such cloths were the product of a time when "the proper rules had not yet been figured out."

This notion reflects general Saramaka perceptions of a progressive refinement in their material life, which includes not only the introduction of outboard motors, aluminum utensils, chain saws, and gas-burning stoves, but also the development of wood carvings with ever finer technical precision, narrow-strip sewing with increasingly consistent bilateral symmetries, and cross-stitch designs which exhibit mathematically perfect regularities within a two-dimensional grid.[13]

Stylistic development in Saramaka cannot be understood purely as a process of innovation, creation, and the introduction of new artistic modes. It must also take into account the various ways in which former styles are disposed—not only through a discontinuance of their production but also through a rejection of the conceptual order within which they were produced and appreciated. George Kubler has written that "Fashions touch the limit of credibility by violating the precedent and by grazing the edge of the ridiculous" (1962:39). He also recognized that stylistic change involves both a selection and adoption of the new and a rejection and disposal of the old.

> The decision to discard something is far from being a simple decision. . . . It is a reversal of values. Though the thing once was necessary, discarded it becomes litter or scrap. What once was valuable now is worthless; the desirable now offends; the beautiful now is seen as ugly. When to discard and what to discard are questions to which the answers are governed by many considerations. [Kubler 1962:77]

In the course of this realignment, at least in Saramaka, that which "grazed the edge of the ridiculous" takes on a central, normatively accepted position, and the "precedent" may in turn begin to graze the edge of the ridiculous. Just as a new fashion may be introduced as an exciting violation of current standards, an old fashion may be phased out as a failure to meet current standards; discrepancies with current trends can both heighten the appeal of a new fashion, and justify the rejection of the old. The embarrassment of Saramakas at my desire to dredge up the attitudes, conceptualizations, and working principles of an old style may reflect the fact that they had rejected the entire aesthetic order that had produced that style, as part of the process of establishing a new order.

Terminological changes represent one of the more effective mechanisms by which art styles are passed out of currency in Saramaka, especially in terms of clothing. Created in the context of Saramakas' enjoyment of verbal play, the labels by which older generations express their disapproval of a new and "outrageous" style and the labels by which enthusiasts exalt its beauty at the height of its popularity are gradually superseded by teasing terms that "dispose" of the style through ridicule and denial of artistic worth. My attempts in the field to understand the Saramaka classification of textile arts produced real confusion until I realized that many terms were temporally specific— direct outgrowths of changing styles and the attitudes that accompanied them through time. For example, the difference between two words for bits-and-pieces breechcloths—*pèndê kamísa* and *awangalió*—was clarified only once I learned that the latter had been coined during the waning days of the style to mock the pretentiousness of anyone who would wear such a busily patterned garment. With *wangaa* indicating extensiveness and complexity of design, and *lió* evoking a swaying motion, the term *awangalió* served to make fun of a man wearing a breechcloth in this style, with the ridiculously elaborate design swinging along behind him, *"lió, lió, lió."*

The history of narrow-strip textiles has also been helped along by such words. In the 1950s and 1960s, when unified bilateral symmetry was the order of the day, the "randomness" of earlier compositions was emphasized by a new term, *apísi-ku-wána* (*apísi* [a white wood] and *wána* [a reddish wood]). Originally serving as a general word for the juxtaposition of unlike materials and as a nonderogatory term for bits-and-pieces clothing, the term was called into service to refer to narrow-strip cloths in which the two sides failed to match. In places where a single cloth pattern "should" have appeared on both sides, the seamstress had instead put in *apísi* and *wána*—some of this and some of that. Partly through its association with a totally outdated fashion, the label *apísi-ku-wána* relegated early narrow-strip textiles to the past and stressed their nonconformance with more current compositional standards. In the 1970s, as cross-stitch embroidery took over Saramaka fashion, *all* narrow-strip textiles became vulnerable to derisive terms. The capes that had, just a decade earlier, been the admired focus for women's artistry and men's formal dress became known as *mòtê kaápu* (motor covers) and *apúku koósu* (forest spirit cloths) since, it was said, they were useful only for shielding an outboard motor from the elements or paying a debt to a forest spirit.[14]

Even terms for the raw materials of fashions reflect changing attitudes. For example, the standard cloth of the 1960s took on a new name when other types of cloth came into style. In the 1970s, Saramakas began to replace the neutral term *avênge koósu* by the term *abáabôò*, an onomatopoeic rendering of the ease with which the cloth tore. At the same time, older Saramakas expressed their disapproval of the new art of cross-stitch embroidery through a term referring to the thick cloth on which it was executed. *Djòdjò*—a word designating worn-out hammock pieces that have been converted into serviceable, if highly unfashionable, skirts for manual chores—became for them a term of derision for the cross-stitch clothing that was the rage among their grandchildren's generation.

In short, changes in the lexicon of description are one of the most telling reflections of the dynamism of Saramaka artistic life, as well as an important tool in effecting that dynamism. Original terms signal the acceptance of a newly created or introduced form, others reflect a variety of attitudes toward it while its popularity lasts, and still others confirm its rejection once it is replaced.

Sewn for Men, Sewn for Women

In Pikilio villages, hand-cranked (or, rarely, foot-pedaled) sewing machines are for men, not women, to own and use.[15] A man buys a sewing machine in a city store in much the same spirit that he buys a digital watch with a calendar function—not so much because he needs its services, but rather as a satisfyingly conspicuous symbol of his economic success on the coast. A man who owns a sewing machine occasionally makes a breechcloth for himself, or hems a cape and decorates it with a few lengths of ribbon or eyelet. He also uses it to provide favors for women. With it, he can hem a woman's skirt quickly, effortlessly, and in perfectly even stitches, and the women for whom this is done never fail to be properly impressed and grateful.

Male-sewn garments, however, constitute a very small portion of Saramaka clothing. Most clothes, for both men and women, are sewn by women, with a needle and thread. And just as men occasionally .machine-sew women's clothes as a way of enhancing their relationships with particular women, women hand-sew men's clothes as a way of reaffirming their love for particular men.

When we look at female-sewn clothing in Saramaka, we see some interesting reflections of the relationship between the sexes. The most striking of these is the relative elaborateness of decorative sewing on men's garments, compared to women's. Although there are some quite beautiful exceptions to the rule, Saramakas have always viewed embroidery as an art intended for men—most often appearing on their capes, but also embellishing their neckerchiefs, breechcloths, caps, hunting sack covers, hammock covers, cartridge bags, and the cloths that sometimes cover their meals until they are ready to eat. Patchwork compositions follow the same pattern, being reserved almost exclusively for men's clothing. Unlike Maroon women in eastern

Suriname, Saramaka women have never embellished their own skirts with more than token embroidery and have no tradition of patchwork art for their own use.

When Saramaka women *do* engage in decorative sewing for themselves, the way in which they plan the designs corresponds to their image of how women's clothing should differ from men's. During the early 1970s, when men were beginning to reject narrow-strip capes in favor of the more fashionable cross-stitch ones, Saramaka women sometimes used their supplies of narrow strips to make skirts for themselves. But in adapting this medium for their own use, women converted it from a high art into a utilitarian, nonaesthetic form. Ideas about symmetry, balance, color contrast, and warp/weft alternation were all discarded, and the strips were hastily juxtaposed without consideration of compositional alternatives. As one woman commented, "When you sew for a husband, you look at how well the pieces 'fit' [go together]. But when you make something for yourself, you just sew all the pieces together."

Technical aspects of clothing also reflect different attitudes toward garments made for men and garments made for women. In the 1960s, for example, the hand sewing on men's capes was usually between ten and fifteen stitches per inch, while the normal edging for a woman's skirt was a visible line of brightly colored thread, three to six stitches per inch.

A Saramaka woman sews her own clothes simply and quickly; she sews clothing for her husband with close attention to technical detail and aesthetic principles. For a gift of decorative clothing is a message of love, and Saramaka women are eager to show their husbands that they care. This understanding about the "meaning" of decorative sewing may go far toward explaining why even the most dedicated young enthusiasts of Heineken T-shirts and store-bought trousers also enjoy outfitting themselves in elaborate Saramaka clothing— from embroidered shoulder capes and breechcloths to brightly colored dance aprons and tasseled calfbands. One type of clothing reflects their success in the outside world, the other their success with women; and of the various aspects of life that Saramaka men care about, these are incontestably two of the most important.

Chapter Seven

Songs and Skirts

Decorative arts are used by Saramaka men and women to express affection and solidarity. By carving a beautiful comb for a woman, a man communicates his love; by composing a handsome patchwork cape for her husband or carving an attractive calabash to set out at his meals, a woman does the same. But when love turns sour, when jealousy intrudes, and when feelings are abused, the decorative arts no longer provide an expressive outlet. In contrast, Saramaka popular songs (*sêkêti kandá*) express feelings that range from love to hate, from joy to despair, and from desire to rejection. And while some *sêkêti* songs reinforce the warmth and passion that are associated with the decorative arts, many more are inspired by interpersonal tensions.

The names that Saramakas create for different patterns of trade cotton provide a related idiom for social commentary, generally of a critical nature. Created largely by women, and used most frequently for either unsewn cloth or skirts, these names focus attention on many of the same interpersonal dramas that fuel the composition of *sêkêti* songs. This chapter examines the complementary ways in which these two verbal forms reflect on the lives of Saramakas, especially women.

Creative Singing

Sêkêti songs are created spontaneously, usually in response to specific incidents. Some express concerns that are shared by others—for example, despair and anger at the flooding of Saramaka villages by the hydroelectric project that was built in the 1960s or condolences to Chief Agbago following an assassination attempt in which one of his houses was burned to the ground. But most are highly personal, referring to the ups and downs of individual relationships. A Saramaka woman once suggested to me that all *sêkêti* songs are either songs of love (*lóbi*), cursing (*kósi*), or hardship (*fuká*)—that they either expressed the passions of a particular love relationship, "poked at" a person who had been spreading malicious gossip, or voiced despair over personal hardships, such as loneliness or poverty.

Sêkêti songs are created and performed by both sexes. But when we look at their content, we find some interesting differences that reflect on the perceived quality of life for men and women. First, women make up these songs more frequently; second, women's songs are more often motivated by feelings of bitterness, despair, and loneliness than are those composed by men. In terms of the emotions they express, about one-half of the songs composed by men may be classed as "positive" and one-fourth "negative." In contrast, those composed by women are about one-fifth "positive" and three-fourths "negative." (*Sêkêti* songs that comment on an incident without expressing either positive or negative affect are rare, but seem to be composed more frequently by men than by women.)

Women are quite explicit, in many of the *sêkêti* songs they compose, about the specific nature of the dissatisfactions they feel in their personal lives. Women most frequently focus their songs of complaint on problems with their husbands, their husbands' relatives, and their husbands' other wives, and they view themselves as relatively impotent in the face of conflicts with any of these people. A woman's husband may fail to provide well for her or he may show preference for another of his wives, but she is acutely aware that if she leaves him she will suffer in terms of material goods and that she may well never have a chance to remarry. A woman's in-laws may spread malicious gossip about her, but if she leaves their village to establish full-time residence in her own village, she loses status in her husband's eyes and weakens her marriage. And a woman's co-wives may make life extremely trying for her, but there is nothing she can do about the fact that her husband enjoys spending time with them. Many women's *sêkêti* songs address these dilemmas, not as general social problems, but in terms of particular situations and individual relationships. Viewed as texts, their cumulative effect is to discredit—with very little room for discussion—the outsiders' popular image of fickle, strong-willed Maroon women holding the "whip hand" in marriages and taking the initiative for most divorces either "on some slight pretext" or "simply because they feel like a change" (Dark 1951:57; Hurault 1961:153).

People compose new *sêkêti* songs most often in solitary and relaxed settings—while paddling a canoe, cutting rice in a field, or daydreaming in a house. I have often seen a person who is sitting idly on a doorstep break into a spontaneous song to comment on the passing scene, and an appropriate way to react to a gift is through a sung expression of delight. Even very young children are actively encouraged to invent *sêkêti* songs. At age three or four, the girl pictured on the dedication page of this book set the name of a kinsman to a little melody, singing "*Peleki-éé, Peleki-oo*," and was embraced and congratulated warmly by everyone around, who interpreted this simple song as the beginning of a promising *sêkêti* career. And children just a few years older enjoy performing their own songs in groups, with soloist, choral response, and rhythmic hand clapping.

Because of the frequency and spontaneity of *sêkêti* song composition, many are quickly forgotten, and even those that become popular have a relatively brief active life. The repertoire of *sêkêti* songs that were being sung in Pikilio villages during 1967–68 was several hundred, but a year or two later, these had all been replaced by new ones that reflected events of more current interest—from love affairs and divorces to gift presentations and petty crime. When asked, Saramakas can still sing the songs of the past decade, and older women derived great pleasure from providing me with nostalgic renditions of songs that were popular in the early twentieth century. But in the absence of an anthropologist's urging, the performance of outdated songs is limited to an occasional brief session at the end of a wake, when most of the participants have already gone home to sleep.

If a person's new *sêkêti* song catches the fancy of others, it is sung and talked about, and eventually presented at a "play"—usually one of the all-night funeral ceremonies in which a member of the community is formally ushered into the realm of the ancestors.[1] In the presence of perhaps a hundred or more people, a carefully groomed and attired performer sings the solo while executing a *tjêke* dance (see fig. 56). A line of women and girls, bent forward at the hips, both provide a steady beat of hand clapping and punctuate the soloist's phrases with a simple choral response. At the end, the performer is embraced and congratulated by others, and another *sêkêti* song begins—either by the same person or by someone else.

For about the past fifteen years, battery-operated tape recorders have also inspired "formal" performances of *sêkêti* singing. Even in the absence of appropriate ritual events, Saramakas often assemble a small group to record the currently most popular songs, complete

Fig. 56. During a community "play," a woman executes the *tjêke* dance and sings a currently popular *sêkêti* song while others provide a choral response and rhythmic hand clapping.

with chorus and hand clapping; they then have them to listen to in the evenings or at leisure periods during the day. Although this practice began as an exclusively male prerogative, a few women have now purchased recorders, and recordings are made by both women and men.

Unlike some genres of Saramaka singing, *sêkêti* songs are composed in the everyday language of Saramaccan, but their verbal style is subtly different. Occasionally a person introduces a new word or phrase that becomes part of *sêkêti* vocabulary more for its sound than for its meaning. *Sêkêti* lyrics also differ from ordinary speech in their greater use of metaphorical words and expressions. For example, various modes of Western-style communication, which Saramakas view partly as foreign novelties, are used as metaphors for irresponsible gossiping. When a nonliterate woman sings that her name is "written down in a book" or when a man who has never used a telephone sings to someone, "Your mother just phoned," they are explicitly accusing another person of spreading malicious rumors (see, for example, songs 21, 22, 33, and 44 in this chapter). Similarly, a faithful wife is often referred to as a nun (e.g., song 4), and a woman may be called Queen Wilhelmina as a compliment to her beauty (e.g., song 3).[2] More idiosyncratic metaphors for particular individuals are also common, and these often take on the status of poetic nicknames (*sêkêti* names) that last for the rest of the person's life (see R. and S. Price 1972*b*).

The actual performance of a *sêkêti* song is a creative act, in which the basic melody and lyrics are repeated many times, with frequent improvisation in the exact wording. Most commonly, terms of address (inserted at least partly for rhythmic effect) may be altered in consecutive repeats (see songs 42 and 43), and some songs in a sense invite performers to introduce variations through the use of words or concepts for which many substitutions are possible (see, for example, songs 23, 29, 33, and 38). The transcriptions in this chapter are of necessity, then, both arbitrary and partial. The fact that some are more fully elaborated than others reflects the unevenness of my field data. Some were recorded at all-night funeral "plays," others were sung expressly for our tape recorder, others were heard but not taped during plays, and still others were elicited during interviews. Thus, although the "core lyrics" of each song were confirmed and elucidated through systematic discussion, the originality of actual performances has not been possible to render. The transcriptions given in this chapter are intended to represent each song's basic lyrics. For some, I also indicate variations that I happen to have heard, but it should be understood that all *sêkêti* songs lend themselves to subtle variations in phrasing, and that Saramakas regard such improvisation as a crucial contribution to the success of a particular performance.

The translations offered below also represent only one set out of the many that could justifiably have been presented. Word-for-word translations would fail to capture the tone of many examples; metaphorical conventions that speak for themselves to Saramakas are often cumbersome to explain (let alone gloss gracefully) to non-Saramakas; and the stylistic "fillers" that contribute to the beauty of many *sêkêti* songs in performance tend not to contribute to the beauty of written English versions. My solution to these dilemmas has been a compromise—an attempt to render each song in intelligible English without totally sacrificing the imagery of the original Saramaccan. A few phrases for which I have been unable to find English equivalents have been left in Saramaccan; some metaphorical expressions have been given literal translations and clarified in notes; and for one song I have supplemented a straight translation with a paraphrased version in an attempt to render both the language and the tone of the original. Each song has been discussed with Saramakas in terms of both its literal meaning and the social situation that inspired it. In the three or four cases in which there was disagreement in the interpretation of a particular song (e.g., with one person saying it was addressed to a certain woman's co-wife and another saying it was an attack on her sister-in-law), I have accepted the version of the person whom Saramakas consider to be more of an authority on *sêkêti* songs.

Finally, my decision not to provide musical transcriptions is based on two considerations. First, this study analyzes *sêkêti* songs as social commentary, for which the musical form is largely irrelevant. Second, recordings of Saramaka *sêkêti* singing are now available (Gillis 1981; R. and S. Price 1974, 1977), and even include performances of some of the songs that are given in this chapter.[3]

Love, Support, and Contentment in Song

Men's and women's love songs are very similar in style, content, and tone. Ranging from straightforward declarations of love to subtle metaphorical compliments, they often include a newly created *sêkêti* name that communicates tender affection. I cite several examples.

A woman from Dangogo, thinking nostalgically about a former husband whom she still loved even though she had remarried, sang:

1. *Soní mi lóbi-éé,*   The thing I love [the love I have],
   Soní mi lóbi-oo,   The thing I love,
   Soní mi lóbi   The thing I love
   Án tá gaándi-éé.   Never grows old.

Another woman's song, respectfully addressing a lover as "that man," declared simply:

2. *Mi lóbi i-éé, dí wómi*   I love you, the man,
   Mi lóbi i-éé.   I love you.
   Kó baasá mi   Come embrace me
   Fu féni tjá gó.   And we'll go off with that.
   Dí wómi-dê, mi lóbi i.   That man, I love you.

A man compared a woman he loved to a queen, and added a further romantic touch by calling to her in a foreign language.

3. *Un sí wán wáka dí a tá*   Do you see that walk she's walking?
     wáka?
   Muyêè, mi kê i.   Woman, I want/love you.
   Wemina kónu-éé.   Wilhelmina the Queen.
   Dí mamzêli-oo,   Mademoiselle,
   Mamzêli sisiyééni,   Mademoiselle *sisiyééni* [Sicilian?],
   Un fá wè?   What about it?
   Un sí wán wáka dí a tá   Do you see that walk she's walking?
     wáka?
   Muyêè, mi kê i.   Woman, I want/love you.

A man from Kampu expanded the standard Saramaka "good morning" (*I wéki nô?* [Did you awake?] or *Fá i wéki?* [How did you awake?]) into a song of admiration for his tall wife.

4. *Gadja mazó, a póbiki búka,*   Statuesque nun, with the mouth of a doll,
   Un fá i wéki-o, mama?   How did you awake, momma?
   Mi wéki-o, mi wéki-é.   I awoke, I awoke [the reciprocal greeting].
   Mama, i wéki hánse sèmbè.   Momma, you awoke [as] a beautiful person.

Sêkêti songs may express affection and sympathy for other people as well as for lovers and spouses. Brothers- and sisters-in-law, for

example, are sometimes addressed in such songs. A woman sang to
her husband's brothers:

5. *Dí ódi i mandá a mi,*   The greeting you sent me,
   Mi tá yéi.   I hear it.
   M'án ó bái sábi sô.   I won't call out to acknowledge it.
   Mi ku i sá míti u mi paká i. You and I will surely meet so I can
                                   pay [thank] you [in person].

Another woman celebrated in song the fact that her brothers-in-
law had bought a new outboard motor.

6. *Déé suági u mi-oo,*   Those brothers-in-law of mine,
   Wán lô suági u mi,   Some of my brothers-in-law,
   Un kó, un bái mòtê-o.   You've come and bought a motor.
   Un tjái mi n'ên-o   Won't you take me for a ride in it
   Túè a déwawe líba-éé.   And bring me up past the Tapawata
                                   rapids.

Many *sêkêti* songs bring greetings to the tribal chief. When Chief
Agbago sent presents of cloth and dishware to a blind and very talented singer from a village on the upper Gaanlio, asking her to perform in his village, she came and greeted him with a new song.

7. *Lío gaamá,*   Chief of the river,
   Mi kó haíka i.   I've come to see how you are.[4]
   Un fá i wéki,   How did you awake,
   Lío gaamá?   Chief of the river?

Later the same day, she made up another new song to honor the
chief, calling out for people to join in the celebration, and referring to
a recently introduced and very popular aluminum cooking pot that
may have been among the presents she had received from him.

8. *Améika galimó,*   American aluminum [pot],
   Kó a kó.   It's just arrived.
   Un kó wái ku mi-é!   Come and celebrate with me!

A man from Akisiamau whose kinsmen had been quarreling with
the chief offered his own personal support in the form of a song that
subsequently achieved great popularity on the Pikilio.

9. *Lánti gaamá,*   Chief of the people,
   M'án tjiká u buusé i-é.   I can't quarrel with you.

After a man tried to assassinate Chief Agbago and burned one of his houses to the ground, a renowned singer from Pempe offered her condolences in a new *sêkêti* song, in which she expressed her horror at the arsonist by referring to him as a German (see note 6).

10. *Mi yéi táa Alumá kó tjumá*	I heard a "German" came to burn
kantóo;	your office;
Sô mi yéi.	That's what I've heard.
Gaamá, mi kó haíka i.	Chief, I've come to pay my respects.
Múndu a zónu!	The world has [such] evil!
Mi yéi táa dí kôndè boóko;	I heard the village was destroyed;
Mi tínga lègèdè.	I thought it was a lie.
Mi yéi táa sobói kó tjumá	I heard a hoodlum came to burn
kantóo;	your office;
Sô mi yéi.	That's what I've heard.
Gaamá, mi kó haíka i-éé.	Chief, I've come to pay my respects.
Zónu dê a múndu.	Evil is in the world.

The chief is not alone in receiving sympathy through song. One man addressed a forlorn woman who had been rejected by her husband, and offered her his moral support.

11. *Gandá muyêè,*	Unmarried woman,[5]
Andí dú i so?	What's bothering you so?
I mánu túè i kaa, nô?	Your husband's thrown you out, has he?
Muyêè, ná kaí dêdè dêdè.	Woman, don't fall down dead.
É sèmbè bi dê	If there were anyone around
De bi sa téi i nóómo-éé.	Someone would surely marry you.

In later performances, his song was prefaced with a melodious explanation of the situation that inspired it:

A dí sáta mámanté,	On Saturday morning,
Dí mi náki téé mi dóu a	When I arrived at the landing place,
lanpéési-dê,	
Hên mi sí mi lóbi, maíngè,	I saw my love [friend], my goodness,
A béndi édi píí.	With her head hanging down.
A dí sónde mámante,	On Sunday morning,
Dí mi náki téé mi dóu a	When I arrived at the landing place,
lanpéési-dê,	
Hên mi sí mi lóbi-o, maínge,	I saw my love, my goodness,
A béndi édi píí.	With her head hanging down.
M'bai hééi-o,	I called out, "Hey there,
Gandá muyêè,	Unmarried woman,
Andí dú i so? . . .	What's bothering you so?" . . .

Many songs express personal contentment without being addressed to a particular individual. Men thinking about a trip to the coast and the money they expect to earn there, for example, may phrase their anticipation in the form of a *sêkêti* song. One man from Akisiamau put his daydreaming about traveling outside of Saramaka territory into a song, mentioning three of the towns where Saramakas have found work (Moengo, Kourou, and St. Laurent).

12. *Dí zámbi gádu bái a Mongo.*	The gods are calling out in Moengo.
Hên seéi bái téé a Kuhú-éé.	They're calling out too in Kourou.
Soolán gádu, un yéi-éé?	Gods of St. Laurent, do you hear?
Wè, djenlelee vunvu-o,	Well, *djenlelee vunvu,*
Wè, djenlelee vunvu-o,	Well, *djenlelee vunvu,*
Gádu, hên tá bái-éé.	It's the gods that are calling out.

Part of the excitement of money-earning expeditions is the encounter with people from other cultures. A *sêkêti* song composed by a man who divides his residence between Godo and Heeikuun reflects the widespread fascination of Saramaka men with foreign languages, through an imitation of the Portuguese greeting of a Brazilian co-worker. (The first four lines are the principal lyrics that are sung many times in succession in the course of the song's performance; the rest represents a "digression" that would occur once or twice, like that given for song 11. I was not able to elicit a translation for *nyénlele.*)

13. *Sinyólu, nyénlele, miíi,*	*Senhor, nyénlele,* child,
Sinyólu, un yéi, nô?	*Senhor,* don't you hear?
Sinyólu, bondia-o.	*Senhor, bom dia.*
Wè, m'án ó yéi môò-éé.	Well, I don't understand any more.
Dí mi náki téé mi dóu	I traveled until I arrived
A Degaa-konde.	At Degaa-konde.
Pootugéi bakáa kó tá bái	A Portuguese [-speaking] man came
Dá m'ódi u sèmbè-ee.	And gave me greetings from someone.
Wè, nô-nô,	Well, now,
Wè, a bái dá m'ódi u sèmbè.	Well, he called out someone's greetings.
A kó tá bái:	He called out:
O sinyólu,	*O Senhor,*
Kumá tá váiwe?	*Como te vai?* [How are you?]
O katé o katé plaatígó.	*O que te pratico* [I am talking to you].
Kutu kutu,	*Escuta, escuta* [listen, listen],
Sinyóó-kónu.	*Senhor,* "king."

Lament, Insult, and Scandal in Song

A large proportion of *sêkêti* songs, especially those composed by women, express such sentiments as sadness or anger. Some of these refer to problems shared by Saramakas in general. In a song composed by a woman from Pempe that became popular in 1967–68, for example, the soloist declared that *Salamáka toónbe* (Saramaka's fallen), and the chorus responded by calling out *Lendema*—Saramakas' name for the man in charge of the construction of the hydroelectric dam that flooded the downriver villages. Another song, composed by a man, joined Lendema's name with that of J. A. Pengel (then the prime minister of Suriname) and lamented the tensions stirred up by the national elections of 1967. And after a 1968 visit by Pengel to Saramaka, during which he was to have been honored by the playing of a *djánsi* drum, the boatmen's inadvertent abandonment of the drum during a stopover in the village of Pempe was criticized in a song that proclaimed, "They escorted Pengel *djánsi*-less [from Pempe to Asindoopo]" (*Déé tjá Pengenen-o sôndò djánsi*).

The woman who offered her condolences to the chief after the 1967 assassination attempt also composed a generalized lament about the state of the world in which such a thing could have happened.

14. *Gaán gádu, yéé-o,*	Great god, listen,
Goón líba-o!	Oh world!
Goón líba téki mi	The world took me
Butá a pikí kuyêè bóto,	And put me in a little calabash boat,
Mi ku déé bêè u mi.	Me and my lineage.
Hên a butá a míndi wáta.	Then it set [it] down in the middle of the water.
Un yéi wán a dú môò a lío.	Listen to another thing that's happened on the river.
Un sí wán a dú môò a múndu.	Look at another thing that's happened in the world.
Múndu a soní-éé,	The world has such [terrible] things,
Múndu a soní-óó, kôndè.	The world has such things, villagers.
Un yéi wán a dú môò a lío.	Listen to another thing that's happened on the river.

But many more songs of lament focus on personal hardship. A man working in Kourou, for example, expressed his real fear of being knifed by fellow laborers from Colombia.

15. *Mi bái helú, déé sèmbè,*   I'm calling out for help, everyone,
    Mi bái helú dá de   I'm calling out for help against them.
    Mi bái helú dá déé Amíngo.   I'm calling out for help against the
        "Amigos" (Colombians).

Many women's songs reflect the loneliness they feel when their husbands go off for several years to earn money outside of Saramaka territory. I cite just two.

16. *M'á ó láfu môò-éé.*   I won't laugh [have fun] anymore.
    Dí wómi dê a Lendema lío.   The man's at Lendema's river [the
        artificial lake].
    M'á ó láfu môò.   I won't laugh anymore.

17. *Dí gaán gádu bái-o,*   The thunder is rolling,
    Nôò mi tá tjalí.   And I feel such sorrow.
    M'án sá andí u mi mêni.   I don't know what to think about.
    Dí wómi dê a Kuhú woóko.   The man's at a Kourou job.
    Dí gaán gádu bái-o,   The thunder is rolling,
    Nôò, mi tá tjalí, miíi.   And I feel such sorrow, child.
    Dí tjúba tá kaí-dê-o,   The rain is falling there,
    Nôò, mi tá tjalí f'ên-o,   And I feel such sorrow about him.
    M'án sá andí mi ó sí.   I don't know what to expect.

Saramakas sometimes express their despair at a lingering illness through song. The following examples, both composed by women, include one song of simple self-pity and another in which the woman's neighbors are accused of responsibility for her condition.

18. *Dí día yabí.*   [Another] day has dawned.
    Ná u mi édi a yabí.   It's not for me that it has dawned.

19. *Sèmbè! Aái, baáa,*   People! Yes, brother,
    Sèmbè, sèmbè-é!   People, people!
    Fá un yéi mi toónbe   When you hear that I've fallen
    Ná u déé zónu u mi.   It won't be from a supernatural
        punishment.
    Sèmbè!   It's *people* [who are causing my
        illness]!
    Aái, baáa, sèmbè!   Yes, brother, people!

Songs complaining about being the butt of malicious gossip are common. One woman sang:

20. *Dí tán u mi a dí lío,*   My life here on this river
    Mi nôò a tjalí dá.   Is only sad for me.
    Lánti wái   Everyone else is quite happy
    Kuma de dá mi gaamá   [Acting] as though they were giving
    môni.   me a tribal chief's salary.

Another woman complained that gossip about her love affairs was being spread as far and as fast as if by airplane. She clinched the image by mentioning the "city chief" (governor of Suriname, in Paramaribo) as another person whose life, like hers, receives quick and thorough coverage in the media.

21. *Yayó u mi paayá*   [Word of] my promiscuity has gone
        out
    Kuma avión.   Like an airplane.
    Fóto gaamá.   City chief.

The most frequent "theme" of *sêkêti* songs is what Saramakas refer to as "cursing" (*kósi*) or "poking" (*tjòkô*). These are songs of persecution that identify specific people as the source of the singer's problems and are often bitter and sarcastic in tone. One *sêkêti* song, composed by a man from Akisiamau, used the suggestive image of a telephone to accuse a fellow villager named Seliso of irresponsible lies, and capped the insult by implicating the man's mother.

22. *Seliso, i mmá telefó-éé.*   Seliso, your mother telephoned.
    Ya, ya, yu mmá.   Yes, yes, your mother.
    Seliso, Seliso,   Seliso, Seliso,
    Yu mmá telefó.   Your mother telephoned.

However, the very great bulk of insulting songs are created by women, and their most frequent targets are husbands, husbands' relatives, and co-wives. Women frequently envision their problems in terms of the combined aggression of both co-wives and husband's relatives, sometimes with the compliance of the husband himself, and over a period of time they may compose a number of different songs that cover the total conspiracy. For example, a forty-year-old woman from Dangogo who had a long and ultimately unsuccessful struggle for power with her co-wife expressed her feelings through a number of songs, of which I recorded four. In one, made up while cutting rice in her affines' horticultural camp, she attempted (at least rhetorically) to elicit sympathy from her husband through exaggerated self-deprecation. In another song that "came to her" after people had convinced him that she was commiting adultery, she called out to the gods in despair about being the victim of ugly rumors. In the third, she accused her husband's family of making life in their village and horticultural camp unbearable. And in the last, she addressed a bitter concession of defeat to her co-wife.

23. *Kiólo-éé,*   Young dandy,
    Wómi án dê a kamía kê mi   There's no other man around who
    môò-nô.   wants me anymore.
    I wánwán sí mi kê.   Only you have ever wanted me.
    Wè, dí fési gaán gádu dá   Well, the face that God gave me,
    mi,
    Dí u hònyò hònyò,   That of a wasp,
    I wánwán sí mi kê.   Only you have ever wanted me.
    Wè, dí fési gaán gádu dá   Well, the face that God gave me,
    mi,
    Dí u mbéti u mátu,   That of a forest beast,
    I wánwán sí mi kê.   Only you have ever wanted me.
    Wè, dí fési gaán gádu dá   Well, the face that God gave me,
    mi,
    Dí u zandibô, wè,   That of a cartoon character, well,
    I wánwán sí mi kê.   Only you have ever wanted me.
    Wè, dí fési gaán gádu dá   Well, the face that God gave me,
    mi,
    Dí u basikáanu,   That of a funeral mask,
    I wánwán sí mi kê.   Only you have ever wanted me.

24. *Dí gádu a dí lío,*   Oh god that presides over this river,
    Mi bái helú dá i   I call out in despair to you
    Dí soní míti mi a múndu   [About] the thing that's happened to
                                            me in the world
    Sôndò mi sábi.   Without my even knowing.

25. *M'án ó téi ên,*   I won't take it,
    Bigá ná mi á dí lío.   Because this isn't my river [home
                                            village].
    Sèmbè sitááfu u tjái,   Accepting punishment from others,
    M'án ó tjái dí f'ên môò.   I'm not going to take *his* anymore.

26. *Kambósa-éé,*   Co-wife,
    Ná wái dá mi môò.   Don't celebrate to me anymore.

Muyêê,	Woman,
I ku i mánu toóu.	You and your husband have a church marriage.
	(Or more freely:
	Co-wife, you don't need to strut around so smugly for my benefit anymore. Woman, it's clear that you and your husband have as monogamous a pact as city people who get married in a church.)

Many women's songs are explicitly directed against particular individuals. I illustrate the tone of these with a small sampling of those I have heard. One woman threatened to leave her husband if he continued to neglect her material needs, singing:

27.	*Mi sá tán*	I can get along
	Sôndò búnu u dí wómi.	Without presents from that man.
	Ma ná mi mánu dí-dê.	But then he's not my husband, that one.

A woman from Godo accused her husband of unjust favoritism toward his other wife and demanded equal attention.

28.	*I pená mi dé ên,*	You've neglected me for her,
	Ma ná pená mi môò.	But don't neglect me anymore.
	U túu da i muyêê.	We're *both* your wives.

A woman from Asindoopo expressed the same complaint in song; in actual performances, the reference to a paddle is changed to a different need (e.g., boat, salt, kerosene, cloth) each time the verse is sung:

29.	*Dí wómi-dê, baáa,*	That man there, brother,
	A púu páda a mi	He's deprived me of paddles
	Dá dí Kalêngi ku Alumá.	To give to the *Kalêngi* and the German [her co-wives].[6]

A renowned singer from a village on the Gaanlio felt neglected by her husband because he spent so few nights in her house. With mock politeness, her song asks the husband if he is in menstrual seclusion (and therefore banned from entering any house except the menstrual hut) and asks solicitously whether she can fetch any supplies for him, to take to the hut.

30. *A kó tá mbéi pantóli*   He's strolling around
    A mi dôò búka   In front of my house
    Kuma ná mi mánu dí-dê.   As if he weren't my husband.
    Na abaáka i dê nô?   In menstrual seclusion, are you?
    Mi sá fuká fên.   I know what hardship that means.
    Kondá dá mi   Just tell me [what you need]
    'M téi sondí dá i.   So I can get things for you.
    Na abaáka i dê nô?   In menstrual seclusion, are you?

Another woman heard that her husband had prepared a special "medicine" to prevent her from commiting adultery. Enraged at his allegedly unjustified suspicions and his recourse to such a dangerous means to control her behavior, she sang sarcastically:

31. *A púu mi a yayó-yéé.*   He saved me from promiscuity.
    Dísi púu mi a môntjo-éé.   This one saved me from becoming a
                                   whore.
    A á mánu fi téi,   When you marry certain kinds of
                                   men,
    Nôò, i án tá yayó môò.   You don't fool around anymore.

One woman cursed her husband in song for repressing her enjoyment of community festivities. Both of them came from the same village; she felt entitled to dance and sing freely as a person born in the village, but he forced her to adopt the more reserved behavior appropriate to a woman who lived there as a wife. In the song, she vows to take her next husband from some other village so she can enjoy herself in her own.[7]

32. *Déé miíi,*   Children,
    Mi ó téi mánu a bóto.   I'm going to take a husband by boat.
    Gandá lóbi án kê u mi wái.   Hometown love doesn't want me to
                                   have fun.
    M'án ó téi lóbi a téla môò-éé. I won't take love on the shore
                                   anymore.
    Lóbi u mi án tá heépi.   This love of mine brings no reward.

Another woman complained in song that her husband continually spread false rumors about her. Like many *sêkêti* songs, this one was intended to be varied creatively each time the main verse was repeated. The references to radio and clarinet represent only one singer's choice from among the many metaphors for crude and malicious gossip that could appropriately be used.

33. *É a gó a baái wáta: ládio,*   If he goes off to a wide river: radio.
    A gó ku mi nê.   He goes with my name.
    É a gó a foóu wáta: kaanêti.   If he goes to the tidal waters:
                                          clarinet.
    A gó ku mi nê.   He goes with my name.
    Baái wáta búka   Whether [at] the mouth of a wide
                                          river [on the coast]
    Ku sumáa lío,   Or a tiny river [the Pikilio],
    Dí wán kódó sèmbè nôò   Just that one person
    Tá dú sondí ku mi sô.   Keeps causing trouble for me.
    M'án a peésa môò.   I can't take it anymore.
    Nê u mi dê a búku   My name [reputation] has been put
                                          in a book.
    Kuma dí óto u gaamá.   Like a speech by the tribal chief.

Many *sêkêti* songs are inspired by the strains of living part-time in a husband's village and, for many women, gardening in a horticultural camp that belongs to his lineage. In these situations, the man's mother, sisters, and mother's sisters represent a collective and potentially hostile authority, against which many women feel impotent and alone. Complaints about a husband's kin as a group are common in *sêkêti* songs; I cite two examples.

A woman from the upper Gaanlio was told by her own kin of some rumors that her husband's kin were spreading about her, and explained that these were responsible for her recent coolness with him.

34. *Soní mi yéi,*   Something I've heard,
    Soní mi yéi,   Something I've heard,
    Soní mi yéi   Something I've heard
    Mbéi líbi tooká-éé.   Is making a change in [my way of]
                                          living.
    Dí soní i tá táki,   The thing you're saying,
    I tínga m'án yéi.   You thought I didn't hear.
    A tjalí dá bêè,   It upset my lineage,
    Hên de kondé ên dá mi.   And they told it all to me.
    Hên mbéi líbi tooká-éé.   That's why [my way of] living has
                                          changed.

A woman from the village of Pikiseei declared in song that her husband's kin were not discriminating against her by living so badly; that was simply the sort of people they were.

35. *Déé mánu bêè,*   Husband's [matrilineal] kin,
    Ná mi un án lóbi.   It's not me you don't love.
    Mánu bêè kabá.   Husband's kin are no good.[8]
    Sô de dê.   That's just the way they are.
    Mánu bêè án lóbi mi-éé. Husband's kin don't love me.

Most songs of complaint about a husband's relatives, however, single out an individual adversary, and this is most often a husband's sister. As we have seen, Saramaka ideology decrees that a woman should enjoy a warm and solidary relationship with her sisters-in-law (in contrast to her mother-in-law, with whom she is expected to be reserved and distant). When friendships with sisters-in-law fall short of the ideal, the frustrations women feel frequently find their way into *sêkêti* songs. A woman from Bendekonde retaliated against the nasty remarks of a husband's sister by sarcastically comparing her behavior to that of a jealous co-wife:

36. *Sísa mái, kambósa,*   Sister-in-law, co-wife,
    Ná i dú-éé.   It's not your fault.
    Mi kó toóbi i-éé.   I've come to "trouble" you.[9]
    Sísa mái, kambósa.   Sister-in-law, co-wife.

A popular song from Akisiamau expressed this same theme more simply.

37. *A buusé mi-éé;*   She's jilted me;
    Sísa mái kó kambósa u mi- Sister-in-law became a co-wife of
    éé.   mine.

Another woman from Akisiamau who took a lover while her husband was in coastal Suriname accused her sister-in-law of driving her to it. Her household supplies had run out and her sister-in-law had refused to share. What else, she protested, could she be expected to do? (Each time the first verse is repeated, the performer inserts a different item that is customarily provided by a husband—e.g., kerosene, salt, and hammock.)

38. *É mi sópu kabá*   When my soap runs out
    I án ó dá mi, sísa mái. You won't give me any, sister-in-law.
    Mi fuká.   I'm in need.
    Mi kê a mánu u mi.   I want a husband for myself.

A woman from Bendekonde composed a bitter song that was addressed, I was told, to her husband's sister, and incorporated a thinly veiled reference to the most powerful threat of all. "Doing a certain thing" (suicide) is the ultimate weapon available to a Saramaka who has been mistreated, for it creates an avenging spirit that will torment the wrongdoer's lineage forever.

39. *I buusé mi-éé;*	You've thrown me out;
I buusé mi-éé.	You've thrown me out.
É ná a pói kaa,	If it's not too late,
Mi sa dú wán soní nòômo.	I will indeed do a certain thing.

Women who are divorced by their husbands often aim *sêkêti* songs at the wives who are kept on. The following example, composed by a woman from Bendekonde, is a bitterly sarcastic celebration of the closeness of her former husband and co-wife. Like the constellations and the seasons, she coos, their love is forever.

40. *Fá a namá ku i dê,*	The way she's pressed up against you,
Fá a namá ku i dê,	The way she's pressed up against you,
Sébitaa ku yái,	From May to January,[10]
Sébitaa ku yái,	From May to January,
Un án ó lúsu môó.	You two will never break apart.

Another woman's song extols the virtues of her ex-husband's newest wife with equal sarcasm.

41. *A dóu a búnu.*	He's arrived at [something] good.
Dí wómi téi sindó muyêè.	The man's taken a "sit-still" [faithful] wife.
Dí wómi táa mi yayó	The man said I was fooling around
Téé án tá yéi m'wootu seéi.	So he wasn't even hearing my words [of protest].
A dóu a búnu,	[But now] he's arrived at [something] good.
Dí wómi téi sindó muyêè.	The man's taken a "sit-still" wife.

Not surprisingly, many of the most piercing attacks are directed at current co-wives. The spontaneous creation of the following song represented the final scene of a dramatic succession of loud verbal curses and physical attacks that involved the singer and her husband, mother-in-law, and co-wife. It addresses a plea for help to *gaán gádu*—the supreme deity of Saramaka cosmology whose voice is heard in the form of thunder—and employs a standard term for a co-wife adversary.

42. *Kabitên, baáa-o. Kéé!*   Headman, oh brother. *Kéé!* [here an
                                 expression of alarm]
    Dí soní míti mi,   The thing that's happened to me,
    Un tá yéi-ó?   Do you hear?
    Dí gaamá-dê,   The tribal chief there,
    Dí soní míti mi,   The thing that's happened to me,
    Un tá yéi, nô?   Do you hear?
    Téé u mi yéi dí gaán gádu   When I hear the thunder roll
        bái
    Mi kái gaán gádu-éé,   I call out to God,
    Mi bái goón líba-o.   I shout out to the world.
    U dí yayó u mi édi   It's because of that slut of mine[11]
    Mi kái ên-éé.   That I'm calling him.

A woman from Bendekonde ridiculed the smugness and self-importance of her husband's newest wife in the following song.

43. *Kambósa, miíi-éé,*   Co-wife, my child,[12]
    Kambósa, baáa-o,   Co-wife, brother,
    A mánu nôò mi ku i míti;   We've only "met" in a husband;[13]
    De án butá i a gaamá-éé.   They haven't installed you as tribal chief.

A woman from Akisiamau accused her co-wife of devoting her life to jealous gossip.

44. *A dí woóko-dê de butá i;*   That's the job you've been given;
    A dí woóko-dê de butá i.   That's the job you've been given.
    Téé i mmá ó gó a kamía   When your mother goes off for the day
    I án ó gó.   You won't go along.
    I ó fiká tá lési búku;   You'll stay behind to "read books";
    Téé a kó,   When she gets back,
    I kondá dé ên.   You report it all to her.

Another woman, who surmised that her husband was growing tired of his other wife, suggested to her that she admit defeat quickly and gracefully.

45. *Adjóisi u gó dá dí wómi*   Saying goodbye to the man
    An taánga môò-éé.   Isn't so hard.
    Adjóisi u gó dá dí wómi   Saying goodbye to the man
    An taánga môò-éé.   Isn't so hard.
    Dí a dá i pási f'i sa gó,   Since he's given you an opportunity to leave,
    Nôò, i gó dé ên,   Just go and say it,
    Nôò, i tooná-éé.   And then be on your way.

I conclude this sampling of *sêkêti* songs with one composed by a Bendekonde woman who finally gave in to her co-wife and took leave of her husband.

46. *Mi pú lái-éé,* I've packed my things,
    Mi pú lái-éé. I've packed my things.
    A dí wán wósu nôò It's just at that one house [the co-
                            wife's]
    I tá kê duumí. That you keep wanting to sleep.

The Naming of Cloths

In 1967, I was sitting and talking with Chief Agbago's ninety-year-old sister Naai one day, when word was brought to her that the chief, who had been in the Netherlands, had arrived safely at the Paramaribo airport. Delighted, relieved, and intensely excited at this news, Naai called out to several of her ancestors in thanks and jumped up to perform a little dance, singing out over and over,

Gaamá sáka a fóto-éé, The chief has landed in the city,
Gaamá sáka a fóto! The chief has landed in the city!

Having composed a satisfying *sêkêti* song, she then exclaimed, "It would be nice if he brought back a cloth for me; I would give it the name *Gaamá sáka a fóto!*"

It is not uncommon for a person to compose a *sêkêti* song and a new cloth name in a single moment of inspiration; and such pairs reflect a general association that Saramakas make between these two verbal genres, which are in a sense formal variants of one another. The similarities between *sêkêti* songs and cloth names include both the ways they are created and used and their subject matter. Like *sêkêti* songs, new cloth names are created spontaneously and frequently, they pass quickly in and out of fashion, they are open to subtle variations in wording, they provide a lively idiom for social commentary, and they are used more actively by women than by men. Even when they are not simultaneously composed, *sêkêti* songs and cloth names often focus on the same incidents. For example, the name of the man whose arson was lamented in songs 10 and 14 was given to a cloth pattern of the 1960s; men's experiences in coastal Suriname and French Guiana, such as those referred to in songs 12–13 and 15–17, figure also in the names of particular cloths; and abrasive encounters between co-wives, such as those in songs 42–46, find their way into many of the phrases by which cloth patterns are designated. However, cloth names comment on social life from a slightly different perspective from that of most *sêkêti* songs, cover a somewhat different (albeit overlapping) range of events, and differ from *sêkêti* songs in focusing on actions more often than emotions.[14]

In contrast to the more general terms discussed in chapter 6 (which distinguish cloths of different width, texture, and durability, cloths used for different kinds of garments, cloths imported to Suriname from different countries, and so forth), Saramaka "cloth names" (*koósu nê*) all designate cloths within one functionally homogeneous domain—the striped trade cotton that is used primarily for women's skirts. The use of the word *koósu* as both the (general) term for cloth and the (only) term for skirt means that *koósu nê* is understood as both "cloth name" and "skirt name."[15] Indeed, the form in which trade cotton is referred to by these individual names is usually either unsewn (*kúakúa*, "raw") or hemmed on three sides as a woman's wrap-around skirt. Many such names refer to a pattern defined by a particular arrangement of stripes of different widths. Others designate specific color combinations as well. When using a name that specifies only the arrangement of stripes, Saramakas may clarify which cloth they have in mind by adding a reference to the dominant color, e.g., "the red version of it" (*bè wóyo f'ên*). Patterns that do not qualify fully for any one name are frequently squeezed into the classification by citing the closest approximation and tagging onto it a qualifying phrase such as "the thin-striped one of it" (*pikí páu f'ên*), "the cross-striped version" (*dóba sitéépi*), or simply "a variation" (*tooká wóyo f'ên*).

Although a few of the names used in Saramaka villages are devised by store owners in Paramaribo, many more are created by Saramakas. The pool of names in use at any one time is on the order of one hundred. The names of the most popular cloth patterns are well known by most Saramakas and are used in everyday conversation. For cloth patterns that have never entered the limelight of fashion, there is less frequent reference to their names, less unanimous agreement on the identity of name and pattern, and less widespread knowledge of etymologies.

The thematic content of cloth names is a true reflection of the wide-ranging fascination of Saramakas with the world around them.

Names are inspired by local, national, and international events—from a co-wife fight in Dangogo to the landing of an American spaceship on the moon. The most common way for a cloth to acquire a name is through association with current events that coincide with its introduction to Saramaka. Historic tribal events, such as an official visit by (then) Princess Beatrix of the Netherlands to the village of Chief Agbago or a meeting between the tribal chiefs of Saramaka and Djuka, are generally commemorated in cloth names. The experiences of Saramaka men outside tribal territory—wage labor opportunities, shortages of particular manufactured products, and the trials of coping with coastal characters and ways of life—are regularly given recognition through association with particular cloth patterns. And the daily life of Saramaka villages—especially at its shocking or embarrassing moments—is also fed into the names of currently available patterns of trade cotton.

The individualization of skirt-cloths through naming facilitates the use of these cloths as symbols of social (most often conjugal) relations. It is true that in certain important contexts Saramakas discuss cloth in terms of sheer volume, much the way they discuss kerosene in terms of barrelfuls, without differentiating the particular patterns of color and stripe that are represented. When a man returns from an extended labor trip, for example, his economic success is customarily glossed by citing the total number of cloths he has purchased and the number that each wife received. But once these statistics have been duly noted and commented on by lineal and affinal kin and others in the region, the cloths begin to take on meaning more as individual pieces. Women are expected to remember the "social origin" of each of their many skirt-cloths (i.e., who gave it to them and on what occasion). Like wood carvings, each skirt-cloth is regarded as a symbol of a particular personal relationship.[16] But the task of keeping tabs on a hundred or more skirt-cloths (all of which are hemmed into identical and virtually undecorated rectangles) is not an easy one. Because of the uniformity of women's skirts (in contrast, for example, to the highly varied shoulder capes that women design and decorate for men), the widths of stripes and the juxtaposition of colors play an important individualizing role. It is the pool of cloth names that codifies these features so that people can talk about them. Cloth names thus provide an idiom for the discussion of skirt-cloths and their social origins, and it is mainly in this context that they are cited. A woman might ask, for example, "Who gave you that *djómbo gogó* [jumping buttocks]?" or comment that "I asked the man [her husband] if he could send me a *límbo muyéè* [clean woman] from the coast."

If we look beyond the existence of cloth names and examine their content (in effect treating them as "texts"), we discover that they reflect upon Saramaka social life in quite another way as well. Not only does the individualization of cloths through naming help women remember who gave them each of their skirts, but the names themselves constitute a creative and lively medium for social commentary about incidents of interest. Cloth names that are primarily descriptive (referring either directly or metaphorically to some aspect of the cloth pattern itself) constitute only about one-fifth of the total pool. The remaining names are nearly all references to "current events" that Saramakas find amusing or otherwise worthy of note. It is this latter type of cloth name that exhibits the most striking similarities with *sêkêti* songs. Several examples may illustrate their tone and content.[17]

A number of cloth names are inspired by events of tribal, national or even international interest.

Améika gó a gádu (American goes to "god")—The first American astronauts landed on the moon.

Kónu faáka (royal flag)—This predominantly white cloth was raised in an ancestral shrine in Asindoopo during the 1965 visit of (then) Princess Beatrix of the Netherlands.

Kónu nyá kasába kúakúa (royalty ate manioc "raw")—A member of the Dutch royal family ate a piece of manioc bread in Paramaribo without first softening it in water or broth.

Binootu toón gaamá (Binootu became chief)—Tudendu, also known as Binootu, was installed as tribal chief of the Saramakas in 1934.

Gaamá baasá gaamá (tribal chief embraces tribal chief)—Saramaka Chief Agbago and Djuka Chief Akoontu Velanti greeted each other.

Gaamá púu faáka [na Aluku] (the chief removes a flag [in Aluku])—Chief Tudendu is said to have removed a tattered banner from an Aluku shrine and replaced it with a new cloth, henceforth known by this name.

Akalali púu wísi (Akalali removed witchcraft)—During the mid-1970s, the Djuka prophet Akalali was gaining widespread renown for his witchcraft purges.

Agbago wáka a opoláni (Agbago traveled in an airplane)—Chief Agbago took his first plane ride to Paramaribo.

Agbago pasá gaán zee (Agbago crossed the big ocean)—Chief Agbago made his first transatlantic flight.

Kaupe (the name of a man from the village of Godo)—On the eve of the first Suriname election in which Saramakas voted, Kaupe set fire to the "office" of Chief Agbago, in an unsuccessful assassination attempt (see songs 10 and 14).

Many other names relate to the experiences of Saramaka men outside of tribal territory and to their efforts to accumulate goods for the return to their home villages.

Kó gó a Lawa (let's go to Lawa)—In the early 1900s, important wage labor opportunities opened up along the Lawa River in French Guiana.
Silaliko ópo lágima (Suralco raised up the poor man)—In the 1960s, the Suriname Aluminum Company provided many jobs for Saramaka men in construction work at the hydroelectric project.
Kónda kabá a Kaise (the necklaces are finished at Kaise)—Kaise, a store in Paramaribo, was out of a certain necklace that a Saramaka woman had asked her husband to buy for her.
Wáta boóko Milanda (water ruined Milanda)—In 1949, a flood ruined a Paramaribo store patronized by Maroons.
Apantu súki (Apantu's sugar)—During a stay in Paramaribo, a village headman from Lafanti was sent by Chief Djankuso (1898–1932) to buy some sugar. When he returned with the container only half full, Djankuso asked him whether he was so poorly paid that he had to steal from the tribal chief.
Amakiti djonkó [a kíno] (Amakiti dozed off [at the movies])—Djuka Tribal Chief Amakiti (1916–31) was taken to a movie in Paramaribo, but fell asleep in the middle. A cloth name and a *sêkêti* song were inspired by this event.
Naili kèê a fóto (Naili cried in the city)—In Paramaribo, a daughter-in-law of Chief Agbago cried all night, standing just outside the house where her husband was spending his first night with a new wife. The next day she urinated on the floor of his house, and they were divorced soon after.
Basiá lási [a gaamá djái] (the assistant headman got lost [at the chief's quarters])—An assistant headman lost his way in Paramaribo, near the quarters of the Saramaka chief.
Nêngè kèê a Sala (Creole cried at Sala)—In the 1960s, a construction boss working near Afobaka on the hydroelectric project lost his job and cried.

Local scandals and humorous scenes are routinely publicized through cloth names.

Abali ábi bómbo (Abali exposed her cunt)—A woman from Masiakiiki, caught stealing a pot in Paramaribo, fell to the ground and spread her legs. There is some disagreement about the reaction of the police who saw this, but the basic incident and the cloth name inspired by it are common knowledge.

Yombe kaí [a taápu] (Yombe fell [on the stairs])—A Bendekonde woman stole something from the mission at Djumu. In her haste to get away, she fell on the stairs leading down to the river.

Aviee boóko Djumu (Aviee caused havoc in Djumu)—A young Bendekonde man stole extensively from a store at the Djumu mission that was owned by a man named Peleki. An alternative name for this cloth is *Aviee kíi Peleki* (Aviee ruined Peleki).

Baáa kíi baáa (brother killed brother)—A Bendekonde man was murdered by his mother's sister's son in the early twentieth century.

Sísa ganyâ sísa (Sister tricked sister)—I do not know the story behind this name.

Mangumuyee boóko Daume (Mangumuyee ruined Daume)—A woman from Daume avoided observance of menstrual seclusion, thus endangering local ritual powers.

Doola kíi Yumbu (Doola "killed" Yumbu)—An older woman, Yumbu, asked a young man, Doola, for a ride to her horticultural camp (possibly because her canoe needed repairs). He then hid from her, and she was forced to stay home.

Gaamá yáka Venipai [a kantóo fu sôsò líbi édi] (the chief threw out Venipai [from his office because of bad living])—An American who had been living in Asindoopo in the early 1970s was asked to leave the village because of interpersonal difficulties with Saramakas.

Asensi kulé [da manungú] (Asensi ran away [from a testicle operation])—A man scheduled to have an operation on his enlarged testicles ran away from the mission hospital.

Basiá kêê [a Kampu] (the assistant headman cried [in Kampu])—In 1978, some young men in Kampu wrestled and inadvertently broke the palm-leaf wall of a house belonging to Assistant Headman Kooi.

Bése kaká a buúku (frog defecated on pants)—A woman carefully laundered her husband's store-bought trousers and laid them on a rock to dry. When she went to get them, she found them soiled.

Mánu gó a dóti (husband went to earth)—A man sat down on the ground; I know no details of this incident.

Síka muyêè bulí gogó (síka woman wiggled her ass)—A woman whose toe was infected from an insect known as *síka* walked in a funny way.

Oposii fútu a sándu (Oposii's feet in the sand)—A crippled man from a Lower River village made peculiar footprints when he walked on the sand.

Pili ganyá kéíki (Pili cheated on church)—A woman from a Lower River village walked out in the middle of a Moravian church service.

Sexual rivalries, both in and out of Saramaka villages, find their way into cloth names as well.

Kpokolo kíi Alena (Kpokolo "killed" Alena)—A woman left her husband for another man.

Baáka muyêè kê gaamá (black woman desires the chief)—A very dark-skinned woman showed a romantic interest in the tribal chief; I do not know details of this story.

Siló a bédi (sloth in bed)—A Lower River woman whose husband bought his other wife a bed commented bitterly that he had a [lazy] sloth in his bed.[18]

Lôndò kíi Gbete (cunt "killed" Gbete)—A woman's promiscuity ruined her reputation.

Djugá úma boóko fóto (Djuka woman "broke" Paramaribo)—A woman caused a scandal by sleeping with many different men. The word for woman (*uma*) here is Ndjuka.

Asikasi kíi Nanete (Asikasi "killed" Nanete)—A man named Asikasi is said to have made love to a woman named Nanete until she fainted.

Afaina gó a bédi (Afaina went to bed)—A woman from the Coppename River made love to an American in a bed (see note 18).

Several aspects of these names deserve comment. First, the cloth itself is not always involved in the incident that inspires its name. In many cases, the only initial link between a cloth pattern and the event after which it is named is their coincidence in time. An event of widespread interest is often commemorated in the form of a name for one of the new cloth patterns that are currently being introduced. And many names are invented expressly in anticipation of future cloth patterns, as in the example cited at the beginning of this section. Second, the majority of cloth names are in the form of a declarative sentence, and almost all are in the third person. As we have seen, *sêkêti* songs tend to express very personal feelings and predicaments; the composer either speaks in the first person or addresses someone in direct discourse. In contrast, cloth names comment on situations from an external perspective, and their phrasing is that of an objective report rather than of empathy or subjective emotion. Third, cloth names are open to stylistic variation. For example, *Agbago wáka a opoláni* (Agbago traveled in an airplane) is also known as *Agbago gó a lókutu* (Agbago went in the sky), and *Gaamá yáka Venipai* (the chief threw out Venipai) is also known as *Venipai kèê* (Venipai cried). This follows a pattern in Saramaka personal names in which, for example, a man named Asipei (mirror) may also be called Lukufesi (look-at-face) and a woman named Sakuima (thresher) may also be called Atasakwe (she-is-threshing); see R. and S. Price 1972*b*.

Some forms can be recycled to fit new incidents, thus constituting a relatively standard mold for the creation of new names. "X killed Y" is used repeatedly to commemorate events in which one person causes problems for another. A common variant, "X tricked Y," is equally adaptable. "X 'broke' Y" is often substituted when a village, rather than an individual, is portrayed as the victim. And "X cried" is used for many cloth names referring to a person's reaction to any kind of misfortune.

The language of cloth names is quite explicit. Specific proper names are generally utilized instead of the elliptical references that lend such a distinctively poetic tone to even the most biting *sêkêti* songs. Names of people and villages document events as local news, not as personal joys and traumas, and these are common, everyday names rather than the metaphorical ones so often created for *sêkêti* lyrics. In cloth names, direct mention of genitals and sexual activity is appreciated, and participants in scandalous behavior are identified without mercy. Many cloth names may also be cited in an expanded form (indicated by bracketed phrases in the examples given) that further specifies details of the incident to which the name refers.

Finally, the events referred to in cloth names tend to be less geographically restricted than those in *sêkêti* songs. Partly because of the strong association of trade cotton with the outside world from which it comes, cloth names make particularly frequent reference to coastal stores and store owners, to construction bosses and fellow laborers, to city women, to cars and buses, to Suriname currency, to imported manufactures, to Western clothes, to beds, and to other novelties of life outside of Saramaka. Even gossip about local people tends to be channeled more frequently into cloth names when it refers to incidents that occur during trips to the coast, and into *sêkêti* songs when it refers to life in Saramaka villages.

The texts of *sêkêti* songs and cloth names reflect a wide range of Saramaka concerns, and offer a particularly important expressive outlet for women. A representative sampling of the conversations women have when they sit with a friend or two on their doorsteps—perhaps sewing a cape, carving a calabash, or breaking palm nuts for cooking oil—would cover the same topics that we have seen in *sêkêti* songs and cloth names, and use much of the same imagery as well. In these conversations—as well as in their songs and cloth names—women do not generally confront the cultural attitudes and social institutions that define (often in rather restrictive terms) their relationships with others. Rather, as we have seen, they address specific problems in the interactions of particular individuals. The final chapter of this book assesses the social consciousness of Saramaka women and the course it is likely to take in the decades to come.

Chapter Eight

Art and Gender

In a thoughtful overview of the contribution of feminist scholarship to anthropology, Michelle Rosaldo argued that the relevance of sexual asymmetries for social scientists is not that they exist, but that they are closely linked—like other phenomena such as racism and social class—with the particulars of women's lives, activities, and goals (1980:417). In this book, we have seen that the lines Saramakas draw between men and women—material, social, and conceptual—are as deeply incised on the arts as they are on subsistence practices, on marriage patterns, or on religious beliefs. Each Saramaka woman's life experience represents in part a response to the attitudes and institutions that define her as a woman. And the creative arts—whether calabash carving, decorative sewing, song composition, body cicatrization, or any other medium—form a dynamic and richly expressive part of that response.

One of the most important cultural contrasts that Saramakas make between men and women is their differential involvement in the wider world. This understanding has left its mark on men's and women's material lives, sexual histories, linguistic patterns, personal styles, and philosophical orientations. It has also been a crucial influence on their respective artistic styles and on the ways that art fits into their social lives.

Saramaka masculinity, in addition to specific expectations regarding sexual virility, hunting skills, verbal eloquence, ritual competence, and so forth, has long depended on an ability to function in "foreign" settings and on an active enthusiasm for dabbling in non-Saramaka culture. Whether in the streets of Paramaribo, the construction sites of Afobaka, the Djuka villages in eastern Suriname, the towns of French Guiana, or the diamond-mining camps of Brazil, Saramaka men must know how to get along in foreign languages, deal with people from other ethnic backgrounds, hold down a job, and make wise purchases for the return home. Men enjoy displaying symbols of this aspect of their lives—mixing into their speech words they have picked up from different languages, decorating their houses with nonfunctional items of Western culture (e.g., light bulbs in villages with no electricity), working the antics of coastal personalities into their songs (see chap. 7), and reminiscing about the novelties of life outside Saramaka, from elevators and supermarkets to prostitutes and motorbikes. Men sometimes consume foods they have imported from the coast with great ostentation. One Dangogo man, for example, occasionally opened a can of evaporated milk and poured it into a cup of coffee—enjoying it especially because of the reaction of his great-grandmother, who considered imbibing the bodily fluids of a cow to be the ultimate sign of the decadence of city life.

In contrast, women's lives have always been envisioned by Saramakas more purely in the context of their home environment. While men often talk about their own alternation between Saramaka and coastal societies, women tend to see their life experience as an alternation between villages and horticultural camps. Women's subsistence activities employ a higher proportion of native materials and locally made tools than do men's. Their houses have fewer manufactured furnishings.[1] Their speech is less sprinkled with foreign terms. Their dress includes fewer store-bought items. Their view of city streets, buses, stores, and other features of life outside Saramaka exhibits a stronger dominance of apprehension over fascination. And while men take pride in mastering appropriate etiquettes and styles of interaction for their dealings with outsiders, women in the presence of non-Saramakas tend either to become very withdrawn or to adopt a loud, crude brashness—both of which reflect their underconfidence and discomfort in such situations.

The different orientations of men's and women's lives vis-à-vis the outside world are reflected quite directly in their arts. In calabash carving, men's use of commercial tools (compasses, chisels, and knives) contrasts with women's use of broken glass. In textile decoration, men's access to sewing machines and commercial thread contrasts with women's use of needles and threads pulled from scraps of cloth. The contrastive artistic styles of men and women also mirror their differential involvement in the outside world. When men decorate a calabash, draw out an embroidery pattern, or carve a wooden object, their designs are rigorously geometric with straight lines, perfect arcs and circles, and exacting symmetry—the very features that they are familiar with from printed signs, machinery, and Western architecture. Women more often produce free-form "organic" shapes with stubby appendages and imperfectly executed symmetries. Even those women's arts whose contours follow straight horizontal and vertical guidelines (such as narrow-strip textiles and cross-stitch embroidery) are subject to the tendency—viewed by Saramakas as typically feminine—to stray occasionally from the perfect regularity of a pattern, for example, by the insertion of an extra bit of embroidery or the reversal of one of two matching strips of cloth. Those few women who teach themselves how to mark out geometric embroidery designs (rather than asking the help of a man or embroidering a more typical woman's design) show pride in their accomplishment, but their behavior is considered by most people to be rather unfeminine. And young girls who show an artistic inclination in this direction (like girls in a traditional community in the United States who aspire to an expertise in physics or construction work rather than in literature or nursing) are made to understand that the precision involved in such designs represents a somewhat unnatural skill for their sex.

In terms of the use of symbolism, too, the contrast between men's and women's arts is clearly related to their differential contact with coastal society. Occasionally (though much less frequently than the literature would suggest), Saramaka men incorporate in their wood carvings a small mark that can be "read" as a specific message (see S. and R. Price 1980a:189). These marks seem to emerge from the same admiration for the idea of literacy that prompted a Djuka man to develop his own "script" in the early twentieth century and that inspired a number of male messianic leaders to "read" inspirational passages from their open palms. Women are well aware of the use of symbolic marks in men's carving, but they are also adamant that the extra elements they add to their finished textiles or calabashes (see, for example, S. and R. Price 1980a: figs. 93 and 255) are, in contrast to the men's, intended only as marks of ownership.

We have also seen that the differential involvement of men and women in the outside world affects the ways in which the arts fit into social life. The long-term absences of Saramaka men from tribal territory are fundamental to the definition of male-female relations and, as a consequence, to the social meaning of the artistic gifts that flow within them. In this society, the value of men's artistry is closely linked with the value of men. The explicit association that women make between particular wood carvings and particular relationships contrasts with the less attentive attitude of men toward the social origins of their decorative textiles, in a way that corresponds directly to the respective concerns of women and men about marriage itself. The insecurities that women express in their songs are the same insecurities that inspire their unbounded joy at receiving a carved comb or food stirrer. And the security that men enjoy in terms of ongoing marriage prospects is similarly related to their more subdued reaction to the artistic gifts they receive from women.

From an anthropological perspective, it should not be surprising that women in Pikilio villages express fundamental dissatisfactions in their personal lives without going on to assess critically the cultural attitudes and institutions that lie behind their difficulties. A Saramaka woman suffering material deprivations because she has no husband, for example, does not wish her culture provided equal money-earning opportunities for men and women; she wishes she could find a husband. Because of their relative isolation from other ways of life, the cultural setting in which they grow up has provided the framework for their social consciousness. Alternatives have traditionally carried connotations of deviance and impropriety for women as much as they have carried a sense of excitement and adventure for men. During my residence on the Pikilio, women reacted with strong moral indignation to stories of Lower River Saramakas who "hid their periods" (*tjubí faági*) in order to avoid the inconveniences of menstrual seclusion. They expressed resentment about their husbands' sexual freedom in the same culturally prescribed rhetoric that their grandmothers had used. They never failed to distinguish their husbands' meals from their own through rigorous attention to special details such as smoothly mounded rice and carefully chosen calabash bowls. And they were bringing up their daughters to expect the same satisfactions and frustrations in life that they were experiencing.

As early as the mid-1960s, however, there were signs of a gradual shift in Saramaka tolerance for women venturing into the outside world, and this shift is beginning to influence the ways in which women think about themselves and their society. At that time, the issue of whether to allow a woman to join her husband for an extended stay on the coast was debated daily on the Pikilio—in gossip sessions, in oracle consultations, and in prayers to the ancestors. The decisions then being reached were almost always negative, but the pressure for change was strong, and just a few years later Pikilio women began to be sent off to Kourou, where their husbands were providing labor for the French missile base. Since the 1960s, the number of Saramaka women who have experienced more than a several-day glimpse of the world beyond their own has increased greatly, and men no longer have exclusive access to the language, money, and experiences of coastal life.

This change promises to affect Saramaka gender constructs as fundamentally as the introduction of money has begun to affect economic life in the interior. For, as women's experiences begin to open up to the outside world, life in their villages begins to be seen from a new perspective. During their trips to the coast, women are exposed to different cultural models: their neighbors are often Creoles or East Indians whose understandings about everything from marriage to cooking contrast with their own; they need to be able to interact with market women and schoolteachers; menstrual periods become a private rather than a public concern; standards of dress and personal modesty are adjusted; and in countless other ways the skills and assumptions that were unchallenged in their childhood are set in the context of a cultural continuum. After nearly three centuries as the most isolated members of Africa's human legacy to the New World, Maroon women are casting interested glances at the mainstream of Caribbean life. The currents they see there have the familiarity of historically related traditions, but they are also raising questions, posing choices, eroding certainties, and suggesting changes that women in the interior have never before considered.

Notes

Chapter 1

1. For a discussion of some of the stereotypes that outsiders have created of Maroons, from Noble Savage to rapacious outlaw, see R. Price 1976:44–45.

Chapter 2

1. This is the form of the rule that I witnessed on the Pikilio. Discussions that I overheard at the time indicated that in some regions there were quite different details that varied according to the infant's sex, but the basic principle of symbolizing sexual identity at the birth itself seems to be observed throughout Saramaka.

2. Ironically, it is when boys are in the exclusive company of men that they learn the "female" tasks that they will occasionally need to call upon as men (e.g., when all their wives are away from the village or secluded in the menstrual hut and their kinswomen are not filling in). Whenever men travel to or from the coast, the youngest able boy (typically about ten to twelve years old) is given primary responsibility for carrying water, cooking, and washing dishes. And when a young boy eats a meal with the men, he is expected to sweep the floor afterward.

3. The strength of this preference for a man to steer a canoe was epitomized by an elderly couple who lived in the Niukonde section of Dangogo, on the east side of the Pikilio. Although the husband was almost totally blind, the wife would help him into the rear of the canoe and then direct from the front, telling him where to head and how to steer around rocks, and finally guiding him to the landing area across the river.

4. Saramakas' descriptions of same-sex friendships are noticeably lacking in intimations of homosexual practices. More generally, Saramaka men and women present an image of their sexual activities that is exclusively heterosexual and genitally focused, though men learn about other "foreign" possibilities, from oral sex to homosexual relationships, during their stays outside of tribal territory.

5. Even people who saw this case as a social scandal expressed tolerance and amusement on a more personal level. As one older woman remarked philosophically, "Well, each person has her own cunt!"

6. Although women sometimes work in only one skirt (e.g., when har-

vesting or pounding rice), two layers are more usual, and there is an explicit prohibition on wearing only one skirt when cooking food for a man's meal.

7. Although most people grow up among their matrilineal kin, some are raised in their father's village and other alternatives are also possible. When a woman marries someone from her own village, she may or may not have two houses—one in her kin group's neighborhood and another in the area where her husband lives. For a social structural analysis of Saramaka residence patterns, see R. Price 1975.

8. This description of menstrual seclusion applies quite generally to Upper River Saramaka, but there is also variation from one village to the next on a more specific level. A particular ritual, for example, may engender a permanent prohibition against menstruating women approaching the site where it was conducted. When a woman visits a new husband for the first time, her sisters-in-law are always careful to lay out these local rules as part of her introduction to life in their village.

9. Of all the adaptations that Richard Price and I made to Saramaka customs during our fieldwork, it was the observance of menstrual seclusion that people most often used rhetorically as proof of our respect for their way of life. Even more than speaking their language or being washed by their gods, my trips to the menstrual hut became an "emblem" of our Saramakanization.

10. People claimed that it would be theoretically possible for a postmenopausal woman to be possessed by a *komantí* god, but I know of no actual cases.

11. "Hunger is killing me" (*Hángi tá kíi mi*) refers to a shortage of rice. "[A shortage of] meat/fish is killing me" (*Gwamba tá kíi mi*) means that there is nothing (except vegetable sauces) with which to flavor the rice.

12. Although this romantic image of camp life is unanimously upheld, many women are in fact frustrated by interpersonal tensions during those years when they are gardening with affines and co-wives in a camp belonging to their husband's lineage (see chap. 3).

13. Note that the naming of cloth patterns permits (and encourages) a similar "individualization" in discussions of imported trade cotton (see chap. 7).

14. This description refers to the processing of *maipá* palm nuts, which are the most frequently used. There are slight variations in the preparation of other palm oils such as *awaá* or *maká*. Peter Kloos, a Dutch anthropologist who works with coastal Caribs, reports that Suriname Indians (whose ancestors first introduced Maroons to the processing of local palm nuts) now buy cooking oil in stores, viewing the making of oil as too time consuming.

15. This service, known as "looking after the belly/pregnancy" (*lúku bêè*) may also be performed by someone other than the man with whom conception took place, for example, if the latter dies or the woman claims that someone else made her pregnant, but Saramakas believe that the wrong man's semen during pregnancy can cause serious health problems for the child during infancy. People may also attempt to compensate for an absent

father's semen through ritual steamings during pregnancy (with the woman straddling a special water-and-leaf mixture into which a red-hot axe head has been dropped) and ritual washings of the baby once it is born.

16. Saramakas explain some restrictions as a symbolic distancing from anything having to do with death; hammering, for example, is associated with the making of coffins and shoveling with the digging of a grave. They see others as a protection from supernatural aggression; the ghosts of deer and tapirs are considered powerful enough to take revenge on an unborn child, and a new marriage creates tensions and jealousies that could also endanger the pregnancy. The woman must observe the child's "father's prohibition" because the fetus is being nurtured through her body, and avoid the *nduyá* fish because its mouth movement resembles that of a baby suffering from respiratory distress. The woman's use of cold water to wash her genitals is seen as a way of opening the vaginal passage and facilitating the birth. It thus represents the complement to her use of heated water at other times, which is said to tighten the vagina and enhance lovemaking. Other, more idiosyncratic, prohibitions arise during the course of each pregnancy in response to specific problems, the involvement of particular gods and spirits, and so on.

17. Of the various forces that may attempt to thwart the healthy birth of a child, "avenging spirits" (*kúnu*) are seen as the most active, for the goal of each is the destruction of a particular matrilineage (see R. Price 1973; S. Price 1978). Until divination can provide a more specific explanation, any miscarriage or stillbirth is generally assumed to represent the effort of an avenging spirit associated with the woman's lineage. My own childlessness during our first two years of fieldwork and a miscarriage toward the end were interpreted by some Saramakas as proof that our society, like theirs, was plagued by avenging spirits.

18. Although certain women are known for their ability to assist with pregnancies and births, they undergo no formal training. Rather, women with other kinds of ritual expertise slowly accumulate experience as midwives by being consulted on particular problems, and shift very gradually into the role of a "woman who delivers with people," usually when they are postmenopausal.

19. In the case of "special births" (twins, breech births, a child conceived before its mother has resumed menstruation after an earlier birth, and so on), the rituals are more complex and take place over a longer time.

20. See R. Price 1975:117–25 for a social structural analysis of the distribution of children to "foster parents."

Chapter 3

1. For a fuller summary of this tale, see S. and R. Price 1980a:187.

2. The meals that the men of a particular neighborhood eat together often last for an hour or two, as gossip, hunting adventures, sexual exploits, conjugal problems, and assorted philosophical reflections are traded in a relaxed, congenial setting. The notes of Richard Price, who participated in

Dangogo men's meals regularly for two years, provide a crucial complement to the women's conversations that I heard in other settings.

3. A person whose death is attributed to hostilities with someone else may become an avenging ghost that attacks the lineage of his or her enemy. The lineages of the two principals are then linked by a relationship which makes marriages between their members especially vulnerable to supernatural aggression.

4. For a fuller version of this tale, see R. Price 1983a:13−14.

5. A recording, transcription, and translation of the Saramaccan historical narrative from which this is taken is included in R. and S. Price 1977.

6. Men enjoy passing critical judgment on the culinary success of particular dishes. When one woman carelessly served monkey meat that did not include any bone, a man inquired sarcastically what kind of animal was made without bones in its body. Another conversation dealt with the subtle distinction between asking "Who brought this peccary here?" (registering disapproval) and "Who cooked this [peccary] dish?" (expressing satisfaction). The seasoning in meat, fish, and vegetable sauces is also invariably noted. My own daily contributions to these meals were tasted cautiously and skeptically for a number of months, and recommendations for improvement patiently transmitted, before my cooking was finally considered suitable for more than token consumption.

7. A kin group's efforts at persuading wives to live and garden with them are part of a larger, politically motivated drive to maintain a maximal resident population. They exert pressure on their own women not to abandon them for long periods in a husband's village, on their men to return as promptly as possible from coastal work trips, and on all adults to have as many children as possible raised locally rather than with relatives in other villages and neighborhoods.

8. Although this discussion is phrased in terms of the man's close family, it applies only slightly less forcefully to his classificatory kin as well. For example, behavior expected of a husband's mother also tends to be appropriate for his mother's sisters, who are referred to by the same kinship term.

9. Men who are alternate generation affines address each other as *máti* (friend) and may engage in stylized joking about sharing a wife.

10. A century ago, it was possible for a Saramaka man to live partly in his wife's village, but this practice has been considered unacceptable since the early twentieth century; see R. Price 1970a; 1975:111−15.

11. During the 1960s, there were two co-wives in Dangogo who became unusually close friends. They would wear matching skirts, braid their hair the same way, cook in the same pots, and carry food to their husband's meals together. But it was clear that part of the satisfaction they derived from this relationship was their power vis-à-vis the man's third wife, who was placed in a very poor position to compete for his attention. Saramakas also cited a similar arrangement in the village of Akisiamau several decades earlier. Two women are said to have slept in the same hammock when they wanted to

"deprive" (*pená*) their husband, which infuriated the man and resulted in an unusual degree of domestic power for the women.

12. For a description of this introduction among the Djuka Maroons, see van Wetering 1966.

13. This name translates literally as "buttocks to the knees," and is understood by Saramakas as lavish praise of a beautifully ample rear end.

14. Individual men adopt different positions on dealing with a wife's adultery. Many take pride in the fact that they have never accepted an adultery payment, and others are reluctant to organize a beating because of the possibility that the man will die and become an avenging spirit directed against their lineage. Kin groups also vary in their policy on beatings versus payments. Most are known to favor either one or the other, but there are also rare lineages that prefer to take no action and others that take a payment and then make no objection if the husband organizes a beating in addition. Beatings often result in serious injuries, and attempts by tribal chiefs to regulate the techniques and weapons used have been only partially successful. In the 1940s, a man from Soola died from head wounds inflicted with a broken chisel. Other men have been permanently scarred by hawk and rodent claws, knives shaped into bracelets, locally made rubber whips, and rings with protruding prongs. Blackjacks and small sacks of shot (held in the fist to add weight to the blows) have also sometimes been used. From a Saramaka perspective, however, the most powerful weapons are the ritual preparations. The case of a man from Pempe who spent three months in the forest performing ritual washings before confronting his wife's lover is recognized as extreme, but most debilitating beatings are credited to the use of some kind of ritually prepared aid. (Saramakas have always used such powers in adultery cases; see R. Price 1983a:96–97 for a description of an eighteenth-century man named Abampapa who readied himself for a fight with his wife's lover by smoking a ritually prepared pipe.)

15. This factor is commonly glossed as a shortage of salt (*sátu pená*), reflecting two important aspects of a man's contribution to his wife's material needs—coastal imports (of which salt is one) and meat and fish (which are heavily salted when cooked). One woman who was asked by a kinswoman about her new marriage, for example, responded by commenting, "I was so poor in salt that I just decided to go out and find myself a husband."

16. This sample included all female members of the local lineages who had received their skirts of adulthood; twenty-eight out of seventy-two of them were over the age of forty-five.

17. The implications of this situation for the exploitation of Saramaka women by outsiders are discussed in S. and R. Price 1980b.

Chapter 4

1. Curtin describes a somewhat more developed system of cloth-currency in seventeenth- and eighteenth-century West Africa, where values could be

figured in terms of named fractional parts of the basic cloth unit (1975:237–38).

2. The trends that I describe for the 1960s and 1970s on the Pikilio took place somewhat earlier in many downstream villages.

3. I was unable to elicit an etymology for the expression *nyá papái*, which translates literally as "eating stems/reeds," and which normally refers to a woman's failure to reciprocate gifts from her husband.

4. Although there were some cases in the early twentieth century in which a girl was declared a virgin on her wedding night, Saramakas insist that this no longer occurs. However, the traditional examination of the hammock for blood, conducted by the man's brothers, is still carried out, and the girl's willingness to identify her first lover determines whether the husband stays for the rest of the night or leaves on the spot and returns only several days later after a special request has been made by her family.

5. For further discussion of the Saramaka concept of revenge, see R. Price 1973 and S. Price 1978.

6. The next most important context for the exchange of goods is funerals. The offerings of food, liquor, and other goods that a person provides at the funeral of a relative and the possessions that are assigned by coffin divination to particular mourners serve to reaffirm symbolically the whole range of interpersonal relations in the society. We will also see how the gifts exchanged between a husband and wife can later take on special significance in their respective funeral rites.

7. Men sometimes make a cape or breechcloth for themselves and women may provide some of their own fish, but in both cases these are lower-status products than those supplied by members of the opposite sex. A male-sewn garment lacks the hand sewing and the careful composition of women's examples and women's fishing techniques (with small hooks, makeshift cloth nets, and traps made from bottles) yield only second-best varieties of fish. The idea that "both men and women cook," which has been advanced (apparently for currently fashionable ideological reasons) by Counter and Evans (1981:96), is also misleading. Although it is true that men may prepare their own meals when no women are available (for example, when they are traveling in all-male company to the coast or serving as hired guides/boatmen for outsiders such as Counter and Evans), Saramakas view cooking as a task that should, if at all possible, be performed by women.

8. These covered baskets (*pakáa*) are usually bought from Suriname Indians, but they are occasionally made by Saramakas in the same style. For a typical example, see Ahlbrinck 1931: plate 158.

9. The hammock covering used by Suriname Maroons is in fact made of trade cotton rather than netting, and its principal function is to provide protection against vampire bats rather than mosquitoes.

10. The man who supplied this list volunteered the observation that "Women have no need of sugar and should not receive it in large quantities. The man should keep it himself and dispense it to them in small amounts when they need it for special purposes."

11. Alarm clocks are used almost exclusively for clandestine sex, since a man risks an immediate beating if he does not leave the woman's house before her neighbors begin to wake up, at dawn. Men who feel more secure sleeping lightly, rather than trusting their fate to a mechanical device, cite stories of women who have trapped lovers into marriage by smothering their alarm clocks. There are also other kinds of protection that can be used to avoid being caught with a lover. For example, certain ritually prepared bracelets, purchased in Djuka villages, are said to prevent dogs from barking when the man enters or leaves the woman's village. And some men employ a special procedure for hiding their canoe—towing a local canoe upstream, tying their own there, and returning to the main landing place with the other canoe, which will not arouse suspicion.

12. I neglected to ask if the same procedure is used for a woman—that is, whether a widow emerges from mourning by being dressed in clothes she had given to her husband as a marriage present.

13. There are, of course, differences among individual married women in how well their husbands provide for them, but this variation is minimal compared to the gap in material wealth between married and unmarried women in general.

14. A man whose wives are all away from the village or in menstrual seclusion may occasionally eat somewhat less regularly than usual, but it is a more common occurrence for a man to be offered more meals than he wishes to eat in the course of a day, because of both help from his kinswomen and the open invitation among male friends and relatives to share meals.

15. The amount of labor involved in, for example, sewing a cape and carving a tray is quite comparable. Differences in numbers of textiles owned by men and numbers of wood carvings owned by women do not, then, reflect the labor involved, but rather differences in the ratio of makers to owners (low for wood carvings, high for textiles).

Chapter 5

1. The Herskovitses describe a woman marking a calabash design with a knife before carving it with a piece of broken glass (1934:219), but I never saw this or heard of it during my own stays in Saramaka.

2. See S. Price 1982 and S. and R. Price 1983 for discussion of the botanical identification of African "calabashes." It would take many paragraphs to list all the botanists, art historians, museum curators, and ethnographers who have contributed in diverse ways to my understandings about the African and Amerindian influences on Maroon calabash art. I am grateful to all of them, but here wish to acknowledge in particular the generous help I received on Amerindian materials from Peter Rivière and the late Douglas Taylor.

3. This word may have been learned directly from Indians in Suriname. But it is also possible that it was first learned by Portuguese slave masters (and their slaves) in Brazil, who then migrated to Suriname and established the

plantations along the Suriname River from which many of the original Saramakas escaped.

4. Research conducted by Richard Price in Saramaka villages, museum collections, libraries, and archives in the 1960s suggested for the first time that Saramaka decorative wood carving represented a relatively new art in the mid-nineteenth century (1970b). Since then, this finding has been confirmed through further investigation, and we can be even more certain now than we were a decade ago that there was little if any Saramaka decorative wood carving before that time. The most recent supportive evidence comes from Peter Neumann's examination of the collections made by Moravian missionaries beginning in the eighteenth century, which included no decorative wood carving "older than the midst of the nineteenth century" (Neumann, personal communication, 1982).

5. A few such calabashes from the 1880s do reflect careful planning and technical skill. For examples, see S. and R. Price 1980a: figs. 222–24. In terms of numbers, however, these represent a distinct minority.

6. The designs on some Matawai calabashes (as well as a very few from Saramaka) are formed with thin gouged lines, but a collection of Matawai examples made in the 1970s by two Dutch anthropologists, Chris de Beet and Miriam Sterman, consist solely of designs that are indistinguishable from the "scraped" forms of modern Saramaka carving. The Kwinti no longer carve calabashes (Dirk van der Elst, personal communication, 1979), and I know of no documented examples from that tribe in museum collections.

7. Similarly, Holm has demonstrated the sensitivity of Northwest Coast Indian artists to the contours of ground areas ("negative space") and has traced the origin of certain of their figures to the gradual standardization of these (back)ground areas. That is, particular shapes (in painted wood, weaving, appliqué and silverwork) which began as carefully controlled backdrops to the design have evolved, over time, into elements of the design itself (1965:57, 80–82).

8. There are now some situations in which new calabashes made by a recognized carver are treated as a marketable commodity. When a woman's husband is planning a trip to Paramaribo, for example, she may prepare some bowls and ask a well-known carver to decorate them so they can be taken to the coast and sold in tourist shops.

9. Saramakas have no term for carving executed in the eastern Maroon style, with both edges scraped on the outside, and of the several thousand calabashes I have seen, only one documented as "Saramaka" included this kind of carving (see S. and R. Price 1980a: fig. 232 [5g]). I strongly suspect that this one example, with its wide border characteristic of eastern Maroon calabashes, was made by a woman from one of the eastern tribes who lived with a Saramaka husband in the village of Ganiakonde, where it was collected.

10. Symmetry has been an alternative in women's calabash carving ever since the nineteenth century, but it was not until the past few decades that it came to be thought of as a design requirement.

11. Melville Herskovits, irritated by the "questionable ethnography and

pseudo-psychological conjecture" behind Dark's study, immediately published a corrective (if cryptic) summary of male-female relations and artistry among Maroons, based on his own brief first-hand experiences in Suriname (1951). In response to Dark's portrayal of Maroon marriage and divorce, he commented that "Mrs. Herskovits and I . . . found no evidence of this sort of social chaos." Of the alleged "difference in temperament" between men and women, he remarked that "there is no evidence of such difference known to me, either in the literature or in my own field experience." And he pointed out that an interest in innovation and novelty is in fact more characteristic of men than of women in Maroon society. See also Dark's reply (1952).

12. My commentary on Dark's analysis of Maroon "personality configurations" is in no way intended as an attack on Dark, but rather as a caution about the power of any observer's social and cultural environment to color his or her perceptions of other societies, especially in the absence of long-term fieldwork. It seems unlikely that Dark's paper, published in 1951, would have reflected the same perspective if he had written it in 1981. And the idyllic feminism that Counter and Evans imagine to exist among the Maroons (with men and women sharing political responsibilities and domestic chores and with women fashioning the rules of menstrual seclusion as a way of liberating themselves periodically to relax in the company of other women) is every bit as much a product of its time (1981: 92, 96, 133). The idea that a convergence of Maroon and Western gender constructs has colored our understanding of Maroon men's and women's arts is developed also in S. Price 1983, which summarizes evidence from various chapters of this book.

Chapter 6

1. Archival documents show that, prior to the 1762 peace treaty with the government, Saramakas requested, among other things, thirteen hats with gold trim, twenty sacks of beads, and one hundred thirty pairs of gold earrings, as well as unspecified amounts of copper bells, jackets, and trousers (R. Price 1983*b*:212, 237).

2. In the remainder of this section, I draw on accounts of clothing from the various Maroon tribes, since it is not until the 1960s that stylistic differences from one region to another begin to be reported. Saramaka fashions probably differed subtly then, as they do now, from those of other Maroons. But the main lines of the descriptions that are available in this historical literature would in all likelihood have applied to all the groups.

3. Such syntheses were an important aspect of clothing among Maroons throughout the Americas. A 1599 painting by the Indian artist Adrián Sánchez Galque, for example, depicts Maroon "chiefs of three villages . . . on a treaty-signing visit to Quito, dressed as Spanish gentlemen, bearing lances, and wearing Amerindian-style gold nose- and ear-plugs" (R. Price 1979: 418).

4. The "crochet" stitch that Saramakas use to fashion calfbands is identical to that of Indians in the Guianas. For an illustration, see Roth 1924: 105 and plate 9. It is executed with a sharpened umbrella rib, and the size of the

bands is controlled by the use of a cylindrical form—most commonly a bottle or a carved wooden substitute (see S. and R. Price 1980a: fig. 148). Saramaka "knitting" is executed with two reeds, each about 1 centimeter wide and 8 to 10 centimeters long, that are pointed at one end and split at the other; it rarely exceeds a centimeter or two in width. (For Amerindian equivalents, see Roth 1924:104–5 and Ahlbrinck 1931:119, 444–45.)

5. The most important sources have been Japan, the United States, and the People's Republic of China.

6. Female mediums of snake gods, for example, wear a white cloth tied around the head and another across the breasts during possession.

7. The continuation of the thin cloth was due, in part, to the fact that women, who always wear two skirts at a time, considered a double layer of "thickies" unacceptably hot.

8. Museum documentation on this cloth (no. H2475) includes no date and lists as the provenience simply "Suriname"; however, the H of the catalogue number indicates that it belonged to the large Haarlem collection which was transferred to the Koloniaal Instituut (now the Tropenmuseum) in 1913, and the embroidered design matches van Panhuys's description.

9. The sewing on these cloths was remarkably fine, sometimes surpassing thirty-five stitches per inch. This may be compared, for example, to Amish patchwork quilts, on which the most highly skilled seamstresses "often 'put in' twenty stitches per inch" (Bishop and Safanda 1976:6).

10. Embroidery pattern books have come from a variety of sources. Those I saw in the field ranged from American publications showing Santa Clauses and angels to a French booklet illustrating seventeenth- and eighteenth-century Turkish saddlebag trimmings.

11. The cloths to which this generalization applies are all modern (1950s and 1960s) Upper River examples. Early narrow-strip compositions and those from other regions were often planned according to quite different principles. See S. and R. Price 1980a:73–76.

12. Adolsecent girls' aprons replicate these principles, but are limited to three-piece constructions. Generally, the center piece is a wide strip cut from the weft and flanked by warp strips or pieces of solid color cloth. For an example, see S. and R. Price 1980a: fig. 52.

13. One man, discussing wood carving styles of the past with Richard Price, compared turn-of-the-century techniques in that art to the contemporaneous state of automobile technology. While conceding that early versions of both carvings and cars were interesting as curiosities, there was no doubt in his mind that very similar strides had been made in the refinement of both. This contrasts with Saramakas' view of their supernatural resources over time. Here, they envision a gradual deterioration of the originally impressive store of knowledge that had allowed warriors to evade bullets or determine the location of the enemy and had enabled some ancestors to fly or to assume the forms of a variety of animals.

14. Some derogatory terminology is independent of stylistic change. During the height of narrow-strip textiles, for example, a narrow-strip cape could be referred to as an *akpánsópu* (it cuts the soap), meaning that its

connecting seams, so crudely turned under that they formed a ridge, cut into the bar of soap when the cloth was washed at the river. The term was often used as an expression of modesty by the woman who sewed a particular cape and referred to the technical skill represented by that one cloth rather than to the status of narrow-strip sewing as a whole.

15. There were a few exceptions to this rule in the late 1970s.

Chapter 7

1. For a discussion of Maroon "plays," see S. and R. Price 1980*a*:169.

2. Note that the (common) association of Queen Wilhelmina (Konu Wemina) with exceptional beauty—in both popular songs and names for cloth patterns—is based largely on a romantic attitude toward Dutch royalty, since awareness of the late queen's personal appearance does not generally constitute part of Saramaka experience.

3. Songs 1, 11, 13, 14, 16, and 42 are included on a Folkways record (R. and S. Price 1977). The following are part of a collection on deposit at the Archives of Traditional Music, Indiana University (R. and S. Price 1974): songs 3, 6, 8, 9, 12, 17, 18, 22, 23, 30, 31, 32, 34, 36, 45. The total corpus of *sêkêti* songs from which examples have been chosen for this chapter numbers 178.

4. *Haíka* means "to listen to," but it is also the verb used for visiting—especially making a visit of sympathy to someone who has suffered any personal misfortune, from illness to a death in the family.

5. *Gandá* means "[one's] village." It is used to connote an opposition with other places where one might be, such as a horticultural camp or a husband's village. Thus, *gandá muyêê* (woman in her own village) refers to a woman who is, at least temporarily, without a husband.

6. Women could explain the term *Kalêngi* only as "a very evil kind of person"; *Alumá* (German) is used to associate the second co-wife's behavior with atrocities such as those of World War II.

7. This is not a new problem for Saramaka women. As we saw in chapter 3, elders recounting the 1762 celebration of peace with the colonists include the song of a woman complaining that her jealous husband locked her in her house during the singing and dancing. Each of the two women with whom I discussed this song in the field rendered it as *Mi ó téi mánu a bóto* . . . (I'm going to take a husband by boat. . .). However, the only recording that I have of this song is by children, who sing it as *M'án ó téi mánu a bóto* . . . (I won't take a husband by boat. . .). Because the rest of the song declares that "I won't take love on the shore [i.e., in my home village] anymore," I have assumed that the children's performance was an aberration of the song as it was originally composed.

8. I am not certain about the meaning of this line, which translates literally as "husband's kin are finished." It may be a shortened version of the common expression of disparagement, *kabá a sôsò*, which means finished in the sense of "come to no good" or "morally degenerated."

9. "Troubling" a person is the way Saramakas customarily refer to a man

sleeping with another man's wife. Its (sarcastic) implication here is that the singer has intruded on the other woman's "marriage" with her own brother.

10. *Sébítaa* is the name for the fifth lunar month. *Yái* means both January and New Year's.

11. *Yayó*, which can be used as either a noun or a verb, means both prostitute and promiscuity (see songs 21, 31, and 41). *Yayó u mi* (roughly translated as "that slut of mine") is generally understood as a term for the speaker's co-wife.

12. As in many songs, the rhetorical address terms that extend two of this song's phrases ("child" and "brother") are inserted for rhythmic/stylistic reasons, and do not imply kinship relations.

13. The concept of "meeting" in a particular situation is significant to Saramakas, especially women. Women invariably comment on who they "met" with in the menstrual hut, in pregnancies, in having husbands from a particular village, or in being divorced at a particular time. Saramakas often indicate closeness of age by commenting that two women had "met in an [adolescent] apron." And "meeting" in something significant is the basis for the special relationship in which two people (usually women) address each other as *síbi*, from "shipmate."

14. The commemoration of a single incident in both a song and a cloth name appears in most cases to involve independent or simultaneous inventions rather than borrowing from one medium to the other.

15. The association of *koósu* with women's skirts is also reflected in a term frequently used for "wife" in the context of particular relationships. Although the word *muyêè* is used for "wife" in both an impersonal sense (e.g., *a tjiká u á muyêè*, "he's old enough to have a wife") and in women's personal names (e.g., *Apentimuyee*, "Wife-of-Apenti"), a slightly more respectful way of referring to a particular man's wife is as his *koósuma* (cloth- [or] skirt-person).

16. Skirt-cloths occasionally take on individualized associations in other ways as well. A skirt worn during certain kinds of rituals, for example, must thereafter not be worn by a woman in menstrual seclusion.

17. For another sample of Saramaka cloth names, including a number of "descriptive" names, see S. and R. Price 1980a:82–83.

18. At the time these cloth names were made up, the idea of using a bed rather than a hammock was very much a novelty.

Chapter 8

1. A woman who has been well provided for by her husband(s) may own a large number of imported buckets, pots, enamel bowls, metal spoons, teakettles, and so forth. See S. and R. Price 1980a for one example from Djuka (pl. IV) and another from Saramaka (fig. 23a,b). In general, however, the ratio of locally made to imported furnishings is much higher in women's houses than in men's.

References Cited

Ahlbrinck, W.
  1931   "Encyclopaedie der Karaiben." *Verhandelingen der Koninklijke Akademie van Wetenschappen te Amsterdam, Afdeeling Letterkunde,* Nieuwe Reeks, 27:1–555.
Bates, Henry Walter
  1873   *The Naturalist on the River Amazons.* 3d ed. London: John Murray.
Beet, Chris de, and H. U. E. Thoden van Velzen
  1977   "Bush Negro Prophetic Movements: Religions of Despair?" *Bijdragen tot de Taal-, Land- en Volkenkunde* 133:100–135.
Bishop, Robert, and Elizabeth Safanda
  1976   *A Gallery of Amish Quilts: Design Diversity from a Plain People.* New York: Dutton.
Bonaparte, Prince Roland
  1884   *Les habitants de Suriname: notes recueillies à l'exposition coloniale d'Amsterdam en 1883.* Paris: A. Quantin.
Bouyer, Frédéric
  1867   *La Guyane Française: notes et souvenirs d'un voyage exécuté en 1862–63.* Paris: Hachette.
Breton, Père Raymond
  1647   *Relations de l'Ile de la Guadeloupe.* Tome 1. Reprint. Basse Terre: Société d'Histoire de la Guadeloupe, 1978.
Brunetti, R. P. Jules
  1890   *La Guyane Française: souvenirs et impressions de voyage.* Tours: Alfred Mame et Fils.
Bunzel, Ruth L.
  1929   *The Pueblo Potter: A Study of Creative Imagination in Primitive Art.* Columbia University Contributions to Anthropology 8. Reprint. New York: Dover Publications, 1955.
Cassidy, F. G., and R. B. Le Page
  1967   *Dictionary of Jamaican English.* Cambridge: Cambridge University Press.
Cateau van Rosevelt, J. F. A., and J. F. A. E. van Lansberge
  1873   "Verslag van de reis ter opname van de Rivier Suriname." In W. R. Menkman, "Uit de geschiedenis der opening van het Surinaamsche binnenland," *De West-Indische Gids* 27 (1946): 182–92, 289–99, 321–43.

213

214   REFERENCES CITED

Coster, A. M.
1866   "De Boschnegers in de kolonie Suriname: hun leven, zeden, en gewoonten." *Bijdragen tot de Taal-, Land- en Volkenkunde* 13:1–36.

Counter, S. Allen, and David L. Evans
1974   "Djuka Counterpoint." *Newsweek* 84, no. 19:4, 8.
1981   *I Sought My Brother: An Afro-American Reunion.* Cambridge and London: MIT Press.

Crevaux, Jules
1879   "Voyage d'exploration dans l'intérieur des Guyanes, 1876–77." *Le Tour du Monde* 20:337–416.

Curtin, Philip D.
1975   *Economic Change in Precolonial Africa: Senegambia in the Era of the Slave Trade.* Madison: University of Wisconsin Press.

Dalziel, J. M.
1955   *The Useful Plants of West Tropical Africa.* London: Crown.

Dark, Philip J. C.
1951   "Some Notes on the Carving of Calabashes by the Bush Negroes of Surinam." *Man* 51:57–61.
1952   "Bush Negro Calabash-Carving." *Man* 52:126.
1954   *Bush Negro Art: An African Art in the Americas.* London: Tiranti.

Eilerts de Haan, J. G. W. J.
1910   "Verslag van de expeditie naar de Suriname-Rivier." *Tijdschrift van het Koninklijk Nederlandsch Aardrijkskundig Genootschap*, 2ᵉ serie, 27:403–68, 641–701.

Fermin, Phillippe
1769   *Déscription générale, historique, géographique et physique de la colonie de Surinam.* Amsterdam: E. van Harrevelt.

Gillis, Verna
1981   *From Slavery to Freedom: Music of the Saramaka Maroons of Suriname.* New York: Lyrichord Discs.

Heeckeren, Godard P. C., van
1826   *Aanteekeningen betrekkelijk de kolonie Suriname.* Arnhem: C. A. Thieme.

Herskovits, Melville J.
1930   "Bush Negro Art." *The Arts* 17, no. 51:25–37, 48–49. Reprinted in *The New World Negro*, edited by Frances S. Herskovits, pp. 157–67. New York: Minerva Press, 1969.
1951   "Bush Negro Calabash Carving." *Man* 51:163–64.

Herskovits, Melville J., and Frances S. Herskovits
1934   *Rebel Destiny: Among the Bush Negroes of Dutch Guiana.* New York: McGraw-Hill.

Holm, Bill
1965   *Northwest Coast Indian Art: An Analysis of Form.* Seattle: University of Washington Press.

Hostmann, F. W.
1850   *Over de beschaving van negers in Amerika door kolonisatie met Euro-peanen.* Amsterdam: J. C. A. Sulpke.
Hurault, Jean
1960   "Histoire des Noirs Réfugiés Boni de la Guyane Française." *Revue Française d'Histoire d'Outre-Mer* 47:76–137.
1961   *Les Noirs Réfugiés Boni de la Guyane Française.* Mémoires de l'In-stitut Français d'Afrique Noire 63. Dakar: Institut Français d'Afrique Noire.
1970   *Africains de Guyane: la vie matérielle et l'art des Noirs Réfugiés de Guyane.* Paris and The Hague: Mouton.
Jobson, Richard
1623   *The Golden Trade, or a Discovery of the River Gambra, and the Golden Trade of the Aethiopians.* Reprint. London: Dawsons of Pall Mall, 1968.
Joest, Wilhelm
1893   "Ethnographisches und Verwandtes aus Guyana." *International Archives of Ethnography* 5, supp.
Johnston, Harry H.
1910   *The Negro in the New World.* London: Methuen.
Kahn, Morton Charles
1931   *Djuka: The Bush Negroes of Dutch Guiana.* New York: Viking Press.
Kappler, August
1854   *Zes jaren in Suriname: schetsen en tafereelen uit het maatschappelijke en militaire leven in deze kolonie.* Utrecht: W. F. Dannenfelser.
1883   *Nederlandsch-Guyana.* Winterswijk: Albrecht.
1887   *Surinam, sein Land, seine Natur, Bevölkerung und seine Kultur-Verhältnisse mit Bezug auf Kolonisation.* Stuttgart: J. G. Cotta'sche Verlagsbuchhandlung.
Kersten, Christoph
1770   "Letter of 12 February." In *Die Mission der Brüdergemeine in Sur-iname und Berbice im achtzehnten Jahrhundert,* edited by F. Staehelin, Vol. 3.1:137–39. Herrnhut: Vereins für Brü-dergeschichte in Kommission der Unitätsbuchhandlung in Gnadau, 1913–19.
Koch-Grünberg, Theodor
1910   *Zwei Jahre unter den Indianern: Reisen in Nordwest Brasilien, 1903–05.* Berlin.
Kubler, George
1962   *The Shape of Time: Remarks on the History of Things.* New Haven: Yale University Press.
Lamb, Venice
1975   *West African Weaving.* London: Gerald Duckworth.

Lelyveld, Th. van
   1919/20   "De kleeding der Surinaamsche bevolkingsgroepen in verband
            met aard en gewoonten." *De West-Indische Gids* 1:249–68,
            458–70; 2:20–34, 125–43.
Martin, K.
   1886   "Bericht über eine Reise ins Gebiet des Oberen Surinam." *Bij-
            dragen tot de Taal-, Land- en Volkenkunde* 35:1–76, plus 4 plates.
Muntslag, F. H. J.
   1966   *Tembe: Surinaamse houtsnijkunst.* Amsterdam: Prins Bernhard
            Fonds.
Naipaul, Shiva
   1981   "Suriname: A Tableau of Savage Innocence." *GEO* 3
            (March):74–94.
Panhuys, L. C. van
   1899   "Toelichting betreffende de voorwerpen verzameld bij de
            Aucaner Boschnegers." In *Catalogus der Nederlandsche West-
            Indische tentoonstelling te Haarlem:*74–82.
Price, Richard
   1970*a*   "Saramaka Emigration and Marriage: A Case Study of Social
            Change." *Southwestern Journal of Anthropology* 26:157–89.
   1970*b*   "Saramaka Woodcarving: The Development of an Afro-
            american Art." *Man* 5:363–78, plus 6 plates.
   1973   "Avenging Spirits and the Structure of Saramaka Lineages."
            Bijdragen tot de Taal-, Land- en Volkenkunde 129:86–107.
   1975   *Saramaka Social Structure: Analysis of a Maroon Society in Surinam.*
            Caribbean Monograph Series 12. Rio Piedras: Institute of Car-
            ibbean Studies of the University of Puerto Rico.
   1976   *The Guiana Maroons: A Historical and Bibliographical Introduction.*
            Baltimore and London: Johns Hopkins University Press.
   1979   *Maroon Societies: Rebel Slave Communities in the Americas.* 2d ed.
            Baltimore and London: Johns Hopkins University Press.
   1983*a*   *First-Time: The Historical Vision of an Afro-American People.* Bal-
            timore and London: Johns Hopkins University Press.
   1983*b*   *To Slay the Hydra: Dutch Colonial Perspectives on the Saramaka Wars.*
            Ann Arbor: Karoma.
Price, Richard, and Sally Price
   1972*a*   *Kammbá:* The Ethnohistory of an Afro-American Art."
            Antropologica 32:3–27.
   1972*b*   "Saramaka Onomastics: An Afro-American Naming System."
            Ethnology 11:341–67.
   1974   *The Music and Verbal Arts of the Saramaka Maroons of Suriname.* A
            field collection on deposit in the Archives of Traditional Music,
            The Folklore Institute, Indiana University, Bloomington. 117
            tapes, plus transcriptions.
   1977   *Music from Saramaka: A Dynamic Afro-American Tradition.* New
            York: Folkways Records.

Price, Sally
   1978   "Reciprocity and Social Distance: A Reconsideration." *Ethnology* 17:339–50.
   1982   "When Is a Calabash Not a Calabash?" *Nieuwe West-Indische Gids* 56:69–82.
   1983   "Sexism and the Construction of Reality: An Afro-American Example." *American Ethnologist* 10:460–76.

Price, Sally, and Richard Price
   1980*a*   *Afro-American Arts of the Suriname Rain Forest.* Berkeley: University of California Press.
   1980*b*   "Exotica and Commodity: The Arts of the Suriname Maroons." *Caribbean Review* 9, no. 4:13–17, 47.
   1983   *Ensayos Sobre Arte Afroamericano.* Santo Domingo: Museo del Hombre Dominicano.

Riemer, Johann Andreus
   1801   *Missions-Reise nach Suriname und Barbice zu einer am Surinamflusse im dritten Grad der Linie wohnenden Freinegernation.* Zittau und Leipzig.

Rochefort, Charles César de
   1665   "Histoire naturelle et morale des îles Antilles de l'Amérique." Translated in *The history of the Caribby-Islands*, by John Davies. London: Thomas Dring and John Starkey, 1666.

Rosaldo, M. Z.
   1980   "The Use and Abuse of Anthropology: Reflections on Feminism and Cross-cultural Understanding." *Signs* 5:389–417.

Roth, Walter Edmund
   1924   "An Introductory Study of the Arts, Crafts, and Customs of the Guiana Indians." *Thirty-eighth Annual Report of the Bureau of American Ethnology:*25–745.

Sack, Baron Albert von
   1821   *Reize naar Surinamen, verblijf aldaar. . . .* Haarlem: Erven F. Bohn.

Schumann, C. L.
   1778   "Saramaccanisch Deutsches Wörter-Buch." In *Die Sprache der Saramakkaneger in Surinam,* edited by Hugo Schuchardt, pp. 46–116. *Verhandelingen der Koninklijke Akademie van Wetenschappen te Amsterdam* 14, no. 6. Amsterdam: Johannes Müller, 1914.

Spalburg, J. G.
   1899   *Schets van de Marowijne en hare bewoners.* Paramaribo: H. B. Heyde.

Staehelin, F.
   1913–19 *Die Mission der Brüdergemeine in Suriname und Berbice im achtzehnten Jahrhundert.* 3 vols. Herrnhut: Vereins für Brüdergeschichte in Kommission der Unitätsbuchhandlung in Gnadau.

St. Clair, Thomas Staunton
    1834   *A Residence in the West Indies and America*. Vol. 1. London: Rich-
                ard Bentley.
Stedman, Captn. J. G.
    1796   *Narrative, of a Five-Years' Expedition, Against the Revolted Negroes of
                Surinam . . . from the Year 1772, to 1777.* London: J. Johnson and
                J. Edwards.
Voorhoeve, Jan
    1959   "An Orthography for Saramaccan." *Word* 15:436–45.
Wetering, Wilhelmina van
    1966   "Conflicten tussen co-vrouwen bij de Djuka." *Nieuwe West-
                Indische Gids* 45:52–59.
Zerries, Otto
    1980   *Unter Indianern Brasiliens: Sammlung Spix und Martius
                1817–1820.* Staatlichen Museum für Völkerkunde München,
                Band 1.

Illustration Credits

Jacket and cover photograph. Dangogo, 1968. Photo by Richard Price.
Dedication photographs. Dangogo, 1968, 1974, 1978. Photos by Richard Price.
  Fig. 1. Drafted by the Photographic and Illustrations Department of the Johns Hopkins University.
  Fig. 2. Dangogo, 1968. Photos by Richard Price.
  Fig. 3. Upper Pikilio, 1968, and Dangogo, 1974. Photos by Richard Price.
  Fig. 4. Asindoopo, 1978. Photo by Sally Price.
  Fig. 5. Dangogo, 1968. Photo by Sally Price.
  Fig. 6. Upper Pikilio, 1968. Photo by Richard Price.
  Fig. 7. Pikilio, 1968. Photo by Richard Price.
  Fig. 8. Pikilio, 1968. Photo by Richard Price.
  Fig. 9. Dangogo, 1968. Photos by Richard Price.
  Fig. 10. Carved by Tebini of Kampu, ca. 1960. Photo by David Porter.
  Fig. 11. Dangogo, 1978. Photo by Sally Price.
  Fig. 12. Carved before 1968. Photo by Richard Price.
  Fig. 13. Carved before 1978. Photo by Sally Price.
  Fig. 14. Carved before 1968. Photo by Sally Price.
  Fig. 15. Rijksmuseum voor Volkenkunde, Leiden: (*a, c, d*) 370-381 (collected before 1883); (*b*) 2777-19 (collected in Lower River Saramaka, 1885). Photo by Ben Bekooy.
  Fig. 16. Tropenmuseum, Amsterdam: A 6034a (collected before 1889). Photos by Sally Price.
  Fig. 17. Musée de l'Homme, Paris: 81.34.13 (collected by Jules Crevaux in Aluku, 1876–77). Photos by the Musée de l'Homme.
  Fig. 18. Rijksmuseum voor Volkenkunde, Leiden: 951-16 (collected before 1893). Photos by Ben Bekooy.
  Fig. 19. Musée de l'Homme, Paris: 35.72.74 (collected in Aluku before 1935). Photos by the Musée de l'Homme.
  Fig. 20. *Left:* collected in Asindoopo, 1976; *right:* collection of John D. Lenoir, New York (collected in 1970s). Photos by Antonia Graeber.
  Fig. 21. Surinaams Museum, Paramaribo: H1066 (collected in Dritabiki). Photo by Antonia Graeber.
  Fig. 22. Carved in Pempe, 1970s. Photos by Antonia Graeber.
  Fig. 23. Carved in Godo, 1970s. Photo by Antonia Graeber.
  Fig. 24. Carved by Seesee, upper Gaanlio, ca. 1970. Photo by David Porter.
  Fig. 25. Carved by Basulio of Godo, early 1970s. Photos by Antonia Graeber.
  Fig. 26. Carved by Keekete of Asindoopo (*top*) 1960s and (*bottom*) 1978. Photos by Antonia Graeber.
  Fig. 27. Carved by Keekete of Asindoopo, before 1978. Photo by Antonia Graeber.
  Fig. 28. Carved by Keekete of Asindoopo, before 1978. Photo by Antonia Graeber.

Fig. 29. Carved in Asindoopo. Photo by Antonia Graeber.
Fig. 30. *Left to right:* carved before 1968, carved in Soolan before 1976, carved before 1979. Photo by Sally Price.
Fig. 31. Carved before 1976. Photo by Antonia Graeber.
Fig. 32. Carved in Asindoopo before 1950. Photo by Sally Price.
Fig. 33. Carved in Asindoopo before 1950. Photo by Sally Price.
Fig. 34. Carved by Keekete of Asindoopo, probably 1950s or 1960s. Photo by Antonia Graeber.
Fig. 35. Carved before 1967. Photo by David Porter.
Fig. 36. Carved by Dofia of Asindoopo, late 1960s or early 1970s. Photo by David Porter.
Fig. 37. *Left:* carved before 1968; *right:* carved in Pempe before 1976. Photos by David Porter.
Fig. 38. Probably carved 1940s to 1950s. Photo by Antonia Graeber.
Fig. 39. *Left:* provenience unknown; *right:* carved in Pempe ca. 1978. Photos by Antonia Graeber.
Fig. 40. Drawings by Sally Price.
Fig. 41. Dangogo, 1968. Photo by Sally Price.
Fig. 42. Dangogo, 1968. Photo by Sally Price.
Fig. 43. Sewn by Bo, probably around 1900. Photo by Richard Price.
Fig. 44. Sewn by Bo or Apumba, probably 1900–10. Photo by Richard Price.
Fig. 45. Sewn early twentieth century. Photo by the Photographic and Illustrations Department of the Johns Hopkins University.
Fig. 46. Drawing by Sally Price, redrafted by the Photographic and Illustrations Department of the Johns Hopkins University.
Fig. 47. Sewn 1920–40 by Peepina of Totikampu (Lower River Saramaka). Photo by Antonia Graeber.
Fig. 48. Collected in Dangogo, 1978. Photo by the Photographic and Illustrations Department of the Johns Hopkins University.
Fig. 49. Sewn in Godo ca. 1940. Drawing by Margaret Falk, after a field sketch by Sally Price and a field photo by Richard Price.
Fig. 50. Drawings by Sally Price, after field photos.
Fig. 51. Asindoopo, 1976. Photo by Richard Price.
Fig. 52. From Eilerts de Haan 1910: plates 23 and 24.
Fig. 53. Drafted by Margaret Falk, after a drawing by Sally Price.
Fig. 54. Drafted by Margaret Falk, after a drawing by Sally Price.
Fig. 55. Collected in Dangogo, 1978. Photo by the Photographic and Illustrations Department of the Johns Hopkins University.
Fig. 56. Dangogo, 1968. Photo by Richard Price.

Index

Abortion, 34
Adultery, preventative measures and sanctions against, 47, 58, 68–69, 77–78, 182, 205
Aesthetic principles: in calabash carving, 100–101, 108–16; in gardens, 32; in men's and women's designs, 110, 119, 122, 145–46, 196–97, 208; in textile arts, 145–46, 152–62, 164–65
Affinal village, woman's role in, 47–52, 57, 180, 182–83, 202, 204
African arts and material culture, 93–94, 129, 159, 205–7
Ahlbrinck, W., 206, 210
Aluku Maroons, 68, 123, 126, 130, 136. *See also* Eastern Maroons
Amerindians, xii, 92–94, 129–30, 202, 206–7, 209–10
Appliqué, 142
Aprons: adolescent girls', 15–18, 20, 86, 125, 129, 140, 142, 210; men's, 71, 142, 165

Baskets as symbol of marriage, 51–52, 70, 72–73, 80, 206
Bates, H. W., 92
Beads, 12, 20, 127, 128, 209
Beet, C. de, 135, 208
Betrothal, 15, 18, 23, 47, 71
Birth, 12, 14, 21, 35–36, 59, 65, 90, 201
Bishop, R., 210
Bonaparte, Prince R., 128
Bouyer, F., 124
Breton, Père R., 92
Brunetti, R. P. J., 128

Bunzel, R. L., 119

Calabash decoration: history of, 92–100, 112, 114–16, 118, 208; men's, 89, 91, 95–99, 119, 122; regional and village styles of, 99–107, 121, 208; specialization in, 101–8, 113–14, 116–17, 208. *See also* Aesthetic principles; Naming
Calabashes: African, 93–94, 207; in meal service, 46, 86; processing of, 87–89, 92–93, 207; ritual uses of, 35, 87, 90
Calfbands, 71, 130, 132, 157, 165. *See also* Crocheting
Cassidy, F. G., 94
Cateau van Rosevelt, J. F. A., 128
Central Maroons (Kwinti, Matawai, Saramaka), xi–xii, 100–102
Christian missions, 8, 24, 66, 125–26, 146, 192. *See also* Schools
Cicatrization, 17–18, 20, 23, 32, 40, 121
Cloth: African, 159, 205–6; as currency, 64, 205–6; imported, 74, 76, 124, 129–35, 143, 147–48, 156, 188–89, 210; locally made, 123, 130; terminology for, 134–35, 163–64. *See also* Appliqué; Embroidery; Imported goods; Naming; Patchwork; Weaving
Colors. *See* Aesthetic principles
Cooperation, artistic, 99, 104–7, 110, 144–46
Coster, A. M., 127, 130